Whatever Happened to
Barry Chambers?

Whatever Happened to Barry Chambers?

Barry Kay

The Book Guild Ltd

First published in Great Britain in 2019 by
The Book Guild Ltd
9 Priory Business Park
Wistow Road, Kibworth
Leicestershire, LE8 0RX
Freephone: 0800 999 2982
www.bookguild.co.uk
Email: info@bookguild.co.uk
Twitter: @bookguild

Typeset in Adobe Garamond Pro

Printed and bound by CPI Group (UK) Ltd, Croydon, CR0 4YY

ISBN 978 1912881 550

British Library Cataloguing in Publication Data.
A catalogue record for this book is available from the British Library.

MIX
Paper from
responsible sources
FSC
www.fsc.org   FSC® C013604

To Rosy and Penny.

CONTENTS

Everything described in these memoirs is true. For the sake of the narrative I have dramatised scenes and recreated conversations. The names of certain individuals have been changed to protect their privacy.

London, January 2019

2010

Prologue

Several years have passed but still I have not been back to visit her grave. The pain, confusion and embarrassment of the funeral overwhelmed me. Everyone else thought it went off well, very well – "Just what she would have wanted," they said.

"Why are you burying my mother in a Jewish cemetery?" I wanted to cry out. But I knew she wished to be buried alongside Harry Reuben, husband number three. Harry Kay, husband number two, my stepfather, was, weirdly, just a couple of rows along, within kicking distance. My real father, Tony Chambers, husband number one, had been forgotten years ago.

The cars arrived at the Liberal Jewish Cemetery in Willesden. The family assembled in the brick building where the rabbi said prayers in Hebrew. I tried to follow them in the translation. He then said some words about my mum: "A dignified woman, devoted to her loving family…"

Then it was my turn. I kept it brief. "I remember what a stunner she was," I began. "All the masters at my boarding school turned their heads when she came to visit. I was so proud to have such a beautiful mother." I mentioned her success in the rag trade, her style, the tears, sadness and laughter, the larger-than-life behaviour.

Her coffin was wheeled to Harry Reuben's graveside on a contraption like a pram. Relatives and friends processed behind. I had remembered this curious sight from Harry Kay's funeral, ten years previously.

I read the inscription:

IN CHERISHED MEMORY OF HYMAN REUBEN
(HARRY)
WHO PASSED AWAY ON THE 29TH JANUARY 1984
AGED 76
WILL ALWAYS BE REMEMBERED BY HIS WIFE JOAN,
STEPCHILDREN PENNY AND BARRY, AND HIS MANY
FRIENDS
SHALOM

Stepchild! That was outrageous. I grabbed my sister's arm. "Where's Dad's grave?" I said, almost choking. We walked around two rows and turned to the left. There was the simple grey marble headstone with the inscription:

IN LOVING MEMORY OF
HARRY KAY
DIED JULY 27TH 1990
AGED 75
SADLY MISSED
BY FAMILY AND FRIENDS

Rage boiled up inside me. "Look, Penny. We aren't mentioned." But Penny was too upset to answer.

Mum was responsible for this. True to form, she had airbrushed history.

1944

End of Normal Childhood

"Where are we going, Mummy?"

There was a pause. Then she said, "What a nice part of town this is. Wouldn't it be lovely to live here?"

We arrived. The little car turned into and chugged along the drive. My mother rang the bell on the imposing door.

A lady, small in stature and plain – no one was as beautiful as my mother – opened the door and gave us both a smile.

"Hello, Matron," said my mother. "I am sorry if we are a bit early."

"Not at all. Come away in." She looked down at me. "You must be Barry. Why, you're just a wee bairn. How old are you, dear?"

"Four and three quarters," I said shyly.

"Here are his things," said my mother, nervously handing over a small suitcase and my green ration card. She then crouched down, her face close to mine. "Barry, I want you to stay for a while with this nice lady, who you are to call 'Matron'. She will look after you."

As I was about to cry, she kissed my face gently. "I won't be long, darling, just a few days. Trust me. You will like it here. You will find other boys to play with. Everything will be all right, I promise." With that she got into her Austin 7 and quickly drove away.

Matron took my hand, smiled and said, in her gentle Scottish accent, "Come and see your room and meet the others."

She took me up a wide staircase and into a small dormitory which had a window overlooking the front drive. There were three boys lying on their beds reading. They were older than me, about six or seven. I was told their names. They raised their eyebrows and then, without saying a word, carried on reading. Were they there just for a few days too, I wondered? I was confused and frightened. Where was my mother, and why was I being left with this strange lady in this big house? Why were these boys so unfriendly?

I was to spend many hours by that window, weeping and waiting for my mother's return. I did not see her again for two months, but it would be many years before I was told the truth of what had happened to our family. It was the end of my normal childhood.

2010

The Document

I have been known as Barry Kay for most of my life, but I was born Anthony Barrington Chambers in 1939 in Northampton, England.

"Why did you call me Barrington?" I asked my mother.

"Oh, we just liked it," she replied. "There was a sports commentator called Barrington Dalby. We thought it was such a lovely name."

"So I'm not related to Sir Thomas Barrington of Barrington Hall?"

"You should be so lucky," my mother said, laughing.

"And obviously you didn't call me Tony."

"Obviously," she said, but quickly changed the subject as she always did when my real father's name was mentioned.

A few months later, my mother died. She was ninety-two, quite impressive considering her severe, chronic bronchitis after years of smoking. Would I ever know the truth of what happened during the early weeks of 1944? Those secrets had gone with her to her grave. A few days after her funeral, however, when we were clearing out her small flat in Marble Arch, we found something surprising. Amongst the piles of papers – old receipts, insurance documents, letters from the council, tax returns, and so on – and tucked deep inside one of the drawers was a large envelope containing several sheets of foolscap in Mum's handwriting. I did not take much notice of it at first as there was so much to sort out. I just stuffed it in my briefcase to read later.

Sitting at home that evening, tired and sad, I mulled over the funeral. I was still uncomfortable about my mother being buried in a Jewish cemetery. I told myself that these thoughts were irrational, because that was what she wanted. But the old feelings of insecurity came flooding back. The past was catching up with me again. What a journey my mother had made – from Eva Gertrude Pearcey, born in 1918 in a poor home in Peterborough, to her reinvention in London as Joan Kay, famous fashion designer and elegant Jewish lady.

It was then that I remembered the foolscap document. There were about twenty pages, all in her neat, confident hand. It must have been written quickly because it was punctuated with dashes instead of full stops, as if her thoughts had been flowing so fast she had hardly had time to write them down. At first glance I thought it was a short story. I remembered that she had wanted to write "the story of my life". Maybe this was it, or the start of it.

The first few sentences had been scrubbed out but I made out the words *Today I am fifty-five years old...* Whatever this was, it must have been written in 1974. As I read on I realised that this was indeed the start of an account of her early life. I felt both nervous and excited. Maybe I would discover things about her that I did not know. It began:

> *Can you imagine a row of terraced cottages in a provincial town, and a small girl we will call Eva...*

I thought back to Grandad and Grandma's tiny 'two-up two-down' with its smell of fried bacon and carbolic soap, and the clanking of railway wagons from the marshalling yards, and the two of them sitting there in silence.

> *It was a household of extreme poverty. Poverty has great fear...*
> *The General Strike of 1926 when I was eight years old made life even worse. My father was a kind man who left school at eleven – he could hardly read or write. My mother was a*

*hard-working Victorian lady with an outward show of dignity.
She worked hard, repairing clothes and household linen at
night – but always nagging my father about money. He had
four shillings a week pocket money, and would go to a working
men's club, drink a pint of beer and sing Harry Lauder songs.
I would sit with my mother, who always had a hard expression
on her face – and my father came home at 10.10pm exactly,
feeling happy. He would invariably be greeted with "That's all
you are good for, drinking beer" – I had a dreadful fear of my
mother so I always took her side.*

I put the document down for a moment and smiled. So, *my* mother,
whom we had just buried, had a great fear of *her* mother just as I,
her son, was frightened of her.

I then read that my mother's talent for clothes- and dressmaking,
a gift which brought her considerable success, had been apparent
from quite an early age.

*Once I made my mother a frock. It was easy for me to put
a pattern together from a length of cheap material and work
on it on the old sewing machine my mother had bought. She
was delighted. It was one of the few happy moments in my
childhood. I left school at fourteen years and worked as a cashier
for ten shillings a week. After that I moved to Woolworths as
a salesgirl, then to a waitress job. I did piecework sorting tulip
bulbs, and for a while worked in a jam factory. I was earning
almost as much as my father. But how could I escape from my
oppressive surroundings? There was only one way – marriage!*

Her interest in boys started early. My mother grew into a beautiful
young woman. She was tall, about five foot ten, with fine features
and a high forehead and cheekbones. Her sister, my Aunty Joan,
told me once that by the age of sixteen Mum had developed an
almost perfect figure.

Mum then described the boys she met as a teenager, local lads who worked in a scrapyard and taught her to drive. At seventeen a young man proposed and gave her a ring which she showed off to her friends. But she decided he was 'too ordinary' and gave it back to him.

It was about this time that my mother decided she did not like the name Eva. When asked her name by a young man at a local dance she quickly replied, "Joan", her sister's name. It stuck, and from then on, outside of the family in Peterborough, that was the name she asked to be called by.

It was now 1936, and Mum writes about her achievements and how she met my father:

I was aged eighteen years and I found a new job as a demonstrator for Darling Washing Machines. I was earning over five pounds a week, much more than my dad. Now I could take my mother anywhere she wanted. It was at the washing-machine company that I met Tony Chambers, the area manager. He said he was thirty-seven and a widower. He was well dressed, charming and handsome, and allowed me to borrow his car any time he was in Peterborough. He bought me a dress, which thrilled me. My mother and father liked Tony. If they had any doubts about him they kept them to themselves. Within three months we were married.

She described the wedding:

It took place on a sunny August day. We were married at Peterborough Town Hall. My mother stayed at home to look after my sister Joan, who was then about three years old, and also to prepare the reception, which was like a children's tea party but with a small wedding cake. There was no alcohol; Mum would have thought it extravagant.

I have a photograph of the wedding, taken with an old Kodak Brownie. It is the only photograph I have of my father. Mum looks radiant. She is wearing a smart suit, pinched at the waist, a white blouse with a double white corsage, and her right hip is thrust forward in a proud pose. Tony looks immaculate with razor-blade creases in the trousers of his light grey three-piece suit, a club tie and a carnation buttonhole. He is about my mother's height, but slim with a strong, square face and a high forehead. Grandma is on Tony's left, looking nervous.

I once asked my mother what her honeymoon with Tony Chambers was like. She was surprisingly forthcoming, telling me how they could not wait to get away from her parents' house. They had a four-hour drive to London and stayed in a hotel in the Marble Arch area. Of course she had never been to a hotel before – everything was new and exciting. She felt like a film star. The linen sheets and room service particularly thrilled her. Tony seemed to know the hotel and had probably stayed there before, but Mum did not mind or ask too many questions because they were married now. She told me she was a virgin on her wedding night, but the first time was an anticlimax. I remember her telling me she was disappointed because "that was all there was to it".

They went to live in Dunstable in a house 'like a mansion' with 'wonderful furniture' and all sorts of labour-saving devices. For the first time she had a bathroom. My mother sounded ecstatic, and wanted *her* mother to have the same luxuries.

After a year or two Tony and Eva moved to Northampton. I still remember that house, even though I was a very small child when we lived there. It was called Treeways, and was set back from the road. It had a long garden. I was born in June 1939. Mum said 'the days dragged on' during the pregnancy. It was a long, hot summer. Tony was often absent, either with the Home Guard on manoeuvres or away on business.

During the early war years they were not much affected by shortages. Tony Chambers was a bit of a social climber, and possibly a Freemason. Sometimes his friends made remarks which hurt my mother and were probably aimed at her lack of education and her Peterborough accent. Despite this and the war, there was nothing in her account to suggest that my mother and father had anything other than – as she said herself – a happy marriage.

I went back to Peterborough from time to time to see my parents and help them financially as much as I could. I was proud of my new status. After all, I had come up in the world. I had a husband, a son, a car, a washing machine and friends.

One day in late February 1944, however, something happened that was to change her life, and mine, forever. The doorbell rang. My mother opened it to find a well-dressed, middle-aged lady on the doorstep.

"I'm Mrs Chambers," she said. "I believe my husband lives here."

1944

Madeley House

Rage, betrayal, bitterness – the words spluttered out onto the page. It was impossible for Mum to express the awful shame she felt. *How could I have been so naive? Why didn't I ask Tony more about his first wife?*

Mum had been in too much of a hurry to leave home and get married, to leave the house of poverty, to escape. Only eighteen, she was confident but unworldly. *Why didn't I see this coming? Why was I so stupid?* The hurt was deep, very deep.

So here she was, a young woman of twenty-five with a four-year-old child, who had just discovered that her husband was already married. Her instinct was to leave the house immediately and return to her parents.

> *I don't recall what happened next other than that I picked up my son and a few clothes, got into the car and drove straight home to my mother in Peterborough, exhausted. Mothers have a way of knowing what to do. She gave me a glass of sherry, put me to bed and called the doctor.*

Mum's account describes how a Dr Wilson came to the house. He comforted her as best he could, advising her to move on with her life and try to forget the past. As far as her young son was concerned his suggestion was to try to see if I could be accepted as a boarder at the local grammar school. He promised to make enquiries.

Remarkably, my mother readjusted her life quickly because within two weeks she had found a job as the manageress of a dress shop in Rushden, a nearby market town. I was deposited at The King's School Boarding House.

Although I had no recollection of the dramatic events which had happened in Northampton a few weeks before, I was old enough to sense that something was wrong. At my grandparents' house, before she took me to The King's School, my mother would weep uncontrollably. At other times she was tense and angry. My continual questioning probably made matters even worse. I would keep asking why we had not returned to Northampton. I wanted to know where my father was. When I didn't get answers from my mother I asked my grandmother and grandfather, but was met with embarrassed silence. They tried to divert me by suggesting stories or games. Eventually I learned that my persistent questioning only led to unpleasantness. If I wanted my mother to love me, to cuddle me, I had to stay clear of any mention of my father, or Northampton.

The King's School, or the Peterborough Cathedral Grammar School as it was known then, was the best in town. It was for boys only, and at that time had a junior and a senior school. Boys boarded for a number of reasons. Some had parents in the armed or colonial services; others such as myself were from broken homes. The fees were more affordable than at public schools. The boarding house, Madeley House, was a large Edwardian building with a handsome façade, about two hundred yards from the main school. Day boys referred to it as the 'Pig and Whistle' – or just 'the Pig'. There were at least twelve spacious public rooms, servants' quarters, two large kitchens, a butler's pantry, and several bath and shower rooms.

My mother gave the impression that it was straightforward to get me admitted, but I learned later that this was far from the case. The school took boys from the professional and impoverished upper-middle classes, with preference given to those who had a clerical, military or academic background. Tony had served for a short time in the First World War but apart from that we had no connection with the armed forces, and certainly none with the church or academia. On the other hand, it was wartime and life in general was topsy-turvy. My mother was a determined woman who fought hard to get her own way. She aroused sympathy and used her charm unashamedly. This did not alter the fact that I was not yet five years of age and too young even to start lessons. My mother hoped that the matron and staff would look after me at the boarding house until I was old enough for classes that September.

In 1944 parents were charged tuition fees as well as board and lodgings, although they were quite modest. Nevertheless, this was a problem. My mother did not know how to suddenly find the extra money, or what sort of financial settlement Tony Chambers would agree to.

In any event, there was a formal procedure for admission to the school, something my mother was unprepared for. Normally applications were in writing and submitted several months in advance. The offer of a place depended on a successful interview with both the prospective pupil and his parents. My mother was confronted with a situation of which she had no experience. Characteristically, this did not deter her. She was a person of decisive actions and demanded immediate results. Dr Wilson had suggested The King's School as the solution, and as far as my mother was concerned that was the answer. All she had to do was convince the staff.

In 1944 the acting head was Mr Walter Francis Fairfax Shearcroft; the actual headmaster, the charismatic Harry Hornsby, was away on active service in the Far East. Mr Shearcroft was a quiet, scholarly gentleman who had written an erudite text on the origins of matter and related topics. He had reluctantly agreed to see my mother and for her to plead her case, but he was unprepared for her charm offensive and probably had never met anyone who would not take no for an answer. And so this reserved, elderly man was confronted by a young, pretty, theatrical lady who was determined to get her young son accepted. "Shearcroft didn't stand a chance," one of the older schoolmasters was alleged to have muttered at the time, adding, "We will never know exactly what went on in his study."

My mother had an ally in Lillian Hay, the matron of the boarding house. She was to become an important person in my life – a surrogate mother, almost. Mrs Hay was small in stature, but handsome with a kind nature and engaging smile. My mother's story had affected her deeply. She had also had an unhappy marriage and was separated from her husband, and saw her two sons only occasionally. Lillian was a principled lady with natural authority. If there was an injustice she had no hesitation in speaking out. Looking after me until I was ready for school was not an imposition, she had declared, pointing out, accurately, that the boarding house was vulnerable in terms of local educational support because in 1944 it housed only twelve boys, less than half the number that could be accommodated comfortably. This argument finally overcame opposition from the redoubtable Miss Wigner, head of the junior school.

Ruth Wigner, together with two other teachers, ran the junior school with efficiency and dedication. She was slim, of medium height, and wore a permanent severe expression. There were about eighty pupils attending the junior school, and a long waiting list. There was opposition to me jumping the queue, however deserving I may have seemed to be. Eventually, however, I was accepted largely because of Lillian Hay's insistence.

And so it was that my mother took me to Madeley House (*I dressed him in a rust-coloured outfit*, she wrote, somewhat whimsically). Unfortunately I was given no explanation, or prior warning, of what was about to happen to me.

After I was shown my bed in the dormitory where the three other boys were, Matron tidied away my few possessions and we went on a tour of the house. Lillian took my hand and I was taken to the spacious dining area, the games and prep room, and the maids' quarters at the back of the house. In the kitchen I was introduced to 'Cook'.

"Blimey," said Cook. "He's a bit young, isn't he? Taking in evacuees, are we?"

Lillian Hay ignored her remark. "His name is Barry, and he is missing his mother."

I must have started howling again, because Cook looked embarrassed and bent down, trying to wipe my eyes with her grubby apron.

"Would you like a sugar lump?" she said with a smile.

"Yes, please," I sobbed. We became friends after that.

Although it was cold, Matron took me into the garden. She explained that the lawn had originally been a tennis court, and told me the names of the trees at the back of the garden. The only one I remember is the mulberry. In years to come this would become my favourite spot for climbing and hiding from bullies.

As the days went by I kept on asking Matron where my mother was and when she would be coming back. Naturally, she could only give me evasive answers. This was not in her nature as Lillian Hay believed in honesty and straightforwardness.

The housemaster, Roland Jermy, also tried to cheer me up. He was a small, balding man with fine features and a bushy moustache, who laughed and chuckled as he talked. He helped Matron distract me with jokes and games. As the days passed and there was no sign of my mother returning, I became inconsolable. I would run to the same spot by the dormitory window where I could look along the drive, desperately hoping that my mother would appear. That would be my default position for the next few weeks. I would rush there every time I was lonely or upset. Sometimes I would panic, convinced she was dead in an air raid as, even in Peterborough, we could hear the German planes overhead and the sounds of distant anti-aircraft guns.

My mother told me later that she had phoned the boarding house a few days after leaving me there, but was advised by the matron not to visit for at least two months, but to send sweets and a present in a week or so.

Gradually I accepted the situation. Like a prisoner serving a long sentence, I eventually calmed down and began to adjust. During the day the house was quiet because the other boys were at school. I would usually play with Matron or one of the maids, sometimes going with them for a walk in the park opposite. My mother had not provided me with adequate clothes; there was a national shortage and rationing. In those 'make do and mend' days I had several hand-me-downs, mostly from a boy called Norman Andrews. Andrews (we did not call boys by their first names unless they were special friends) was about three years older than me and made it clear that I had usurped him in Matron's affections. I was called 'Matron's little pet', and taunted by the others. I longed for them to like me, and I started to become cheeky with the staff. Luckily they were too wise to take much notice of my childish behaviour. Matron continued with the task of turning me into a well-mannered, well-spoken child and gave me an informal preschool education. Looking back, I realise how privileged I was to have had such individual attention. In time I settled in and became more secure. Lillian Hay was always there to comfort me when I wept for my mother.

One morning in May, alone in Matron's room reading a comic, a boy shuffled in and said, rather sulkily, "You've to go downstairs. Someone's here to see you."

My heart bounded. I jumped up and ran down the big staircase. There was my mother. I burst into tears. All was confusion: joy in seeing her; anger at her leaving me for so long with no explanation.

"You are looking pretty, Mummy," I managed to say through my tears. My mother was wearing a colourful frock and a wide-brimmed hat.

"Do you like it, darling?" Then she picked me up and kissed and hugged me in a slightly possessive way, as if indicating to Matron, *Even though I left him with you, he is still my son.* After putting me down she twirled around, seeking my approval of her outfit. I fell silent. I did not know what to say.

"Have you been a good boy?" she said.

"Yes," I mumbled, choking back tears.

"And did you miss me?"

With that Matron intervened, seeing that I was distraught. "He missed you very much, Mrs Chambers. Now come away and we will have some tea."

During teatime my mother and the matron talked in whispers, but I heard that I was to be taken back to my grandmother's house for the weekend. My little case was packed and my mother and I set off in the Austin 7.

"Will Daddy be at Grandma's house?"

My mother abruptly stopped the car and looked at me crossly. "Barry, your father is wicked. He is a bad man. You are not to speak of him again. We are never going back to the house in Northampton. He and I are getting divorced."

I did not know what 'divorced' meant.

"You will have to stay at the boarding house meanwhile; you can come to see me in Rushden during the holidays."

I was pleased to see Grandma, Grandad and Aunty Joan. They had missed me, but my grandparents had been too shy to visit the boarding house. Aunty Joan was then about eleven. She was always kind, and we would become close over the years. She took me out to play at the local recreation ground. I was happy.

But after a short while the atmosphere in the house became tense. My mother was restless, talking quickly and in a loud voice. Suddenly she picked me up, gave me another hug and announced, "I have to go to Rushden and work."

"You have only been back a couple of hours!" Grandma exclaimed.

"I just can't stay here any longer. There is so much to do. Please take Barry back to school." With that my mother gave me a quick hug and kiss, strode out of the house and drove away. Our reunion had lasted only a few hours. I was dismayed.

Grandma was angry. "This is too bad," she said, putting on her faded blue coat and securing her hat with a long pin. "Barry, I will take you back to school."

We walked across town together. Grandma tried to soothe me, pointing out that things were not so bad. "Everything will be all right after the war. It won't be long now. Last week our soldiers invaded France, and soon they will be in Germany and that will be the end of Hitler and his gang. After that we will have lots of parties and games. Everyone will be happy."

"A boy at the boarding house said that after the war we will all get a bit of Hitler to eat. Is that true, Grandma?"

Grandma looked astonished and then smiled. "No, it is certainly not true. There wouldn't be enough of him to go round."

We both laughed.

1944–1945

Rushden

Dr Wilson's advice, that my mother should try to forget the past, urged her on. Slowly she began to see recent events more as an opportunity than a calamity. Following up on the advertisement she had seen in the local newspaper for a manageress of a dress shop, Mum phoned Rushden from the local post office and was called for an interview with a Mr Archie Kaufman, who owned several shops in the area.

Archie, an unmarried, middle-aged man, was immediately captivated by my mother. She, in turn, was fascinated by him. In Northampton, Mum had developed an affection for a neighbouring family called the Winklemans. They lived in constant fear of an imminent invasion and had shocked my mother with the horror stories coming out of Nazi Germany. Mum became intrigued with all things Jewish. This interest was more than curiosity. It had somehow taken a hold on her to the extent that she wanted to become a student of Judaism. Archie became her enthusiastic mentor.

In the document we found after my mother died, she had written:

Archie was the most wonderful person I ever met. He found me a flat with a bathroom and gave me more than enough money to educate my son, and all the clothes I ever needed. I wanted so much to learn about Jewish people. He taught me everything, good and bad. I learnt about various traditions in relation to religion, food and hygiene, and the meaning of Jewish holidays. He was my Pygmalion.

Archie became a father figure and enjoyed mentoring my mother. In any event, she became more and more fascinated by Judaism. For her it was a new world, almost exotic; a culture so different and so much richer than what she had previously experienced. Archie and his family probably knew about the break-up of her marriage but were kind and non-judgemental. Thus, my mother underwent a transformation and, after a while, began to act as if she *was* Jewish and wanted people outside of the family to *accept* she was Jewish. Being a bit of a drama queen, she found it exciting to masquerade as a Jewish lady. She could hide behind the mask; shield herself from the past. No more talking down to her. No more whispers about her betrayal by Tony Chambers.

Her job as a manageress was going well. My mother was confident. Her knowledge of dresses and fashion was proving useful. Under Mum's supervision Archie's shop was thriving, and he was delighted.

Archie had an elderly mother and a married sister. They invited Mum to their home for Shabbat dinner. *This was going to be the big test. I was going as a Jewish girl and he gave me full marks on the first Friday night. It was like a stage setting, and I was an actress.* The family were not particularly *frum* (meaning that they did not observe all the rituals and customs). My mother describes how, with her few Yiddish words and phrases taught by Archie, she acquitted herself well, enthusiastically joining in the lighting of the candles, the 'Shabbat shaloms', and the traditional hugging and kissing.

Mum became a regular visitor at Archie's home, and before long his mother set about matchmaking. As far as my mother's own romantic intentions were concerned, she wrote, *I was twenty-five and he was about fifty-five… after a while the relationship between me, Archie and his family was closing in on me… I was not mentally prepared for this. I wanted time to think.*

Reading all this in her document and learning about Archie Kaufman for the first time, I wondered what my mother actually told him about me and Tony Chambers. How was my existence explained to Archie's family? Although I have no recollection of meeting Archie, I still have memories of Rushden from the school holidays of 1944 and 1945. What I remember more than anything else are the Americans.

This is how my mother wrote about one of them:

There was a tall, handsome American soldier called Paul Fink. He was about my age, and Jewish to his fingertips in appearance and mannerisms. We enjoyed conversation and sex... a wonderful combination! After about two months he said he had written to his parents about me and told them that I would be a perfect wife and we intended to get married. They had replied saying we could be married again at their synagogue in Cleveland, Ohio, as we had planned a wedding in Rushden before Paul left for Germany. When I eventually told Paul I was not really Jewish he laughed and said, "Who the hell cares?" I took him to see my parents in Peterborough and for the next few months we visited them regularly. We took them lots of food (I think the PX stores suffered badly!). My parents and all the neighbours were never short of food.

What did they intend to do with me, I wondered? Was I also to go to Cleveland, Ohio? How was I explained to Paul's parents?

After a few months working for Archie, my mother decided to branch out on her own and opened a dress shop on Rushden High Street. She called it Joan's Dresses and Separates. The shop was set up and paid for by Archie and Tony Chambers, so my father must have made some sort of financial settlement, but Mum does not give any details.

Paul Fink also seems to have helped:

He took half a dozen GIs to paint the shop and the flat upstairs. It was all great fun. Paul then applied for a wedding licence, hoping we could get married after he returned from Germany. His commanding officer was against it, but he eventually got permission. He gave me a beautiful ring bought with money he had somehow managed to get from the US. He left for France in October 1944, but after he had gone I didn't really miss him. I had met several other Americans whose company I enjoyed as well. I sent Paul a long letter returning the ring.

I do have one recollection of Paul. I was back from school, and he was with my mother in the flat above the shop. He had a fine, smooth uniform with shining buttons and two rows of ribbons. Mum said, "Darling, come along and say hello to Paul. You will like him. He is Jewish."

"What is Jewish?" I said.

"Jewish, you know. He is a Jew."

I think I must have blushed and run away. Sometime later when we were alone I said to my mother, "How can that soldier be a Jew? Jews live in Palestine and have brown skin." (I was remembering the pictures in our children's Bible.) "My teacher said they killed Jesus."

I can't remember my mother's reaction. She probably did not think it was worthwhile explaining these things to a five-year-old.

The next man in her life was not Jewish at all. His name was Major Arthur Wigg.

His family were from the Newcastle area and his regiment was stationed near Rushden. We had a whirlwind romance. He took me back to meet his mother and sister in Newcastle. They lived in a beautiful country house. I was invited to stay on after the major was called back to his regiment. I needed a holiday. The family had a Jewish friend, a fighter pilot on leave who would 'pop by' from time to time. On the last night of my stay he took me out for dinner. I played the Jewish girl.

"Does Arthur know you are Jewish?" he said.

"You tell them if you think I am," I said to him.

"Well, it's the last day of your holiday. I think they should know."

"All right, I will tell them tomorrow, but only because you think I am."

I told Arthur's mother I was Jewish. She looked surprised. I then returned to Rushden. A few days later Arthur sent me a lovely ring; by that time he had been posted to Italy and so it was brought to me by one of his friends. Then I got a letter from Arthur's mother. It was affectionate and she said how much she had enjoyed having me to stay. But she was quite direct. She did not want Arthur to marry a Jewish girl.

Mum went into a fit of rage. Her first experience of anti-Semitism. I wonder how she got it out of her system. In her usual confrontational way, I would imagine. Intemperate letters were sent, and phone calls made to Arthur and his mother. *I hate that type of person*, she wrote. Thirty years later and she was still angry. Poor Mum, I thought. How confused she must have been.

What are my own recollections of those Rushden days? I remember the shop with its rows of dresses, and our flat above with its sitting room and leather sofa. I slept in a tiny room at the back which had a gaslight. Sometimes my mother would put me to bed and read a story to me, or just chat. I cannot recall having any friends, although the American soldiers and airmen (there always seemed to be a few in the shop) would sometimes sit on the floor and play with me. The one I remember vividly is Hank. Why did Mum not mention him in her writings? Did he just come under the heading of *several other Americans whose company I enjoyed*? When I first read my mother's account my heart raced because I hoped I would learn more about Hank. Handsome Hank, with his thick, black, curly hair, who lifted me high up to the ceiling. I would piggyback on his leather flying jacket and march up and down wearing his hat. Sometimes he was a lion, sometimes I was a tiger. He taught me to play Snap, and Snakes and Ladders, and told me about New York and its skyscrapers. Everything in America was the biggest in the world!

Hank was stationed at Podington, a large American airbase a few miles from Rushden. I wonder how many flying missions he made. Sometimes he came to the flat looking tired and did not want to play with me. He would just collapse on the sofa and fall asleep. Mum said I should leave him alone, but I just kept poking him with my fingers, trying to wake him. Then I balanced playing cards all over him. He turned and they scattered everywhere. Half awake, he shouted at me angrily. I did not understand. Why did he want to be alone with my mother? She said they wanted to "talk about the war". Why couldn't they talk about the war with me?

At Christmas in 1944 Santa Claus was exceedingly generous. I was given a fort with a hundred soldiers, and a toy yacht. The yacht was huge, about fifteen inches long. It had three sails. It was not as interesting as the fort because we only had a small bath to sail it in. I played with the fort for hours, often with Hank. But Hank was getting more irritable. Sometimes he would play with me, but more often he was moody and just wanted to sleep.

Years later I learnt that crew members of American bombers had to fly twenty-five missions before they could return home to the US. Their life expectancy was only eleven missions. If the stress got too much they were given amphetamines during the day and barbiturates at night. It must have been hell to raid Germany during the daytime and face the flack and the German fighter planes. If they got hit with firepower they could burn to death. Incredibly, airmen like Hank would often have to fly on raids twice a week. I learnt that the B-17s had no comforts except that the crew had to wear warm suits heated like an electric blanket. If they malfunctioned airmen would freeze to death as the temperature at thirty thousand feet was fifty degrees below zero. Sometimes their oxygen masks clogged up with ice and they would suffocate. Added to that were mid-air collisions, landing in the sea and loss of fuel. If they survived a mission the chances were that many of their buddies would not – the death of a friend could be unbearable. Did Hank tell my mother all this? Probably not. He would have wanted to forget, and Mum, well, she just wanted to have fun.

Two girls helped my mother in the shop. One was called Sonia, a refugee, but I did not know what that meant. She was kind and often took me shopping, or for a walk. Mum loved her shop and getting to know people in the gown business. From time to time she would go to London to collect stock. Years later, she told me about those trips. The train would take ages. It was always crammed with soldiers and there were frequent stops. During the day Mum would rush from one wholesaler to the next, collecting boxes of dresses. She was anxious to get to Marylebone Station and catch the train back to Rushden before dark. Sometimes she was caught up in an air raid and had to spend hours, sometimes all night, in a shelter. I never got the impression she was frightened. I think she found the war exciting.

It was a comfort to my mother that her parents and I were safe in Peterborough. The only casualties of war she knew were the airmen. During Easter of 1945 when I got back to Rushden for the holidays I sensed that something was wrong. Where was Hank? Mum said nothing. Sonia cried and came across the room to give me a hug. Another lady said that Hank was "in heaven". Mum abruptly changed the subject, saying she had a treat for me but I was to wait until the shop closed. I accepted the situation. I could play with my fort and my yacht by myself for a while.

I set off upstairs to find my toys. They were not in the cupboard. I looked everywhere, but to no avail. My mother eventually came upstairs.

"Where is my fort and my yacht?" I demanded.

She sat me on her knee and spoke in a quiet, serious voice. "Barry, this is a terrible war. There are lots of boys and girls who haven't got a mummy and daddy. They have no food and hardly any clothes."

"Where are these children?" I said. "I haven't seen any."

"They are in Germany," said my mother, beginning to get exasperated. "They wander around the streets of the bombed-out towns, tired and hungry."

"But what has this to do with my fort and yacht?"

"I have given them away to children who need them more than you. You must accept this, Barry, and be grateful for what you have. Don't cry. Let's go to the pictures tonight. We will see Rita Hayworth and I will buy you some sweets with coupons I have been saving up."

The thought of having my mother all to myself helped to dry my tears. Soon I had forgotten about Hank, and the fort and the yacht. We would chat about Rita Hayworth and always agree that although she was pretty, she was not as beautiful as my mother.

A few days later I came back to the flat after a walk with Sonia. There were stairs from the street which went directly up to the flat. I was told to go up alone as Sonia was needed in the shop. As I reached the top of the stairs I heard raised voices. I entered the room and there was Tony Chambers, my father. I had not seen him for several months. He gave me a sheepish grin and then turned to my mother to continue the argument. It was about money. Tony was accusing her of being un-businesslike.

"I sent you a lot of money," he said. "It should have been enough."

"It *was* enough!" she yelled back.

"Then why did you sell the fort and the yacht I gave him?"

1944–1945

The Pig and Whistle

Madeley House dated from the 1880s. It had been built by the Reverend Charles Richard Ball, who reigned over his Christian household, reading morning prayers for the servants each day after breakfast. The property went into decline after his death. In the mid-1930s, before it became The King's School Boarding House, it was a sanatorium.

I remember how in awe I was, the first time I went there with my mother. There were the coloured glass panels in the porch, and inside was the imposing hall leading to a broad staircase and a sturdy wooden gallery. How many times as a small boy would I look down at the tiled floor and its pink star patterns? Little did I realise that this large Victorian house with its stone mullions and leaded glass panes would be my home for the next thirteen years.

The house was generally shabby. The rooms were sparsely furnished with old pine tables, benches and rickety chairs. On the first floor there were three dormitories. Each one had five or six beds with hard iron frames and thin mattresses. In winter there was little heat. When it was raining hard, several buckets had to be placed strategically in the hall and gallery to catch the dripping water. The huge boiler in the cellar was fed with coke twice a day and required frequent de-clinkering – a task I got quite good at when I was older.

As the weeks and months passed I accepted the strict routine. The day began at 7.15am after the rising bell sounded. There was a general rush to the bathrooms. These were too few and too small to accommodate us all, and so we lined up, shivering in our pyjamas. We washed our hands, face and neck, brushed our teeth, combed our hair and polished our shoes before going downstairs. It was the worst time of the day. Would I be tidy enough? Would I be late? Would I be punished? It was also prime time for bullies. Sometimes my shoes would be hidden, my neatly combed hair ruffled, or my tie pulled down.

Breakfast was at 7.45am, with a warning bell five minutes earlier. Nails and shoes were inspected and general tidiness assessed by a prefect before entering the dining room. We sat on benches at long wooden tables waiting for Mr Jermy to enter and say grace. The food would arrive on large platters, with each boy being allocated a small sample of whatever was on offer; a piece of bacon, an egg, a half-slice of fried bread. On Sundays there were tiny kippers. Standard fare was lumpy porridge from a large tureen. There was an adequate supply of bread and margarine, but no marmalade or jam (boys were expected to supply their own). We drank weak, milky tea from cracked mugs. Strict silence was observed at all meals.

Mr Jermy sat in some splendour at the head of the first table. He had a tablecloth, a silver coffee pot, a toast rack, silver cutlery and a linen napkin with an ivory ring. Unlike the rest of us he was served hot, crispy toast. His crunching could be heard all around the room. A particular source of envy was his bowl of marmalade, which he dipped into from behind the *Daily Telegraph*. If Mr Jermy was moved by current events he did not seem to show it. The war was not discussed. One morning in early June he told us, gravely, that all bicycles were to be inspected for roadworthiness during the dinner break. He failed to mention that a few hours previously the Allies had landed on the Normandy beaches. After the various domestic announcements he would slowly fold his newspaper. Another short grace would end the meal and we were released to prepare for school.

We went off to make our beds and generally tidy up. For the matron, who rose at six each day, this would be her busiest time.

Many problems needed attention: torn clothing, a sick boy, a child in distress after receiving a letter from home, a lost homework book, a grumpy cook, and other items both trivial and more serious.

In September of 1944 I joined Year 1 of the junior school. Lillian Hay was quite emotional, waving me goodbye dressed in my new uniform – a grey flannel jacket, jumper, socks, short trousers, and a grey-and-maroon cap and tie. An older boy accompanied me down the road to the main school. There the strict and unsmiling Miss Wigner would take us in charge and the day's lessons would begin with prayers and hymns. Miss Wigner was a competent and confident pianist. We sang rousing favourites such as *Fight the Good Fight* or *Eternal Father, Strong to Save*, all in keeping with the mood of the time. The prayers were for our brave soldiers, sailors and airmen. We prayed for King and Country and deliverance from our enemies. We were told we had nothing to fear because Jesus would save us.

By and large I enjoyed the lessons, at least in the junior school. Sums and writing were easy since I had been well prepared by Lillian Hay. On Friday afternoon we had Cubs supervised by the beautiful Miss Beaumont with her dark skin, blue eyes and slender body. I managed to survive PE even though I was small and weedy. My birthday being in June, I was always the youngest in the class and usually ignored by my classmates. Sometimes Miss Wigner would play the piano for us. On these occasions she would lose her half-frown and become pensive. Many years later I discovered that Ruth Wigner was of German extraction. During those war years she must have been constantly sad and anxious.

My mother telephoned once a week, usually on a Sunday evening. None of the other boys' parents rang, which I found awkward. The old-fashioned telephone, shaped like a table lamp with the earpiece hung on the side, was set in a tiny closet at the end of the hall. Matron disapproved of these calls, feeling they were far too extravagant, and she did not understand why my mother did not write more often, like the other parents. In any event, Lillian

Hay did not like the telephone and always got a bit flustered when the operator said, "Please stay on the line; you have a trunk call from London."

It was on the telephone when I usually broke down, sobbing endlessly into the mouthpiece. "I hate it here. Nobody likes me," I wailed.

"Don't be silly," my mother would say. "The matron is a wonderful and kind person. Surely you have everything you need. And don't upset *me*," she would add. "How can I work to pay for your school fees if you keep telling me you are unhappy?"

"But I want to live with you at home. Why can't I?"

"You know that is not possible."

"Why isn't it possible?" I sobbed.

Changing the subject, my mother would tell me what she was wearing, which did not interest me. *She does not want me at home*, I thought, *because I am in the way. Why am I in the way?* It did not make sense.

Matron always sensed I was upset after these telephone encounters and gave me a hug, attempting to console me. It was never enough. I ran away from her, wanting to be alone. I did not want to show any weakness in front of the other boys. Crying was an invitation for teasing and bullying. Instead I would cry myself to sleep, but as quietly as possible, hoping the others would not hear me. Often another boy would be sobbing. Then I didn't feel quite so alone.

Agonising homesickness and longing for my mother was always with me. When she began to write instead of telephoning, her letters were just marked *Barry*. When the postman dumped all the mail on the large hall table my post would be quickly grabbed by Lillian Hay because she knew other boys would want to know why my letters were not addressed to Master Barry Chambers. After my mother married Harry Kay in 1946 she wrote *Barry Kay* on the envelope; she could never bring herself to write Chambers. The school had told my mother that it would be better if she continued to use my real father's name to avoid confusion for the staff and embarrassment for me. Mum ignored this. Having reinvented herself, she was going to reinvent me. Even in the document I found after her death, my mother could not bring herself to write the name Chambers correctly, referring to Tony as Tony Chalmers.

1946–1947

Enter Harry Kay

The dress shop did not last long. By the end of 1945 my mother was tired of Rushden. She loved London. After each trip to the capital to buy stock she had become more excited about the possibility of living there. The war had ended. The Americans were going home and life in Rushden was dull.

Initially, she rented a small bed-sitting room in Nottingham Place in the Marylebone area. At school holidays and half-term I would be put on the train at Peterborough and my mother would meet me at King's Cross. I cried with relief when I saw her. During the long holidays I returned my ration card to her, but at half-term we were given tiny packets by the school cook. These contained a weekend's supply of tea, butter, margarine, sugar and cheese. My mother thought it absurd for the school to go to all this trouble. She did not appreciate that it was the law in those strict rationing days that children either took their ration cards or, if only away for a few days, were entitled to proportionate amounts of these basic groceries. Other boys' parents were grateful for what little extra they could get, especially if they had large families. My mother, on the other hand, was contemptuous of those who adhered strictly to rules, and fearful that a knob of butter could stain her dress. So she just laughed when I handed her the package and promptly threw it away.

Nevertheless, like everyone else, Mum had to register her ration card with tradesmen in the nearby shops in Paddington Street.

I was soon running errands to the baker shop where a kind lady would carefully cut out the coupons. She would hand over the loaf together with a crust or bun just for me.

I was overwhelmed and frightened by London. There were bomb sites everywhere. Sometimes a long row of houses would be reduced to rubble. Pink willowherb colonised the dead buildings. Compared to Peterborough, the main streets were crowded. Some people were still in uniform, and there were unfamiliar black faces. It seemed as if almost everyone was smoking, or wished they were smoking. Not only tramps, but respectable-looking people would occasionally stoop to pick up a cigarette end. My mother was hardly ever without a lighted cigarette, sometimes with an ebony or silver holder. When we drove around in her little Austin 7 the interior of the car would be thick with smoke. I coughed and felt sick.

I was fascinated by the barrow boys with their displays of shining, tempting fruit. They were always looking over their shoulder in case a policeman appeared and moved them on.

Mum wrote:

In 1946 I came to London hoping to find a Jewish businessman who would marry me. Quite a hard task! One day when Barry was home from school we went to Marylebone High Street to buy a radio as mine was old and broken. The shop owner, a Mr Harry Kay, obligingly offered to come around to my flat to install the set. He stayed on, talking for about three hours. As he was leaving he offered to take Barry to a football match the following day, and also invited both of us for dinner. I was thrilled. I had met a tall, handsome Jewish man who owned a business and who was clearly taken with me. It was the most wonderful thing that could happen to us. Barry loved every minute of his holiday with Harry Kay. I loved Harry for his gentleness. We were married ten weeks later.

The marriage took place in Chelsea Town Hall on 26th October 1946. I have never seen a photograph of the event and I do not know who was there. In 2016, out of curiosity, I wrote away for a copy of their marriage certificate. It records that Harry Kay, a thirty-two-year-old bachelor and radio dealer, of Flat A9, Sloane Avenue Mansions, married Eva Pearcy (not Pearcey?), a twenty-eight-year-old spinster. So my mother did not describe herself as Eva Chambers, divorcee. Why did she spell her maiden name incorrectly, dropping the second E? Was this just carelessness or an attempt to fudge the issue of Tony Chambers, fearful that the authorities would catch up with her regarding her previous bigamous marriage?

What about the wedding itself? Who would have been there? Harry's parents were Orthodox Jews. They would have seen through Mum immediately. His sister Betty may have come along, and maybe Harry's dodgy Welsh friend Leo Marle. Who would Mum have asked? Not me – that would have been impossible. How could she explain me and keep up her Jewish pretence? What about her sister Joan, who would have been only fifteen and still at school? Maybe my mother said, "Let's elope; it will be so romantic." Someone in the register office would have been the witness. The happy couple would probably have gone for a wedding feast – but where, in 1946? In the summer of the following year they did have a belated two-week honeymoon in Viareggio. A photograph from the time shows my mother in a bikini, looking happy and glamorous.

I heard the news of the marriage at school a few days later, and I think I felt happy. My mother was correct in saying that I loved being with Harry Kay in London during those early days. I was desperate to be like the other boys at school and have a proper father. Anyone without a father needed a good excuse. Being killed in the war was acceptable, but divorce was not. For me, not having a father – or rather, having a father who had been 'blotted out' – was a source of deep embarrassment. My mother told me repeatedly that my real father was wicked. No reason was given, but I must never speak of him. Harry Kay was now my father, and I was to call him

Dad. So I could now go back to school and tell the other boys that I did in fact have a father. Unfortunately, they were unimpressed.

"You can't just come back after the holidays and say you have found a father," one of the nastier ones remarked.

I insisted, tearfully, that he was wrong. Not only did I have a father, but we also had a new home. I would have preferred it had we lived in a house rather than a small flat (all the other boys lived in houses), but this would have to do. Anyway, it was London and things were different there. "Everywhere outside of London is provincial," my mother would often remark.

The emotional precariousness of my situation was brought home to me one day when Miss Beaumont, our form teacher, gave us an exercise in which we were asked to write down our different roles as we went about our daily tasks. She gave an example: "Yesterday I was a cyclist, a cook, a companion, a pedestrian and a shopper, as well as a teacher, of course. What are all the different roles that, say, your father might have played yesterday, or indeed any other day?"

We chewed on our pencils and looked at the ceiling. Some boys began to write. This, I thought, could be my chance to impress my peers and Miss Beaumont with my account of Harry Kay. I wanted to say that he was, well, heroic, but all I could write down, or at least what I thought I wrote, was that he was a friend. The exercise books were gathered in, and Miss Beaumont studied them and suddenly let out a shriek of laughter.

"Barry Chambers says his father is a fiend!" she exclaimed.

The class convulsed into fits of giggling. Miss Beaumont thought it was so hilarious that she felt compelled to share the story with her colleagues. When news of the incident got back to Lillian Hay, the matron, she did not think it at all amusing and reminded Miss Beaumont of the special sensitivity of my situation. Thanks to Lillian Hay, the teasing subsided, but only after several days of torment.

I told Dad about the 'fiend' incident the next time I was home from school. He thought it was amusing. But then, he saw the good side of everything. Everyone liked Harry Kay. He was kind, gregarious and loved to chat. It was not surprising that he had so many friends, because he was interested in other human beings and was an attentive listener.

Harry was born in 1914, the son of Solomon Kay, a leather manufacturer and an Orthodox Jew. The family name was Kruschinsky. They were from the Ukraine and had fled to England after the 1905 Kiev Pogrom. Harry had a sister called Betty who was kind to me, although she was suspicious that my mother and, therefore, I were not Jewish. Academically Harry seems to have done well as a boy. He attended St Marylebone Grammar School and was awarded a scholarship to the London Polytechnic but did not take it up. Instead he left school at sixteen because he had to earn money. For a while he was a bookie's runner, something I did not know until he died in 1990. As a young man he was left wing politically and joined the Communist Party in the 1930s. He got involved in anti-fascist rallies against Oswald Mosley and his Blackshirts in the East End. By the time he met my mother his politics were less radical, but he was still a committed socialist and an admirer of Clement Attlee and the new Labour government.

Harry was twenty-six years old when war broke out. Although a tall, well-built, handsome man, he was also a bit of a hypochondriac. As a child he had contracted rheumatic fever, and he had a heart murmur which exempted him from military service. Instead he served in the London Fire Brigade. This seems to have become his 'university', because when he and his companions were not fighting fires they held political discussions and writing groups, and performed amateur dramatics. One photograph embedded in my memory is of Dad playing King John, wearing a ludicrous beard and a cardboard crown. He never talked about his experiences in the Blitz. When questioned about that time he would become pensive. I think Dad must have witnessed some terrible scenes.

Harry Kay's best friend was a larger-than-life Welshman called Leo Marle. Like my stepfather, Leo was tall and muscular. He had thick, curly black hair and a fruity, musical accent. They seem to have been quite a pair. Mum did not care much for Leo. She was suspicious of his previous bachelor life with Harry, thinking he was a bad influence. She was probably right.

They made frequent trips to the film studios in Pinewood and Ealing and signed on as extras in crowd scenes; Dad mentioned *The Lady Vanishes* and *Fanny by Gaslight*. A highlight was Dad's appearance in *The Man in Grey* starring James Mason; he had a small part in the opening scene as a bidder at an auction. One day the director singled him out and asked him to breathe heavily into a microphone for as long as he could. When the film was released he heard his voice in a scene where the heroine was in labour!

Dad was a laid-back sort of person who was not easily roused and tried to avoid arguments. He was contemptuous of the police because he said they had sided with the Blackshirts during the East End riots. He had witnessed police brutality first hand and believed that they were all basically anti-Semitic. Even as a seven-year-old I realised there was something slightly dodgy about my stepfather. I did not understand his lack of respect for authority. After all, at school we were taught to always obey policemen, and indeed anyone in uniform. Dad took the opposite view. Take the circus incident, for example.

It was 1947 and as usual I went home from school by train for the Christmas holidays. Mum and Harry met me at King's Cross Station. I noticed there were posters everywhere for Bertram Mills' circus at Olympia. It looked wonderful.

"Can we go to the circus?" I blurted out.

"Impossible," said Mum. "It has been sold out for months, and anyway it's far too expensive."

"Hold on," said Dad. "I can get tickets."

"Can you?" Mother was doubtful.

"Of course."

"I hope you are not raising the boy's hopes without good reason."

"You just see," he said.

A few days later Dad announced, "Right, we are going to the circus. Get your coat. We are off to Olympia."

My mother, who at that time was seven months pregnant, showed little interest and preferred to stay behind.

When we entered the vast Olympia arena, Harry began to look anxious. "Actually, I haven't got any tickets," he mentioned casually. "But don't worry. I know a man who will find us some."

I was desperately disappointed and started to cry. Dad told me to wait by one of the entrances to the big top. Then I saw him in the distance, talking to one of the attendants who was splendidly uniformed with medals and gold braid. Although I did not know it at the time, Dad was doing his usual routine. He was trying to convince the official that even if the event was sold out, there were always a few unoccupied seats for one reason or another. According to Harry, it was just a matter of a discrete transfer of cash and we would be let in. My mother told me later that this strategy almost always worked. Unfortunately, on this occasion it did not! I could see the official looking very cross and shaking his finger at Dad. After a while he wandered back, a shy grin on his face, explaining that he had arranged to collect the tickets here at Olympia but had been let down. "Never mind," he said. "We will see something."

Suddenly the band started playing and there was a huge roar from inside the tent. The show had started. I was now in floods of tears, but as we ambled around the perimeter of the big top we found ourselves at the mouth of the main tunnel leading into the ring. After a while the lights lowered and the audience fell quiet. There were lots of gasps. At this point Harry grabbed my hand and said, "Let's go in." I was terrified, but longed to see something of the circus. He pulled me down the tunnel, almost to the edge of the ring. Nobody noticed us as all eyes were fixed on the ceiling. A man was riding a bicycle upside down and trapeze artists were flying through the air.

We stared up for a good five minutes and then the show up by the tent ceiling ended and the floodlights were directed to the tunnel where we were standing. Before my dad could drag me away, horses and riders in beautiful uniforms galloped past a few feet in front of us. Four strongmen followed carrying dumb-bells. There were dwarfs dressed as babies, a bear riding a scooter, and brightly coloured clowns. A huge stagecoach appeared, pulled by six white horses. There was hardly room for it to get along the tunnel. Dad and I pressed our backs hard to the wall of the tent. We were lucky not to get trampled.

Suddenly the same uniformed man that Harry had dealt with previously shouted at us from the other end of the tunnel. "'Ere, what do you think you're doing?" At the first opportunity we made a quick exit.

When we got to safety, Dad said triumphantly, "Well, you can tell your mother you went to the circus after all."

Had I, I thought? It was true I had seen some of the circus through the 'back door', and that it was thrilling. But we did not have proper seats – that was cheating. We had only spent a crafty few minutes in the big top before being chased away. This was not 'going to the circus'. It was underhand. I could not tell the boys back at school, or the boarding house staff, what we had done. They would have thought that sneaking into a circus tent without paying was deceitful. I decided to keep quiet about the whole episode. I was not going to boast about my visit to Olympia; on the contrary, I felt ashamed.

As far as I remember, Mum and Harry's first year of marriage was happy, although life was hard in those post-war years and the restrictions and rationing were wearisome. Harry introduced Mum to horse and dog racing, which she found exciting. For a while Harry was an agent for Keith Prowse, the theatre ticket agency, and so they managed to get into several West End shows either free or for very little. Mum loved glamour and the high life, dressing up and going out. It must have been restrictive for her when, after just a few months of marriage, she became pregnant.

The pregnancy did not go well. Apart from being uncomfortable, Mum was needy and complaining. Just before I went back to school there was a frightening domestic scene. Her mood swings, always in the background, were getting worse. Arguments usually began with unfounded accusations phrased in the most hurtful way. Mum would accuse Harry of infidelity, lack of affection, incompetence and worse. Then she would get violent and throw objects. Harry had no idea how to deal with these outbursts. If he stayed around he would be humiliated and attacked physically. If he left the flat he would dread what she might do if left alone. There was no question of calling for help because apart from the fact that they did not know any of the neighbours, there was the shame of having someone in the family who might have a mental illness. Mercifully, things usually calmed down after a few hours, but each episode would inevitably be followed by a low period when my mother would sit with her head in her hands, occasionally looking up to light another cigarette.

Although I did not appreciate it at the time, being just a young boy, my mother was showing signs of manic-depressive, or bipolar, illness. For women with this predisposition there is a high probability that pregnancy will trigger episodes of mania and/or depression. Things would get worse after my sister's birth.

1947

Christmas

"One of the joys of being a Christian is Christmas," Miss Wigner liked to exclaim when we were in junior school. This statement heralded the Advent countdown and Bible stories of the shepherds and the three wise men.

Lillian Hay, on the other hand, was not particularly interested in the religious side of Christmas, even though her father was a Scottish minister. But she enjoyed taking me to Sheltons, the local department store, to see Santa Claus. I was told to go into his grotto and sit on his knee and tell him what I wanted for Christmas. I was frightened. Father Christmas was holding me too tightly. I could smell the beer and cigarettes on his breath. I kicked and screamed and ran out. Lillian looked disappointed. Nevertheless, she made Christmas fun and exciting. We made paper chains from old newspapers and smelly glue heated by the fire. Decorations were hung, presents were made, carols rehearsed and the Christmas party prepared for. I was taught to knit and managed to make a cotton dishcloth for my mother. She was thrilled. In fact she cried when she opened it and gave me a long hug. I did not understand why it had made her so emotional.

The Christmas carol concert was a big event. Parents came along and I had a solo to sing; one verse of *The Holly and the Ivy*. I was so anxious at the rehearsal that I wet my trousers. It was all right on the night; my mother was there, dressed extravagantly as usual. Other boys' parents stared at her, partly with envy but mostly with disapproval; after all, clothes were strictly rationed. Where did she obtain the material for such a lavish get-up, they must have wondered?

The end-of-term Christmas party was a triumph of ingenuity over austerity. We ate jam tarts, blancmange and jelly. Mr Jermy lifted me up on the table and asked me to sing. I gave them a rendition of *You Are My Sunshine*, my mother's favourite. The audience roared their approval. Lillian Hay beamed. Others recited poetry or played a party piece on the piano. At a critical moment we all tiptoed down the hall without making a sound and, at the signal from Mr Jermy, gave a hearty three cheers for Cook and the kitchen staff. Everyone was happy. When we broke up and went home on about the 20th December, Miss Wigner reminded us that the school festivities were just a prelude to all the wonderful things that were going to happen on Christmas Day.

I loved the run-up to Christmas, although as the years went by I learned to be apprehensive about Christmas Day itself. At the boarding house we were swept up in the excitement generated by matron, who enthused about Santa Claus (whom I believed in until I was about seven or eight). On the other hand, the junior school mistresses, particularly Miss Wigner, reinforced the Christmas story, and there was usually a nativity play in which I took a small part. So I returned to my mother and Harry in a magic cloud, thinking of baby Jesus and expecting that *all the bells on earth shall ring on Christmas Day in the morning*.

In the Rushden days, before my mother met Harry, Christmas was a fairly happy time, particularly the year I was given the fort and the yacht. There were parties above the shop and the coming and going of American airmen, all of whom showered me with 'candy'. When I was eight my mother and Harry moved into a small, rented basement flat in Luxborough Street, just off the Marylebone Road across from *Madame Tussaud's*. It was there that my mother's moods became my main source of anxiety. They became more florid. Christmas was an added strain for her to cope with. To be fair, she did pull out a few stops. Oranges, dates, nuts and Christmas crackers would appear, and usually there was a small tree with decorations. On Christmas Eve I waited for the snow to fall and for the sound of celestial angels singing carols. On the day itself my expectation was that church bells would ring out loudly, people in the street would hold hands and dance in circles, and mince pies and nuts would be handed out at street corners whilst everyone wished each other a merry Christmas.

The reality was different. When I peered up from the window of our basement flat it was usually overcast and drizzling. The few people in the street would walk by briskly with long faces and their heads down. On the other hand, Father Christmas did visit; my stocking was filled with a paper pad, pencils and crayons, a comic and an orange. By my bed was a large parcel, to which a message was attached. It was written in red lipstick in large capital letters and read:

Dear Barry,
    I have brought you presents – but your mother paid for them. Be a good boy.
    Love, Father Christmas.

My main present that year was a dartboard with six darts, three red and three blue. I put it on the floor against the wall and practised hitting the bullseye. My aim was poor, and the darts were quite blunt and did not stick well. But it was fun. Just as I was throwing a dart particularly hard, my mother, who was seven months pregnant, came into the bedroom. It missed her leg by a few inches and impaled itself on the skirting board.

"What a crazy present to buy him," she shrieked at Harry. "He will have someone's eye out in no time."

"Don't be silly. The boy has got to learn."

"Got to learn? Got to learn?! He nearly stabbed me."

"You have to be very careful with these darts," Dad said. Coming past her into the room, he gave me instructions on how to hold and throw them. "Put the flight in front of your nose and never throw from further back, otherwise you will hurt someone."

It was good advice, but difficult in practice. The dart would often leave my hand too soon and go flying upwards to the ceiling. My father looked pained, and from his expression it was clear that he too was having second thoughts about the wisdom of buying me this present.

There was no time to be wasted, however, because the Christmas dinner had to be prepared. We were having guests – Dad's radio business partner Mr Gross, with his wife and their son Ahron. They were expected about twelve. Although it was 1947, a time of considerable austerity and rationing, Harry had managed to procure a turkey; admittedly a small one, but a rare treat nonetheless. My mother, who hardly ever entered the kitchen, was nevertheless surprisingly skilled at cooking traditional meals.

The guests arrived. I did not know Ahron well, having only met him briefly a couple of times at the radio shop. I told him excitedly about my dartboard and the possibility of a game in my bedroom when we had finished dinner. The roasted turkey was produced, held aloft by my mother and then gently placed in the middle of the table amidst squeals of delight. Harry's eyes bulged as he seized the carving knife and fork with glee. Ernest Gross looked on with a dignified smile.

"You and I will have the legs, Ernie," said Harry.

"No, no. Give them to the boys," replied Mr Gross.

"Absolutely. Quite right," chimed in my mother.

"Of course the boys must have the legs," added Mrs Gross.

Harry gave a gruesome grin of disbelief. His hands were almost trembling with disappointment as he set about carving.

Little was said during the meal and it was a relief when Ahron and I were excused from the table and repaired to my tiny bedroom for our game of darts. All was going well and, mostly, we managed to hit the board. But the darts got blunter and the feathers started to disintegrate. Whilst aiming, and out of frustration, I suddenly pulled my arm right back behind my ear and hurled the truncated arrow towards the board. But it left my hand too soon and smashed into Ahron's spectacles and attached itself to his left temple. He cried out in terror. Luckily the dart quickly detached itself from his skin and slid gently to the floor. A little blood oozed from the superficial wound. The left-hand side of the frame of his glasses was scratched but not seriously damaged.

The howl from Ahron penetrated the whole flat, and his mother immediately rushed in, followed by the others.

"What have you done to my boy?" wailed Mrs Gross. "Darts, is it? What madness, giving a small boy a lethal weapon!" Trembling, she wiped Ahron's bleeding forehead with her handkerchief.

"How could you?" my mother screamed at me. She grabbed all the darts and put them in her handbag.

"Perhaps we should call a doctor," Mr Gross said.

"He will be all right," said Harry, anxious to downplay the damage.

Mrs Gross hugged Ahron tighter, muttering, "My poor boy! My poor boy!" (Ahron would not last five minutes at The King's School Boarding House, I thought, but I was not stupid enough to say that.)

"We must take him home," said a grim-looking Mr Gross, and with that they grabbed Ahron and their coats.

"That is the end of your dart games," said my mother after they left. "These will be confiscated." She patted her bag.

The departure of the Grosses did not seem to upset my parents too much as I knew, from overhearing their conversations from time to time, that they found them tedious.

Harry's preoccupation was with the turkey legs. "How can you have let this happen," he accused my mother, "giving the legs to the boys? I paid good money on the black market for that bird – and you give the legs to two small boys!"

"That's enough," said my mother. "All you think about is your stomach."

The argument continued, with shouting and recriminations. Harry tried to laugh it off, but he never forgot. Twenty years later he was still talking about it.

1948

Leap-Year Sister

My mother's labour and convalescence were stormy. Harry said she was "very hysterical" and needed plenty of calming down. Eventually I received a letter at school informing me that I had a baby sister called Penelope. Mum said her birth was *the most important thing in our lives*. I received the news with mixed feelings. I did not want any dilution of my mother's affection, but on the other hand the arrival of a sister meant we were more like a normal family. The importance of the event was reinforced by a newspaper cutting my mother put in the post for me. The *Daily Mirror* had thought it newsworthy to print a picture on the first page of the five babies born at Queen Charlotte's Hospital, Hammersmith, on the 29th February 1948. 'Baby Kay' was the middle one. That was my first glimpse of my sister, Penelope Ann, a leap-year baby who had made it into a national newspaper on her first day of life.

A few weeks later Matron received a telephone call from my mother asking whether I could come home to London for the weekend. A party had been arranged at the flat to celebrate my sister's arrival. Lillian Hay was not happy about me going home during term time and did not like being put on the spot by a phone call. After all, it was not an emergency or a bereavement. My mother was told it was "quite irregular" but pleaded with Matron, and eventually the housemaster, Mr Jermy, the only one who could give permission, relented and I was given two days off to go home.

The Luxborough Street flat was cramped and dingy and I hated it. On the wall of the gloomy entrance was a timer switch that operated a dim light, making it just possible to see the stairs going down. Inside the flat there was a small sitting room with a tiny spare bedroom at the front. The main bedroom and bathroom were at the back, looking into a dark inner well. Only one person at a time could stand in the mini kitchen.

The party took place towards the end of March. Lillian took me to the station. No arrangements were made to meet me at King's Cross; I was to make my own way to the flat by Underground. Even as an eight-year-old I was capable of doing this. I liked travelling on the Tube. In those days it was easy to negotiate and hardly ever too crowded. When I arrived at the flat and rang the bell, the door was opened by a small man with a dark suit and a foreign accent.

"Who are you, my boy?"

"I'm Barry," I said. "I live here."

"Oh, it's Barry,'" he said, somewhat surprised, as if he was not expecting a small boy wearing a school cap and a blazer.

I pushed past him to find my mother. The flat was crammed full of people. I squeezed through to the sitting room and there she was, holding baby Penny.

"Come and see your new sister," my mother said proudly.

I stared down at the bundle and tried to look excited. Mum gave the baby a little hug and kiss, and then was distracted by one of the guests. I had got her attention for a few seconds only. I wondered why Grandma and Grandad were not there. One or two guests ruffled my hair and joked with me. I wanted to talk about my school and tell them about my teachers.

"Ours is a cathedral school. We go there and sing hymns and psalms twice a week."

Nobody seemed interested. Some seemed oddly embarrassed. There was no one to talk to. Dad said he had to talk to the guests and would chat to me soon. Had I come all the way from Peterborough just to be ignored?

I grew restless and went into the spare room where I slept when at home from school. There was a row of bottles on top of the cabinet. From time to time a guest would enter the room to fill a glass. I looked at the assortment of bottles – gin, cherry brandy, egg flip, brown ale and cider. There were unfinished glasses on the sideboard. Out of a mixture of boredom and curiosity I decided to sample the various drinks on offer. I hated the gin but thought the cherry bandy was quite nice. The egg flip was sickly and had a nasty metallic taste. The brown ale was awful but the cider, which was quite sweet, was tasty. My head began to swirl. A man came into the room.

"Please tell Mummy I am not well."

My mother came into the room and saw me lying down on the bed, crying.

I was drunk.

1948

Harry Hornsby

I was proud of my school. Ruth Wigner told us it had been founded by Henry VIII.

"King's is a grammar school," she said. "In the old days, grammar was not writing and spelling, but Latin and Greek. You will learn Latin and Greek when you get to senior school," she added hopefully.

"Henry was a good king," she remarked. "Before he did away with the monasteries, the people were Catholics. Now we are Protestants, which means we can pray directly to God rather than through the Pope in Rome. The Pope is a foreigner, which is a bad thing!"

Unfortunately the school had a chequered financial history. It was permanently short of money, had few endowments, and on several occasions had been on the verge of insolvency. With little money for improvements, our surroundings were dreary.

In the old days the pupils were choristers and the school was located in the cathedral's Minister Precincts. The dean and chapter provided funding. In 1853 it moved about a mile away to its present buildings in Park Road. We were fortunate to have a large playing field next to the school which was surrounded by handsome horse chestnut trees.

King's took in boarders, which was unusual for a grammar school. When I joined as a four-year-old in 1944, it was still independent. The fees were forty-five pounds a year. There were the usual extras, such as the school uniform and sports kit. My mother's letters invariably contained some reference to the school fees. *I am working so hard to pay them,* she wrote. This may have been so in the early days, although she implied in the document we found after her death that Archie Kaufman, and even Tony Chambers, helped financially with school expenses.

With the Butler Education Act and the eleven-plus examination, tuition fees were abolished but my parents were still invoiced for my board and lodgings, which at the time were thirteen pounds and thirteen shillings per term. Mum did not make a distinction between subsistence and tuition fees. To her they were all 'school fees' – a sort of unfair burden she perpetually had to struggle with.' Of course if I had lived at home she would still have had to clothe and feed me.

My mother never conceded that dumping me in a boarding school at the age of four may have had long-term deleterious effects on me, not to mention the immediate trauma this would have had on any young child. In fact her attitude was just the reverse. She felt triumphant that she had managed to place me in a good school, and from then on, right into my adult life, Mum would expect gratitude from me for her enormous financial sacrifice. It is true that at first she felt anxious about 'the fees', even with help from Archie and my father. Later on, when the business was going well, she could easily afford them. Furthermore, it was convenient for me to be away at boarding school. I did not have to be explained to her Jewish friends.

Every boy was expected to be kitted out with sports clothes – running shoes, sports vest and shorts, socks and so forth. I never seemed to have the full set and often had to borrow from other boys, which I hated because they often refused. I could easily have asked Matron for a chit to take to the school outfitter to get what I needed, but I knew the bill would eventually arrive at home and my mother would kick up a fuss.

In 1948 there were three hundred day boys and twenty boarders at the school. The headmaster, Harry Hornsby, had returned from war service in 1945. He had arrived back in Peterborough in the early hours and, not wanting to wake anyone, slept in a wheelbarrow rather than ring the school bell. Consideration for others was one of the many fine qualities associated with this extraordinary man. Hornsby was every boy's hero: charismatic, enterprising, a keen sportsman, with inexhaustible energy and the gift of remembering every boy's name. Oxford educated, he had taught at Christ's Hospital before taking the headship of The King's School in 1939. During the war he trained Gurkhas in India and Burma, saw active service, was mentioned in dispatches and received an MBE.

Being a small boy in a large school I only once had one-to-one contact with the headmaster. It was his custom to invite boarders, in groups of four, to take breakfast with him and his wife in their flat in the main school building on Sunday mornings. We arrived at his door at 7.30am and sat down to a feast of bacon, eggs and toast – total luxuries in those immediate post-war years.

He chatted to each boy in turn, drawing us out. "How long have you been with us now, Barry? It must be almost three years."

"Yes, sir," I said, delighted he had noticed me.

"Last term Mary and I enjoyed the junior school play. I think it was called *Why the Mice were Blind*, and you were a mouse, or was it a fairy?"

"A fairy, sir."

"Ah, yes, a fairy. What fun it was," he said, looking at me warmly and laughing.

Then, with no more ado, he announced what we had all been waiting for – the game of mah-jong. From a sideboard he produced the magic box with its engraved tiles. Older boys, who had previously been to breakfast with the head, had taught us the elementary rules, so we got off to a flying start. We all knew about a *pung* and a *chow* and how to build the Great Wall of China. I was the East Wind and luckily managed to get a set, and cried out, "Mah-jong!" I was nine years old and will never forget that hour. Curiously, I have never played the game since.

*

Years later, I asked Roland Jermy about his memories of Harry Hornsby.

"He was a remarkable man all right. Everyone looked up to him. The first thing he did when he arrived in 1938 was get the senior boys to dig trenches across the school playing field in case of air raids. He organised billets for evacuees and supervised making blackout frames. A year later, war broke out. He joined up immediately and Mr Shearcroft took over in his absence."

"What was it like at the school during the war years?" I asked him.

"The staff and boys were kept pretty busy," he replied. "Once, a German bomber flew down Park Road. Everyone took cover in the sandbagged corridor of the main school. Even though there was hardly any damage there were numerous air-raid warnings and nights spent on mattresses in the back corridor of the boarding house. When the all-clear sounded Lillian would rush off to make us all cocoa."

Roland was given the job of aircraft spotting. He became quite good at it and taught the Junior Observer Corps how to identify the silhouettes of German aircraft when they came back from bombing Coventry or Birmingham. "The only place they dropped a bomb around here was on the Corporation Swimming Pool," he said with his usual chuckle. "They blew a foreman out of bed with his girlfriend." Suddenly he looked serious. "Thirty-two Old Petriburgians died in the war. The first one was poor old George Rae, the head boy. Such a young life. There's a physics prize named after him."

Roland got back to the subject of Harry Hornsby. "When he came back after five years in the army he had quite a shock. The war had disrupted everything. The school was shabby and ill equipped, and then there were those dreadful winters. You know, in a sense, there were two schools. One was elitist and middle class and harked back to pre-war days, and the other was when it became a grammar school and eventually a comprehensive. When I arrived to teach in the 1930s King's had many of the trappings of a minor public school. Life centred on the cathedral, its choristers and the teaching of Classics. At that time we were semi-independent, and had some fine traditions such as the prestigious King's Scholars who had their fees paid and joined in processions with cassock, surplice and red tassels.

"Much of this was swept aside by the 1944 Education Act and the rise of egalitarianism. This is not generally well known but in 1947, the governors tried to join the Woodward Group, an association of independent High Church schools. Lancing College was their flagship. The whole thing fell through, largely, I believe, because we couldn't pull our weight financially. Instead the school was now open to any boy who had passed the eleven-plus, irrespective of his background. Working-class boys entered a predominantly middle-class world. Harry Hornsby rose to all these challenges because he was a human dynamo and had the common touch. He raised morale, appointed excellent staff and soon had a steady stream of boys going to Oxford, Cambridge and other universities. But he had endless 'fights' with the local education council to get more funding for building and equipment. Eventually it got him down. In 1950 he resigned and accepted the headmastership of Christ's College, Christchurch, New Zealand. Under Hornsby it became one of the most famous schools in the southern hemisphere."

1948

Jesus Loves Me, This I Know

Whilst my mother was at home being Jewish I was becoming more and more embedded in the ethos of The King's School – a community which believed in the Holy Ghost, the Holy Catholic Church, the Communion of Saints, the resurrection of the body and the life everlasting. We were encouraged to pray and follow a Christian way of life. Anglican Protestants were superior to Catholics, we were told, although exactly how was never explained. Jews and Arabs were foreigners, never mentioned except in Bible stories.

Jesus loves me, this I know for the Bible tells me so was a favourite hymn of Miss Wigner's. "What further proof do you need?" she would say. "The least you can do is go to church regularly." As boarders, attendance at cathedral every Sunday morning was compulsory. At 10.45 we lined up in the front drive to have our face, hair, teeth and shoes inspected by either a prefect or Mr Jermy. Each boy wore a clean white shirt with a starched collar. We were each given a penny for the collection. With a prefect in charge, we set off in a crocodile, whatever the weather, for the mile-long walk through the town.

The city of Peterborough was no beauty in the post-war years. (Now it is even more depressing, since in the 1960s it was made a new town with characterless buildings.) Walking the mile or so from our school to the cathedral took us from leafy Park Road into the tatty city centre with its dreary shops and run-down market square. However, once we passed through the gatehouse dividing the cathedral close from the square we could feast our eyes on the glorious West Front, considered to be the most impressive medieval facade in England. Entering the nave, one's eyes looked up to the hand-painted ceiling; "like a carpet in the air," the dean had once proclaimed in a sermon. King's School boarders sat in the carved choir stalls just along from the choristers. We all piled into the wooden seats, making an unholy noise, and received rebukes from the verger.

I envied the choristers. "Why can't I be one?" I had often asked Lillian Hay. She usually replied that I was too young. But one Sunday when we were just leaving the cathedral I spotted the assistant organist gathering up the hymn books.

"I want to be a chorister," I blurted out, and with that started to sing a hymn.

He looked a little startled and then smiled, saying I had a bright, clear voice and that I should discuss my ambition with the school staff. Unfortunately, my further attempts to become a chorister came to nothing. I was told that it was too big a commitment since it involved missing the first lesson at school each morning and other classes on numerous occasions throughout the church calendar. I think the staff probably thought I had enough to cope with.

Over the years I attended 'sung Matins' hundreds of times so the service is quite ingrained in me. The peal of bells would stop at eleven and the choristers, with their red cassocks and white surplices, would process from the south transept followed by the choirmaster and the clergy. The precentor, the dean, the archdeacon and the headmaster solemnly walked to their seats. As I grew older I became more and more moved by the music and the dignity of the service, although I was later intimidated by its Anglican smugness and confidence. As the last chord of the processional music from the mighty organ died down, the precentor's pure voice rang forth, "O Lord, open thou our lips" and the choir responded with perfection, "And our mouth shall shew forth thy praise." The service continued with the Venite and the first canticle of Matins. Peterborough Cathedral was Low Church and Protestant. There was no ritual or incense.

Churches were quite well attended in the 1940s and 1950s, and at school religious instruction was a key element of the syllabus. In junior school Mrs Barnes was our form mistress (always mistresses, never teachers). She was a jolly, stout lady with a loud voice – quite a contrast to the stern Miss Wigner. I enjoyed her Bible stories, which were suitably embellished in her particular theatrical way. Unfortunately she overdid the drama when it came to her description of the wages of sin – hell, fire, brimstone and eternal flames. I was terrified, and trembled with fear. Was it my fault my mother and father divorced? Would I go to hell and burn for eternity? If Jesus loved me, why did he not do something about the bullying, homesickness, cold and hunger?

Hunger struck cruelly at mid morning or mid afternoon; it could also be unpleasant late at night. One day during the summer term of 1948 I thought it a good idea to eat some crab apples from a tree in the garden. We had been warned they were inedible and would give us tummy ache. I must have been pretty desperate, or just wilful, to ignore this. A short time after eating four or six of them I began to have tummy pain and vomited. I continued to vomit for several hours.

Dr Holmes, the boarding house GP, was called. He was anxious and left instructions that I should be closely observed. Matron was by my bedside all night. By the next morning, exhausted and dehydrated, I was rushed to Peterborough Memorial Hospital and admitted to a surgical ward. They thought I had an intestinal obstruction and it was touch and go whether they should operate. I deteriorated a bit further and was put on the 'danger list'. My mother was told to come urgently. She rushed up to Peterborough with Harry Kay. Tony Chambers was also alerted and within forty-eight hours the three of them were looking down at me by my bedside. The doctors remained puzzled. What was the diagnosis?

Mum became uncontrollable and screamed, "Get another doctor! They don't know anything here. Call in a specialist from London." A specialist did come, but from Cambridge. He was an elderly man with a grey moustache and yellow teeth and smelt strongly of tobacco. By the time he arrived I had had an enormous bowel motion and was feeling much better. Nevertheless, for an inexplicable reason, he prescribed a course of penicillin and I endured painful injections for several days.

I learnt later that Tony Chambers and Harry Kay, who had met for the first time at my bedside, had got on rather well. Harry told me that Tony had said that my mother had been "a bit of a handful" and had wished him "good luck with her". Hearing this story from my stepfather years later, I wondered if Tony had been glad to get rid of my volatile mother. Perhaps he had even engineered the unexpected arrival of his first wife on their doorstep in Northampton. Was it a plot to reclaim his freedom? We will never know.

1948–1949

Luxborough Street, W1

For most of my childhood the school holidays were lonely and boring. I still feel angry that so much time was wasted in aimless pursuits. I had no friends my own age and was left to my own devices with little guidance on how to structure my days. Mum and Harry would drive off in the morning 'on business' and did not return until after six o'clock. Mum's parting shot was usually, "Well, Barry, at least you can tidy up. The flat looks dreadful."

So I tidied and washed up, which took about half an hour, and then I willed myself to get out and about. I had to kill time. One way was to travel on the Underground. We were only a five-minute walk from Baker Street Station. I would buy a return ticket for tuppence, enough for one stop, and then I would travel around and around on the Circle Line, or up the Bakerloo Line to Stanmore, Watford Junction or Uxbridge. When I got to the end of the line I crossed over the bridge without leaving the station, so I would not have to show my ticket, and then return to Baker Street. There was something about the movement of the train that was calming. When it stopped at a station and the doors opened for a moment I always felt anxious. I willed the doors to close and when the train started to move off I would feel calmer. These train rides became obsessional. Sometimes I would be more adventurous and naughty and go for longer journeys and, at my destination, squeeze past the ticket collector without paying. I hardly ever got caught, and if I did I only got a ticking-off.

Some days, again feeling bored, I would hang around the bomb site at the back of Marylebone High Street. A landmine had flattened a large area. All that remained was a mass of rubble and the empty shells of two tower blocks. Occasionally there would be other boys to play with, but they were usually unfriendly and called me posh. They dared me to climb up what remained of the stairwell of one of the buildings. One of them boasted he had climbed up to the fifth floor. Desperate to be accepted, I rose to the challenge. Ignoring the notice which said, *Danger: Keep Out*, I started to climb. It was a stupid thing to do and I was petrified. As I ascended the frail staircase I saw inside the empty rooms with their charred furniture and remains of people's lives. Suddenly my foot went through a burnt-out floorboard and I cried out. But I summoned up courage and kept on going up, now at the fourth floor and then the fifth. Trembling with fright, I realised that to prove myself to the boys below I had to go even higher – to the sixth floor, or even the seventh. I clung on to a banister but it collapsed and went hurtling down.

I heard a man's voice shouting up from far below. "Come down, you silly little bugger, before I call the police," he yelled.

I gingerly descended and was confronted by an angry bomb-site warden who gave me an almighty ticking-off. The other boys, meanwhile, were nowhere to be seen. I never played in a bomb site again.

One day I had an experience which nearly brought my travelling on the Underground to an abrupt end. I decided to go to Harrow on the Hill, and on this occasion paid the proper fare. Harry had told me that Harrow was a lovely area with a large park to play in.

The train was empty apart from a man who looked about thirty or forty. He was small and wore a mackintosh and a trilby hat, and started talking to me. He asked what I was doing on the Underground all by myself. I must have said something non-committal. He smiled and said he was a photographer who liked to take pictures of children. When I got off at Harrow he followed me and suggested that we went to a park nearby where he would take some photos of me. I did not feel there was any harm in his suggestion.

We arrived at the park and he got his camera ready. He said he wanted me to pose in what I thought were funny positions, and asked me to take my shirt off. Suddenly I felt frightened. My mother had often said, "Don't talk to any strange men", but I never quite understood why she said this.

Then the man slowly put away his camera and sauntered across to where I was sitting on the grass and sat down beside me. "You are a very pretty boy," he said, and he tried to put his arm around me.

I became acutely embarrassed and was seized with panic. I sprang up and ran. He called after me, and as I turned I saw him quickly following me. I ran and ran, outpacing him until I got back to the station.

I was waiting impatiently for a train to come along to get me back to Baker Street when the man suddenly appeared, out of breath, at the top of the bridge leading down to the station. Just then a train came along. Would he have time to negotiate the ticket barrier and join me on the train? Luckily the doors closed just in time. As the train pulled out he banged on the glass, entreating me to return. My knees trembled. I cried all the way back home.

I told my mother and father what had happened. They both looked alarmed.

"I told you never to talk to strangers," shouted my mother.

"What was he like? Describe him," said Harry.

After a while they calmed down and my mother gave me a lecture on 'dirty old men'.

"No man is ever to be trusted," I remember her saying. I felt more alone and frightened than ever.

My mother was the dominant personality in her relationship with my stepfather. Harry Kay wanted domesticity and tranquillity, but he rarely found them. My mother was ambitious. She craved fame and fortune, and to live life in the fast lane. Eventually she would succeed, but at a price. In the early days in Luxborough Street she spent a lot of time with her sewing machine, dressmaking. She would work for long hours, often into the night, cutting out fabrics on the floor. These bursts of activity could last for several days but were inevitably followed by low periods in which she became argumentative and impossible to reason with. Despite our drab surroundings my mother always managed to look elegant. She would sometimes wear slacks or trousers around the house, but never outside the flat. I remember her fine woollen suits with a pencil skirt split up the side. It helped that she had an hourglass figure, perfect for the fashion of the time. I would see her silhouetted at the window with her wide padded shoulders and high, nipped-in waist.

When it rained there was the novelty of television. Harry brought home a set from his radio shop. I would gaze at the small screen with its flickering images. I watched the same programmes over and over again – *The Demonstration Film*, *London to Brighton in Four Minutes*, or an interlude with a pottery wheel. Sometimes – just to please Harry, who, unlike my mother, would sometimes feel guilty about leaving me to my own devices – I went to museums and art galleries. Being alone and just a small boy, I was too young to appreciate what London could offer. I tried trainspotting because some of the boys at school did it. Although aimless in one sense, there was something exciting about seeing *Mallard*, the streamlined A4-class loco which had broken the world steam train speed record. I would spend hours collecting numbers and underlining them in the Ian Allan trainspotter's book. A new sighting was a 'cop'. Life then consisted of Jubilees, Black Fives, Eight Freights and Jintys.

Another way of killing time was the Newsreel Cinema. There were several of these in the West End. For one and sixpence I could see the Pathé News and cartoons. It was a feast of Tom and Jerry, Pluto, Mickey Mouse and Donald Duck. The shows lasted about one hour but it was possible to stay on and see the programme a second, third or even fourth time. Once a man sitting next to me grabbed my hand and thrust it towards his groin; another time one exposed himself to me in the toilet. I became alert to these dangers, making sure I always sat next to a lady or other children.

In the summer of 1948 Harry took me and his friend Leo Marle to the opening ceremony of the Olympic Games.

"I won't ask how you got the tickets," Mum said. She showed no interest in the event, and anyway, she had a small baby to look after.

"Have you really got tickets?" I asked Dad suspiciously.

At school we had been told all about the Olympics. The head of sports had arranged a showing of the Leni Riefenstahl film of the 1936 games. The introduction has mystical Greek stuff with naked ladies prancing about. Boys giggled uncontrollably. For his initiative the master got a ticking-off from the head. Anyway, I loved all the competitiveness and the sporting camaraderie. We all knew about Jesse Owens and how Hitler snubbed him after he won the hundred metres.

Dad, Leo and I set off for Wembley in the newly acquired family car, a Standard Eight (the 'Flying Standard'). It was a boiling hot day. We arrived and entered the stadium. The atmosphere was thrilling. At first I could not see a thing because I was so small, but I was propelled down to the front on a sea of hands. The handsome John Mark ran a lap of the track, holding high the Olympic torch, and then dramatically mounted the rostrum and lit the flame. Malcolm Sargent conducted the Olympic Hymn; the King saluted, stiff as a rod, for hours on end. The Boy Scouts released masses of pigeons from large wicker baskets. Finally the colourful athletes from all the countries marched past.

When it was all over and we had to drive back, Dad said, "I don't think we have enough petrol to get us back home." He was fairly nonchalant.

I was anxious. "What will happen if we run out of petrol?"

"Well, we will just have to push," he laughed.

Then we did run out of petrol, luckily just by a garage. But Dad had no petrol coupons and the pump attendant was unsympathetic.

"No petrol without coupons," he said.

After an exchange of cash, however, the garage man cooperated and Dad managed to get a gallon. We were saved.

I was still worried. "Isn't it against the law to buy petrol without coupons?" I had heard Mr Jermy say that once at school.

"Remember," said Leo, "rules are there to go around, jump over or crawl underneath." He and Dad laughed.

Before we reached home we stopped off for tea in a café. As we were sitting down an attractive lady entered. She recognised Harry and Leo and they all smiled and chatted. Harry told me she was an old friend that he and Leo had known before he met Mum.

"Best not to mention it to your mother," said Harry.

For some reason, perhaps just for the fun of a conspiracy, I told my mother that evening when she and I were alone for a moment. Mum, who was a bit flaky anyway and still nursing my five-month-old sister, started to question Harry.

"Who was the woman you and Leo were talking to in the café?" she demanded.

Harry was taken aback. "Oh, nobody," he said with a sheepish grin.

The more he tried to brush off the incident, the more insistent my mother became. "Who was this lady and what was your relationship?" she demanded. "How long have you known her?" she kept on asking.

Soon things got out of hand. Mum became excitable, working herself up into a fearful storm. She fired off ludicrous accusations. Harry covered his face with his arms as she began to hurl objects. My crying and distress and threat to run out into the street to fetch a policeman calmed her down. She then subsided into tears.

I was confused as usual. Why should my dad not have a friend who was a lady? He could have invited her back to our flat for tea. Mum would have had another friend. Why did Dad say it had to be a secret that he and Leo had met her by accident in the café? There was nothing wrong with it. I had been there. But here was my mother saying that Harry and Leo were meeting ladies behind her back.

Sometime later Harry asked me why I had told my mother. I had no answer. He realised I couldn't keep a secret and that I would probably always take my mother's side. Trust had been lost. I often wondered how much the relationship between my stepfather and me suffered as a result of that incident.

Penny became quite ill when she was just a few months old. She had a fever with vomiting and was floppy and unresponsive. The local GP dismissed it as a viral infection, but Mum was not satisfied and rushed her round to Great Ormond Street Hospital. She had meningitis. The doctors said they could do nothing, but she was given a new wonder drug, probably streptomycin. Penny slowly recovered but did not start to walk until she was about two and a half, although it is unclear whether this was related to the illness.

We often had a live-in German au pair girl to look after Penny. There was quite a turnover of au pairs. They would sleep in my room and I would have to share with them when I came home from school. My mother regarded the au pairs with suspicion and grudgingly accepted their help so she could get on with her career as a dress designer. Mum could be very vulgar when she was angry or impatient, and would often refer to an au pair girl as "the shiksa", a horrible, derogatory Yiddish term that she used too often. My mother would sometimes set a trap for one of these unfortunate girls if she suspected they were dishonest. Money would be left deliberately in a drawer and my mother would check regularly that it was all still there. One day a ten-shilling note was missing. Mum immediately accused the poor girl of theft and chucked her out of the flat with all her belongings. When Mum told Harry he turned bright red and confessed that he had taken the note because he was short of cash.

One day a new au pair girl arrived at the flat without any luggage, explaining that she would pick up her things later from a friend. She was a German, charming and intelligent, and listened carefully to my mother's instructions. After explaining what was expected of her, Mum walked the girl round to the nursery school where she was to collect Penny in the afternoon. When my mother returned to the flat in the early evening there was no au pair and no Penny, and the phone was ringing. It was the school telling Mum that Penny had not been collected. Looking around, she saw to her horror that the flat had been ransacked. All the drawers were pulled out and their contents scattered on the floor. Mum had had a few valuable jewels of which she was very fond, mostly gifts she had kept from her Rushden days. They had all been stolen. Her first instinct was to contact the police, but Harry would have none of it. He did not ask the police for help – he avoided them! In the end Harry got the blame. Mum went into a rage, and the recriminations which followed left my stepfather trembling. It was all Harry's fault even though he had had nothing to do with employing the girl; it was Mum who found the au pairs by putting advertisements in the classified columns of the *Evening Standard*. Nevertheless, Dad got the blame. Mum was never wrong.

I came home from school shortly after the au pair episode. As usual, I did the swap of surnames from Chambers to Kay. My mother liked to believe that Tony Chambers had never existed. At first this suited me. I did not want to be on the periphery of the family now I had a sister. More importantly, I hated the name Chambers because my tormentors at school called me chamber pot and so I acquired the nickname, Po. It became a source of misery and mental torture. The more I was called Po Chambers, the angrier I became, and the angrier I became, the more I was tormented, this being the nature of some cruel small boys. Being weak and vulnerable, I was constantly picked on.

I longed to have a different surname than Chambers, although I was puzzled that there was another boy in the school called Chambers – some years older than me – who was popular and a good cricketer, who wasn't teased and appeared to be quite content with his name. Nevertheless, deep down I preferred Kay to Chambers. But Kay also had its problems – Kay, Danny Kaye, foreign? Jewish?

By this time Mum had taken on the full mantle of Judaism, at least socially, but how was I to be explained to Harry's parents? They were an elderly, poor and Orthodox immigrant couple who lived in North London and believed that my mother was a 'nice Jewish girl'. They could not have accepted that she was a divorcee with a young child. So it was decided, probably by my mother and Harry, that as far as Moma and Poppa Kruschinsky were concerned, I, like Tony Chambers, also did not exist. Accordingly, I never met them. When Mum, Harry and Penny set off to visit I was easily persuaded to stay at home. They told me I would be bored if I came along. It was more important for my mother to keep up the pretence of being Jewish than it was to be honest to her new parents-in-law about me.

A few days before I was due to return to the boarding house I mentioned to my mother that all my clothes had to be marked with Cash's name tapes, otherwise they would be lost in the laundry – it was a school rule.

"Just write *Barry Kay* on the inside in black ink," she said. "I haven't got time to order name tapes."

"It has to be Barry Chambers," I said quietly, "in Cash's name tapes."

"Stop being a nuisance and get it into your head: there is no Barry Chambers."

1949

London and Peterborough

One Sunday I was left alone in the flat because my mother and Harry were going to 'an affair'.

"What's an affair?" I asked.

"A wedding. Mrs Cuplin's daughter" (or 'tdortta' as my mother would say, trying to sound authentic) "is getting married in Willesden Synagogue and the reception will be held in a classy hotel."

They set off at 9.30. My mother was wearing a beautiful blue halter-neck dress and a patterned shawl to cover her shoulders – "For the ceremony," she explained.

Immediately they drove away I was overcome by the usual bout of loneliness and loss of purpose. What should I do? Where should I go? What would I be doing on a Sunday morning at the boarding house, I asked myself? Of course, I would be going to the cathedral with the other boys and 'thinking about Jesus', as Miss Wigner had instructed us.

St Marylebone Parish Church was nearby. I had passed it quite often. It has a very grand front with eight columns based on the Pantheon in Rome. I decided to go there for Matins at eleven o'clock. Miss Wigner had said we would be warmly welcomed in all Anglican churches, although I did not know what an Anglican was except that, like me, they were Christians.

It was a hot day when I set off. I tried to look my best in a slightly soiled white shirt and grey short trousers. I walked gingerly up the huge steps. Churchgoers swept past me, some looking backwards in curiosity at this solitary boy. As I entered the verger stared at me disapprovingly and told me to take a seat at the back. The nave and transepts were almost full. Everyone was elegantly dressed. The men were in dark suits, most of the women had expensive hats. The children were smartly turned out – some sneered at me. There were bright colours and flowers everywhere. The congregation at Peterborough Cathedral were a drab-looking lot in comparison.

During the service the clergy, wearing far more sumptuous robes than I had seen before, paraded behind a man waving an incense burner. I was amazed. Had I strayed into a Catholic church by mistake? However, the service was familiar and I knew all the hymns. To impress, I sang loudly. Several elderly ladies turned their heads and frowned.

At the end of the service members of the congregation lined up to shake hands with the vicar. I joined the queue, but sensed unfriendliness. A small, rather grubby boy had intruded into their privileged midst and they wished he would go away. When my turn came I grasped the vicar's hand. He recoiled, removed his limp fingers abruptly and regarded me unsmilingly.

"Where do you live?" he said.

"Oh, quite near, in Luxborough Street."

The vicar's eyes bulged. The lady behind me gave a gasp. "Do you mean Luxborough Lodge, the… umm… institution?" (Luxborough Lodge was the grim Victorian building opposite us. It had been a workhouse but by 1949 was an old people's home and refuge for displaced persons.)

"Oh no," I replied. "I live in one of the flats opposite in Cheviot Court."

"Why are you alone? Where are your parents?" The vicar was suspicious.

"They are at church," I said boldly. "They are at a wedding."

"A wedding?! On a Sunday?!"

He, and a small crowd of grown-ups who had been listening to the conversation, roared with laughter. "Jews have weddings on a Sunday," I heard someone say. There was more laughter.

I felt ashamed but I was not sure why. Had I done something wrong? I thought I was doing the correct thing by going to church on a Sunday, just as Miss Wigner encouraged us to do. But I was being made fun of. I did not fit in at this church. Where did I fit in?

During the summer holidays of 1949 my parents received a letter from the school announcing that the matron, Lillian Hay, had married the housemaster, Mr Roland Jermy. The happy couple would be leaving the boarding house to live in a flat not too far away from the school. *The new matron*, the letter continued, *is to be Miss Winifred Trunton, previously governess and housekeeper to the Archdeacon of Oakham. Mr Anthony Parker, presently Deputy-Head of English, will replace Mr Jermy as House Master.*

I did not receive the news at all well – in fact I was angry. Why wasn't I consulted? Lillian Hay was the one who protected me from the older, rougher boys. Did this mean I could no longer escape to her room and sit at her feet by the luxuriant coal fire, feeling safe and drinking cocoa? After all, I had always been her special one. She had always been there to protect me – reliable, predictable, wise and loving. What would Miss Trunton be like? Would she love me like her predecessor?

The headmaster's letter continued: *Since the junior school has now been phased out in accordance with the new Education Act and your son has passed the necessary qualifying examination to enter the senior school he will be offered a place in Form 1. Unless we hear to the contrary we will assume that you are agreeable to him taking up this placement. Under the act tuition fees have been abolished. However the terms and conditions for boarding remain unchanged. The subsistence fee will remain at twelve pounds, ten shillings and sixpence per term.*

My mother, who always had difficulty distinguishing between tuition fees and maintenance, threw her arms up in the air, saying,

"How am I going to pay the school fees? Oh, the sacrifices I make for you, Barry. I work and I work." She would then light a cigarette, inhale deeply and look at the floor.

Harry would try to reason with her, saying that it would cost them both much more to have me living at home. "It's cheap at the price," he said.

As the day of my departure approached it became more difficult to hold back the tears. The car ride to King's Cross Station was an agony. I would howl away in the back seat. My mother looked sad.

"You should buck up and think about the brave Spitfire pilots," Harry said.

"Is that the best you can do to comfort the child?" barked my mother. "What has this to do with Spitfires?"

The pain was eased when Harry produced a two-shilling piece ("to be spent carefully"). It joined the half-crown my mother had given to me the night before, and the shilling donated unexpectedly by Mr Gross, Dad's partner at the radio business. The coins gave me some comfort. How many Wagon Wheels, sherbet fountains and aniseed balls would they buy?

1950

The Lovable Rogue

During another school holiday when I was about ten, and Mum and Harry had taken Penny with them in the car on their daily business trip, I was, as usual, left alone in the flat. I decided to poke around in drawers and cupboards, hoping to find something interesting. There was an old violin in a battered case under the bed in Mum and Harry's bedroom. I remembered he had once mentioned he had started to learn it as a child but did not get very far. There was also an old wind-up gramophone together with several boxes of shellac '78' records, unopened and in mint condition. I broke the seal of several of the jacket covers. None of them seemed to have been played before. What was the point of having so many records if they were not played? Dad had never mentioned he liked classical music and I had never seen him play the gramophone. The records were mainly Tchaikovsky, Mahler and Wagner, names I had only heard mentioned on the wireless. I liked the composers of pieces we did in the school concerts and the singing competition – Purcell, Handel, Schubert and so on. I did play a few of the records but got tired of winding up the gramophone and did not like the music.

I got up from exploring under the bed and started poking around, looking at the books. I had never paid much attention to the large tomes scattered around the flat. Some sat in the bookcase, others were left in piles on tables. Here was another mystery. I had not seen Harry sitting down and reading, apart from the newspaper. I knew he liked the book reviews because he would sometimes read them out to my mother. She was bored when he did this, although she took an interest in politics and liked to hear Harry's stories of his bachelor days as a young communist and later as an ardent Labour supporter. Harry led her along a left-wing path and she went with him initially. Years later they both became reactionary conservatives.

I picked up a couple of the volumes and skimmed through them – *The Ragged-Trousered Philanthropists*; *Soviet Communism: A New Civilisation?* Gosh! What would the boys at school think if they knew my dad was once a communist? I had overheard one of the masters saying the Russians were worse than the Germans.

I then realised that most of them were library books. Not only was *St Marylebone Public Library* written on the inside covers, but the little tickets in the small wallet which the librarian removed when books were borrowed were still there. How could this be? At school we had a similar borrowing system but no boy was allowed to take out more than one book at a time and it had to be stamped with the date for its return.

I reasoned that my stepfather had simply forgotten to return them because he was too busy. Since the public library was only a short walk away and I had nothing else to do I decided to help him by taking the books back. The library would be pleased, Dad would be pleased, and I would be pleased after he had praised me for being a good and responsible boy. I could tell everyone back at the boarding house about it. So I loaded up about thirty volumes in Penny's big Silver Cross pram and set off.

St Marylebone library (almost as imposing as the church) was an annexe of the town hall and had a grand Corinthian portico with Grecian friezes above. Inside was a huge, domed central space. I loved going there, although I was only allowed in the children's department. When I got to the library I could not push the pram up the steps and so I left it on the pavement and went inside to look for help. There was an attendant at the reception desk.

"Whadya want, son?"

"I have come to return some books. About thirty of them. They are in my sister's pram on the street but I can't push it up the steps."

"What are you doing with thirty books, you little bugger?" he snarled.

"Well, you see, it's my dad. He must have forgotten to return them," I said proudly.

"Forgotten to return them? Nicked them, more likely," he said.

I was alarmed and confused, and about to cry. Reluctantly, the attendant sauntered out to help me. Together we negotiated the steps. Then he grabbed me roughly by the collar and dragged me along a corridor, pushing the pram at the same time, to where a young lady librarian was seated. She was pretty with a grey twinset and skirt. Her hair was tied back in a bun. She gave me a kind smile and asked my name.

"Barry," I said firmly.

"And where do you live, Barry?"

"Luxborough Street. I was tidying up my parents' flat."

"More like the little sod's been thieving books," the attendant said.

"I haven't, I haven't," I sobbed. "It's my dad. He borrowed them. I'm just returning them because he is so busy."

"That's a bleeding laugh if ever I heard one."

"No need for that, Charlie. Leave this to me," said the lady sternly. Examining the books and looking at her colleague, she remarked, "I don't think it's likely that a small boy would be stealing *The Labour Party in Perspective*, or *The Condition of Workers in Great Britain, Germany and the Soviet Union*."

The attendant grumbled and slouched away, muttering something about my needing "a good belting". The lady smiled at me again, realising how distressed I was. She relieved me of the books without asking questions.

"You are a good boy," she said. "Other readers are waiting for these. They will be grateful."

My pride restored, feeling quite puffed up in fact, I sailed back to the flat to await Mum and Harry's return.

Immediately after they returned I told them all about the books, expecting them to be pleased. Instead my stepfather looked frightened and angry.

"What sort of questions did they ask?" he said.

"None. The nice lady was pleased and thanked me. All she said was, 'I expect your daddy is a slow reader', and then she laughed."

Harry looked relieved. He explained that sometimes there was such a queue in the library that he did not have time to get the books stamped and always intended to return them the next day – but sometimes he forgot. He seemed to have forgotten about thirty times, though. I quickly changed the subject.

"Dad," I said, "why do you have so many records under your bed? They all look brand new. Do you ever play them?"

With this revelation he looked even more uncomfortable. "Don't go snooping about the flat," he burst out angrily.

"But I have nothing to do all day," I wailed.

"Go to a museum," he shouted. "Go to a cricket match, go to an art gallery, go to Regent's Park, Hyde Park and the Houses of Parliament – there are a hundred and one things you can do!"

"But I want to have a friend, someone to go with." I was sobbing.

My mother, having only half-witnessed the scene as she was trying on new make-up, walked across to me and gave me a cuddle. "Don't you dare talk to my son like that," she said angrily.

"*Your* son? I thought he was our son now."

"Not when you talk to him like that, he isn't," she responded, quiet but terse.

This time Mum had brought some food back, some cold chicken and salad. She quickly prepared it. I was told to go my room. I was allowed to listen to Arthur Askey and Ted Ray on the radio – my favourites.

I eventually fell asleep, but was woken in the middle of the night. Dad seemed to be walking up and down the stairs, loading things into the car. He made several trips and then there was silence. The next day he sheepishly gave me an extra half-crown to spend and left with my mother 'on business'.

I peered under their bed. All the boxes of records had gone.

1950

The Sport of Kings

The summer holiday of 1950 dragged on. As usual I was left on my own to roam around London, counting the hours until my mother and Harry returned from work. Somehow I got it into my head that Mum and Dad would be killed in a road traffic accident. During the morning this thought would only be in the back of my mind, but as the day progressed I got more and more anxious. By four o'clock I was sweating and trembling with anxiety. The next few hours were purgatory as I paced up and down Luxborough Street, looking around to see from which direction they would return. Mercifully they always arrived back between 6.30 and seven. My mother gave me a quizzical look and asked me if I had been crying or was upset. I denied everything and put on a brave face; after all, they were back and my anxiety had vanished immediately.

"When are we going to have supper?" I asked my mother.

"I can't think about cooking. Harry! Let's go out for dinner."

With that we all got into the car and went around the corner to Paddington Street and the local Italian restaurant. Mum asked me about my day but was not really listening when I tried to tell her. Soon she and Harry were deep in conversation about blouses and dresses, styles and costs, embroidery and sequins. I was ignored and given sixpence to buy some sweets and told to find my own way back home.

During the years we lived in the Luxborough Street flat the postman regularly delivered letters marked *Private and confidential.*

Hardly any of them were opened; they just lay in a pile on the bureau in the living room. When I asked my mother what they were I received an evasive answer. Eventually Harry told me they were bills from their bookmaker. I wondered what a bookmaker was. Did he make books? I did not understand. There were hardly any books in the house after the episode at the library. Dad explained about gambling and what a bookmaker was, and how sometimes he and my mother would win money betting on horses and dogs. Sometimes they lost, but they always broke even.

I did not ask any more questions on the subject although I was aware, even at an early age, that my mother found racing and gambling exciting. Harry shared her enthusiasm and introduced her to casinos when they went to Deauville and, later, when they were more affluent, to Cannes, Juan-les-Pins and even Monte Carlo. For my mother the pinnacle of high living was to rub shoulders with the rich and famous, with champagne and caviar, at a casino in the South of France.

Mum's fondness for horse racing went back to the early days with Tony Chambers. He had once taken her to a 'point-to-point'. Laying a bet, watching the horses run and hearing the sound of thundering hooves sent a thrill down her spine. She was hooked, but did not have a further opportunity to go to a race meeting until after the war when she met Harry. Harry was as keen on the horses as Mum; after all, he had been a bookie's runner when he was a lad. Whether this was his main job at the time I never knew.

The racetracks reasonably accessible from London – Kempton Park, Sandown, Goodwood, Brighton and Lewes – were popular destinations with my parents. Sometimes they would make longer journeys to places like Doncaster, York and Lincoln and stay overnight. Occasionally I would tag along; at least it was something to do. Derby Day, however, was different.

"If you have not been to the Derby you haven't lived," Dad would say. He was right.

The worst bit was actually getting to Epsom Downs. We always went by car and usually found ourselves in a huge traffic jam. The smell of hundreds of pre-war cars, many of which broke down and blocked the road, was unpleasant. Harry got impatient, overtaking in the oncoming lane and oblivious to other drivers shaking their fists at him. If a policeman stopped us he would turn round to me in the back of the car and say, "Barry, try to look as if you are not feeling well."

I obliged, since I was feeling carsick anyway.

"What's all this, sir?" said the officer. "In a bit of a hurry, are we? Why aren't you in the queue like everyone else?"

"It's my son," Dad said, jerking his thumb at me. "He's very poorly. Got to get him to a doctor."

The policeman peered at me in the back seat and then waved us on. When we were stopped again, the performance was repeated.

Eventually we got to the massive car park on the Downs. Walking down to the race track we became enveloped by the crowds of people, the carnival atmosphere, and the gaudiness of the funfair with its carousel, roundabouts, swings, coconut shies, acrobats and fortune tellers. There were jellied eel stalls, ice cream and fizzy drink stands. The noise was thunderous; the funfair, shouting bookmakers, laughter and the jollity of the spectators. To all this were added the smells of oil from generators, candyfloss, cheap perfume, and fish and chips. Crowds formed around spivs selling watches ("They've got no insides," said Harry), tipsters, anti-gambling preachers and assorted speakers on soapboxes ("All con men," said my dad).

As we came down one of the slopes we saw a large black man in a brightly coloured outfit surrounded by a throng of racegoers. He had a headdress of ostrich feathers, coloured trousers, waistcoat and jacket, and a necklace of bones and trinkets. He kept on shouting, "I gotta horse. I gotta horse." He had the patter of a market trader, and his audience howled with laughter.

"That's Prince Monolulu," said my dad. "He's an Abyssinian tribal chief."

"What's he doing?" I asked.

"He's a tipster, he sells tips. You know, which horse is going to win a race."

"How does he know?"

"He doesn't," chimed in my mother. "He just guesses," she added somewhat sourly.

"She's right," said Dad, laughing. "Sometimes he gets it right. If he is wrong he does a runner."

At that moment 'the prince' looked up and, seeing us coming towards him, shouted, "'Allo, 'Arry!"

"How are you, Chief?" said Dad.

"Dad knows an African prince," I said. "Golly!"

"He knows everyone at the races," said Mum, this time smiling.

There was an atmosphere of abandon; everyone was out to have a good time. The crowd laughed and were good-natured. I suggested that we wander around the various stalls, but Mum and Harry wanted to get down to the serious business of betting. They were anxious to size up the horses in the parade and look for the best odds with the bookmakers.

Mum's behaviour at these meetings could be disturbing. She got excited and her eyes sparkled. Strangers talked easily to each other at the races, toffs mixing cheerfully with the hoi polloi. Mum soon had a small entourage of young men around her. She flirted outrageously and Dad was continually yanking her away. Nevertheless they were happiest as punters, unless they lost money – a frequent occurrence, unfortunately.

I was amazed by the tic-tac men standing on steps, towering above the crowd and gesticulating in a sort of private Morse code to someone in the distance.

"What are they doing?" I asked Harry.

"They are telling the other bookmakers how the betting is going so they can adjust the odds if too much money is placed on one horse. When the favourites win, the bookies lose."

I gazed at the sea of bookmakers, some in white coats, most wearing trilby hats, perched on their step-up ladders writing furiously in chalk on blackboards headed with their names, all in jolly colours. Equally furiously, they would keep wiping the board to adjust the odds. "Come along, now. Come along, now. Five to two the favourite," they shouted.

People placed their bets. A man behind the board with a brown coat and bowler hat wrote them down in a large ledger.

Suddenly a huge cheer rang out. People surged to the edge of the race track to witness a procession of open-topped Rolls-Royces. "It's the King! It's the King!" they shouted. "God bless him." They then surged back to get on with the main business – choosing a winner.

I soon noticed that my mother was impulsive and erratic in her gambling. Mostly she guessed a winner on the basis of the horse's or jockey's name; the colour of the jockey's breeches, shirt or hat; attractive odds; or whether the owner was famous (she would never bet on the favourite). My mother was not interested in a horse's track record except in a rather superficial way ("If it won the last race it will probably win this"). On bad days, when Mum had lost more than she could afford, there were recriminations. She would never accept any fault or blame herself. She had a standard reply to any criticism of her reckless betting: "It's all Harry's fault. He took me to the races, encouraged me to gamble and gave me bad advice."

Harry was more measured in his wagering and liked to study form. Mum found this boring. As in everyday life, she took immediate, rather than thoughtful, decisions. Whether Harry was a more successful punter than my mother is uncertain. Probably not! When I asked him if he had won his standard reply was, "I broke even." This usually meant he had lost, especially if he said it with a sad face.

Derby was fun because of the characters and the wealth of other activities besides horse racing. Ordinary race meetings were, for me at least, a bit tedious. Even as a ten-year-old I was better at predicting winners than my parents. One day, when they had lost quite a lot of money at Kempton Park, I showed them a newspaper I had bought that morning in which I had correctly ticked the winners of eight out of the ten races. I had simply chosen the favourites as tipped by the racing journalists. Nevertheless, my mother got it into her head that I had clairvoyant powers, a view reinforced by a popular film at the time called *The Rocking Horse Winner*, in which the hero, a small boy of my age, would go into a trance when furiously riding his rocking horse and splutter out the first past the post of the 2.30 at Epsom. Sad to say, my magical powers did not last as further predications on my part became unreliable. My mother was disappointed. I think she believed I could make the family fortune, or at least become a professional tipster.

1950

Senior School

Seeing me off on the train to Peterborough was as upsetting for my mother as it was for me. Her guilt came to the surface and she started to make promises she would not keep.

"Darling Barry," she would say, "I will write to you every day."

The blast of the guard's whistle, a huge puff of steam, final hugs and kisses, and the train moved slowly out of the station. An hour and a half later it rolled into Peterborough North. Trunks and large cases were piled up on the platform to be sent along later by Carter Paterson. One of the schoolmasters detailed to provide a taxi service would be waiting for us. I did not recognise many of the other boys. Of course the junior school had been wound down. These would be the new intake to Form 1 of the senior school.

We were apprehensive driving through the town to Park Road and Madeley House. This time there was no Lillian Hay to swoop down and hug me; no Roland Jermy with his chuckle to tease me about life in London and ask all about my holidays. Instead there was a gaunt, plain, middle-aged woman in the entrance hall with a dewdrop at the end of her nose, looking like a frightened rabbit. Miss Winifred Trunton, thereafter nicknamed Trunt (but whom we were instructed to call 'Matron'), went on the defensive from day one. Whereas Lillian Hay would smile, Trunt would frown. Lillian Hay would comfort a boy in distress; Trunt would walk away. It was not her job!

By now there were about forty boarders. After tea Mr Parker, the new housemaster, addressed the assembled boys. He was a short man with a high forehead and crinkly black hair. Although his voice was gentle, he spoke with authority.

"I would like to start by giving a special welcome to all the new boys who are probably away from their homes and families for the first time. But this will be your new family. We are a Christian family, and if you trespass God will forgive you, after we have punished you. We are a strict and obedient family, a clean and tidy family, a punctual family and a family which does not speak after lights are out in the dormitories. We are never late for meals. I have little more to say, unless Matron would like to add anything."

Trunt looked startled and shook her head, but then as an afterthought whispered in Mr Parker's ear. Mr Parker looked grave and addressed us once more.

"Ah yes. Matron wishes it to be known that she will not tolerate soiled underwear."

The Carter Paterson van arrived at the boarding house gates and disgorged its contents onto the driveway. We were instructed to unpack our trunks quietly and quickly. The new members of the junior dorm met for the first time and tried to bond. My handicap became apparent immediately. I was the 'baby' of the group. I had passed the eleven-plus but I would not be eleven years old until the following June. I was also small and weedy, and because I had been a boarder for a number of years I had foolishly assumed an air of proprietorship which did not serve me well. The new boys took command, and I was sidelined, ignored and then bullied.

Every boy had a story to tell, although he seldom told it. Some coped with homesickness and loneliness better than others. Martin ('Ginner') Gray, with his confident grin and shock of red hair, was tougher than most. Many years later he confided in me.

"I remember having a small lump in my throat after my mother dumped me at the front door, but it only lasted a minute. I was from a broken home. My parents were continuously arguing, often violently. My mother had told me at an early age that I was simply not wanted. She was having a relationship with her boss at work.

Life at home had become unbearable. Eventually she left and took me and my brother and sister to live with our grandparents who owned a smallholding. They had animals, hayfields, an orchard and outbuildings. I loved it. It was like arriving in paradise. But the idyll was short-lived. After a month I was shifted off to a strict aunt who lived in the centre of Northampton. I think my mother was at a loss as to what to do with me. So she said she would pack me off to boarding school, and that's exactly what happened when I passed the eleven-plus."

Despite his unpromising beginning, life turned out well for Ginner at 'the Pig'. He was a natural leader and sportsman, popular with the staff and older boys. He did not excel academically but this was not a handicap. School life, and later the army, were his happiest days. Being strong for his age, he was eager to show off his athletic prowess.

"I could push you over with two fingers," he would say to me, and often did just that.

Another member of our intake was David ('Chips') Rafferty. His angelic face and chubby features disguised mischievousness. Chips liked to be one of the gang and was up for anything clandestine. He was rarely caught. Although strong and a bully, he and I seemed to get along reasonably well – at least initially. He did not talk much about his family. He had lost his mother and was devoted to his father who, because of his work, could not cope with poor Chips. One Easter I invited him home to our flat in London. My mother was in a good mood and I was pleased to have him to stay because it meant I had someone to play with. I could show Chips around London and get out from under my mother's feet. It was pretty cramped in the Luxborough Street flat and Chips and I had to sleep on mattresses in the living room. The stay seemed to go well and we had fun exploring my favourite haunts and going back and forth on the Underground.

A few weeks after we got back to school I saw Chips laughing with a crowd of boys and pointing at me. He was telling his friends that when he stayed with Po Chambers he had seen his mother naked.

"I was lying in bed, pretending to be asleep," he said to the giggling throng, "when Barry's mother came into the room to fetch something. She had no clothes on!"

Howls of laughter from the boys. I had seen my mother naked many times before, but it must have been a shock for Chips. I felt ashamed but tried not to show it.

John Uzzell, a serious boy with frizzy blond hair, had a typical experience of boarding school life. Years later he told me, "My memories of the first days and weeks have been repressed as they were painful, physically and psychologically. I felt abandoned by my parents and I was bullied. I just survived, but still bear the mental scars."

He had entered the school with great expectations as he was already a cathedral chorister and had impressed the headmaster, Harry Hornsby. But the bullying and misery took their toll and his schoolwork suffered, at least for the first few years. Things looked up as he grew and became physically stronger, and he eventually found success on the athletics field. To the surprise of many of us, John, an essentially gentle and philosophical person, was to become the governor of Bedford and then Durham Prison, also doing a spell as a borstal housemaster.

Trunt did not last long. She was unqualified for the job of matron. In her previous employment she had been a housekeeper looking after the needs of the archdeacon. Now she had to deal with noisy, energetic boys, supervise the kitchen staff and face a mountain of dirty laundry. She eventually crumbled and, unable to cope any longer, would retreat to her room at the least opportunity and become 'unavailable'. The other staff began to complain about her lack of commitment. Dejected and cowed, she left the boarding house after two terms. She was replaced by a stout and sensible lady called Mrs Nicholls. Mrs Nicholls was kind but uninspiring. She commanded more respect than Trunt but had a frosty relationship with the housemaster. The boys were aware of this and played one against the other. Mrs Nicholls too fell by the wayside, lasting for just four terms.

For me, these changes were disturbing. I was no longer the matron's favourite; no longer protected. Being smaller and weaker than most boys I was an easy prey to bullying. This took two forms; physical and mental. Being punched, tripped, head-gripped or put in a half-nelson was routine, as was the 'apple-pie bed' or a beating on the head with a Wolly plug (a sock stuffed with other socks), and the mysterious disappearance of one's clothes and other belongings. Institutional bullying came from the prefects who had a licence to use the slipper for any misdemeanour, however trivial. A boy would bend over in the smelly prefects' study and receive up to six whacks on the backside, the impact of which was accelerated by a running jump before the blow was landed.

More pernicious was the mental torture and taunting I received as 'Po'. I tried to tell my mother in one of my regular calls home but she just laughed and said, "Why do they do it? Chambers is not your name."

Continuous bullying drags one down into despair. Confidence and self-esteem are whittled away. Although we did not recognise it at the time, victims, including myself, were probably on the edge of clinical depression because at times one felt that life was not worth living. Schoolwork suffered. Night-time in the dormitory was hellish because tormentors could act with impunity, out of earshot of prefects and masters. Making friends was difficult because the bullied individual was often shunned by classmates who were frightened that association with him would lead to them being bullied in turn. There was no refuge. Some turned to their parents and were taken away from the school, but many had no parental support – character-building, they would say. Why were some bullied, but not others? The bully readily recognises vulnerability. Those who are self-assured are usually left alone. The bully has his own demons which are often deeply buried. He puts these at bay by tormenting others.

Letters from home addressed to 'Barry Kay' continued to embarrass me. Even the housemaster and matron looked bemused when the morning mail was distributed and my letter was handed to me. On one occasion I overheard Mrs Nicholls ask, "What is this name 'Kay'?"

"He's my stepfather," I blurted out. The other boys sniggered.

The only way to get peace and quiet to read a letter from home was in the lavatory. After locking the door and sitting down I would read my mother's accounts of home life, what she wore, how hard she worked, how my small sister Penny was getting on and other chatty items. When I saw the long row of kisses at the bottom of the page the tears welled up. By this time another boy, desperate to read his own letter from home, would be banging on the door.

We looked up to certain older boys because of their athletic prowess. One hero was Mick Allison, outstanding at everything including rugby, cricket, hockey, boxing and athletics. He could not swim but this did not stop him from winning 'the plunge' at the annual swimming gala. Combined with sporting excellence, he was a 'thoroughly good chap', always kind, laughing and smiling. He was at the boarding house when I arrived in 1944. All the boys and staff admired him. He left at the time the Jermys married and became a day boy.

Another sporting figure with a fine physique was Brian Mason (not his real name). He had deep-set eyes, bushy eyebrows and a large forehead with slicked-back hair. He was not particularly popular and would often be seen alone practising sprinting on the school playing field. As a winger at rugby or hockey he could outrun all opposition.

During the middle of the term there was an unexpected addition to the boarding house. The boy in question had been so unhappy at his previous school that his parents had removed him at half-term. His name was David Pitman and he was to become my best friend. He snivelled and wheezed and became *the whipping boy for everyone's inner Flashman* (a phrase I have 'borrowed' from the distinguished journalist Alice Pitman who wrote a tribute to her uncle in *The Oldie* in November 2015).

Somewhat in awe of his elder brother Robert, then a household name in political journalism, David was both intelligent and maddening. The school and the boarding house were proudly sports orientated. Pitman could not abide physical activity of any kind. He also rubbed up his peers in other ways. For example, our schoolboy politics were conservative – you criticised Winston Churchill at your peril. David was an ardent socialist (his father was a Labour councillor) and thought that Churchill was a war criminal because of Gallipoli and the Bengal famine. To some extent he was recycling the opinions of his brilliant elder brother but he was persuasive and passionate. With his advanced vocabulary he won every argument, and in return received a beating.

At the Pig and Whistle, physical weakness combined with an artistic temperament was a recipe for a life in purgatory. I was sickened and angry with the fighting, bullying and jostling for power. Boarding house boys were becoming feral. What purpose did it all serve? I decided I would try to protect Pitman, even with my limited abilities. David was unusual and made me think differently. I would befriend him. I was intrigued by his hobbies and interests. As well as politics he was devoted to the theatre, the cinema, photography, books and music – particularly nineteenth-century Romantics and Gilbert and Sullivan. He could draw on paper and scraperboard, and wrote plays and stories for young children.

At the beginning of one term David brought back a large package that looked like a bundle of plywood slabs. When assembled it was a toy theatre complete with a proscenium arch and footlights.

"Penny plain or tuppence coloured?" he said.

"Penny what?" I replied

"I have one penny plain, *Hamlet*, and one tuppence coloured, *The Highwayman's Daughter*."

"How about *Hamlet*?" I said.

"Agreed. Excellent. The script is no more than a synopsis, a parody almost, but it will have to do. My brother gave me a record of Laurence Olivier speaking the famous soliloquies which we will use as voiceovers at the appropriate times."

And so, assuming I was as enthusiastic as he was to bring Shakespeare to the likes of Ginner Gray and Chips Rafferty, we proceeded for the next few weeks to use most of our leisure time pushing cardboard figures across the tiny stage. Surprisingly, the production was a success. The housemaster, his assistant and the matron, as well as a handful of curious boys, sat through the production and clapped heartily at the end.

It took me a while to get used to David Pitman's odd personality. At times he was insufferably stubborn and inflexible. For example, he would ask me to sit whilst he sketched me. One minute he was intensely absorbed with the project, but then he would abruptly erase what he had drawn and, with violent, rapid strokes of his rubber, start all over again. If I fidgeted or moved he would cry out in his shrill voice, "Don't move, don't move. Oh my God, you have moved! You have spoilt everything."

When I jumped up to see what I had spoilt there was nothing to see but a rubbed-out page.

David was somewhat uncoordinated, even clumsy. He was hopeless at games and was usually excused because the staff could not be bothered with him. As an asthmatic he always had an excuse. It was expected that every boy, whatever his ability, should partake in cross-country running. David was horrified, saying it was barbaric and dangerous. To get out of it he once lit up a herbal 'asthma cigarette', to the consternation of the games master and the great amusement of the boys. Somehow he did not appreciate he was being provocative.

Apart from a few hale and hearty boys, cross-country running was loathed by the majority. Despite the weather, in freezing temperature or snow, boys would make their way to the starting point at Walton Crossing about two miles outside the city. We had to run two to four miles across ploughed fields and through ice-cold water, mud and slush. Afterwards, exhausted, we put our day clothes on over saturated running gear and set off back for school. Sometimes boys collapsed and had to be assisted into a nearby cottage (prompting angry correspondence from a 'disgusted observer' in the local paper).

Pitman and I managed to escape into our private worlds from time to time but bullies would discover our hideout and smash up whatever we were working on – photography, drawing or the toy theatre. We were often in the depths of despair. Then there was a turn in our fortunes. Mr Parker, Roland Jermy's successor as housemaster, himself a bit of a thespian, seemed to take pity on us. He pulled us to one side as we left the dining room.

"Come here, Pitman and Chambers. You both seem unhappy. I suspect you find it hard making friends with some of the other boys."

This was difficult territory. If we were to admit to being bullied and were so unwise as to tell Mr Parker the names of our tormentors, terrible recriminations would follow. We looked at the floor and remained silent.

He continued, "Matron has pointed out to me that the spare sick bay on the top landing is hardly ever used. I am minded to let the two of you use this as your dormitory room. This will be an experiment, just for a while, to give you some respite. You must both keep a low profile."

"Thank you very much, sir," we said in unison. And so it was decided and we moved in our belongings.

This happy state only lasted a term before the room was reclaimed. Quietly, after lights out, David would tell me about the plays and films his famous elder brother had taken him to see – *Hamlet* and *Antony and Cleopatra* with Laurence Olivier and Vivien Leigh – and the new films from the Ealing studios such as *Passport to Pimlico* and *Kind Hearts and Coronets* (which I hadn't even heard of). With Mum and Harry I only watched Marx Brothers films, Hollywood musicals and Danny Kaye movies. It was not that I did not enjoy them, but David made me realise my horizons were narrow. I felt both ignorant and jealous of David, and that I had missed out on so much. Politics was another of David's passions, not surprisingly as he had been brought up in a radical left-wing family. I was ashamed that I had never heard of the Beveridge Report and its implications. But David set me straight on most issues. Anyway, I had a lot to discuss with Harry when we broke up for the school holidays.

In the following months I began to toughen up a little and started to perform quite well at athletics, particularly in the long and high jump. Even Brian Mason had growled a quiet compliment at me when he saw my silver cup and clutch of certificates at the end of sports day. I was chosen to represent the junior team at the March Sports, an important inter-school athletics event held at the end of the summer term. The whole school would descend on Peterborough East Station for the hour-long train journey across the Fens to March. The grandstand at the sports ground rocked with boys shouting, "Peta-bara, Peta-bara-ra."

The senior hundred yards starting pistol sounded. Mason got off to a slow start but then, like the winged messenger, sprinted forward to a clear win. King's School boys erupted in wild applause. In the two hundred yards Mason snatched victory from the Wellingborough Grammar School champion. He was also the star in the relays. I had my own victories in the junior events, winning the long jump and scraping over five feet to take the high jump. We returned to school, jubilant. On the train back Mason congratulated me, staring at me hard with his faint, superior smile.

Back in the junior dormitory there was much chattering, although talking after lights out was dangerous, running the risk of painful corporal punishment. Mason, on prefect duty and still in his tracksuit, had warned us he would be ruthless. However, I was still excited and continued to retell the day's events in a rather loud voice. The door flung open. Mason had been listening outside. I had been caught red-handed.

"Go to my study," he said.

I followed him, trembling. He locked the door behind us and produced a large slipper. "You can either have six of these, or," he said, grabbing my hand and placing it on his huge, erect penis, "you can wank me off."

1951

Mr Butler

When I returned to the flat at the end of one summer term – I was twelve at the time – my mother told me that Harry had gone away.

"Where has he gone?" I asked.

She gave a well-rehearsed reply. "He has gone away on business and will not be back for some weeks."

Penny had also vanished. Mum said she was being looked after by a friend.

I did not ask further questions. Deep down I was pleased. I could have my mother to myself.

This happy state did not last for long. A man called Mr Butler became a frequent visitor. He was a policeman, a detective inspector. How he came to know my mother was a mystery and I was afraid to ask. He was in his early forties, quite tall and thin, and always dressed in a striped grey suit and trilby hat. Unlike the detectives I had seen at the cinema, Mr Butler did not ask questions. He had an awkward smile, talked very little and was anxious that I should like him. Mum said he was an important person in the police force and that I should be especially polite to him.

Detective Inspector Richard Butler gave me lavish presents, the most memorable of which was an album of cigarette cards containing the full set of football players, cricketers, golfers, boxers, motor-racing drivers and jockeys. These were priceless currency amongst my peers at school and I was amazed that I was the proud possessor of such treasures. At the time, collecting sets of cigarette cards was an obsession. When an adult threw away his empty cigarette packet several small boys would run and grab it, hoping the card inside would be a rare one, or at least one that could be swapped. Anyway, after I was given the album I lost all interest in cigarette cards. The thrill had gone. I owned every card; what was the point in collecting more?

One morning I was sitting in the flat, reading. Mum came back about midday with Mr Butler. She was looking a little restless and excited, and was annoyed I was still around. Suddenly she blurted out, "Why aren't you in the park on such a lovely day?"

"I'm reading," I said, trying to ignore them.

Mum got agitated and Mr Butler looked awkward. She then exclaimed in a loud voice, "Barry. You are looking so pale. You will get sick again if you don't get some sun on your face."

"How do you mean, sick *again*?"

"Well, you were in hospital. You almost had to have an operation."

"But not because of lack of sunshine," I protested.

Mum exploded. "Get out of the flat at once and look up at the sun for at least an hour! Leave now! Don't argue! I am your mother and know what is best for you."

She pointed at the door in fury, her hand trembling. I leapt out of the chair and ran out of the flat. Mum was impossible in a mood like this. It was best to avoid her. I stood on the opposite side of the road and stared up at the sun. Five minutes went by, then ten. My face was burning. I started to amble down the street. Several passers-by looked at me with curiosity. Who was this strange boy walking along the street with his head right back looking up at the sun? After the third or fourth scolding from aggrieved pedestrians I had collided with, I looked at my reflection in shop windows to see if my face was pinker. I had walked up to Marylebone High Street, along Baker Street, back around Paddington Street and returned to Cheviot Court. I then repeated this more slowly, but only forty-five minutes had passed.

Nevertheless, I would take a chance and go back even though I had not stayed out long enough.

Just then I saw Mr Butler emerge from the flat without seeing me. He looked anxious and pulled his hat firmly down on his head, walking away furtively. I wondered if I should run after him and ask whether he thought I could return before the hour was up. But it was too late; he had hurried off. I mounted the steps gingerly, went along the landing and down the stairs to the basement. I was nervous. I knocked on the door. Mum opened it. She smiled at me, looking bright and happy.

"Hello, darling. Where have you been?"

"I have been staring up at the sun, just as you told me to. Soaking up the goodness of the sun's rays so I will not have to go back into hospital. Is my face a different colour? Am I still pale?"

"What a silly boy!" She was doing up the buttons on her blouse. "Now, I will make us a quick cup of tea and then I must fly."

I was left in the flat, alone.

I started snooping around again, hoping to find something interesting to relieve the boredom. The tall walnut bureau was one thing I was forbidden to open. It was always locked but I knew where the key was. I opened it. In the middle drawer there was a stack of letters. Each page was filled with Harry Kay's tiny, neat handwriting which spilled around the edge of each sheet to make sure that no space was wasted. Several letters were left unopened. I read some of them but could not understand much of what was written except *loving you, missing you, can't wait to see you again, oh, my darling*, and similar. Then I looked at the letterhead. It read *HM Prison Pentonville*.

1951

Bust and Boom

I did not know that Harry's radio business had collapsed until I came across a cutting from the *London Gazette* which read, *NOTICE is hereby given that the Partnership heretofore subsisting between Harry Kay and Ernest Gross carrying on business as Radio Dealers at 13, Marylebone High Street, London, WI under the style or firm of "EXPRESS RADIO COMPANY" has been dissolved by mutual consent...* etc., etc.

The demise of the business and Harry's subsequent imprisonment were due to his lack of judgement. Earlier in the year a spiv with whom he had a nodding acquaintance approached him with an offer of new radio sets at a bargain price. It was the usual 'fallen off a lorry' story. Business had been slow and here was an opportunity to make a quick profit. Unfortunately a passing police constable recognised some of the items in the shop window as stolen property. Harry was arrested, convicted of 'receiving' and sentenced to three months in prison. It could have been worse but his wartime record in the London Fire Brigade was taken into account. His partner, Mr Gross, denied all knowledge and escaped a custodial sentence.

The investigating officer was Inspector Richard Butler. Shortly after my mother had bundled me out of the flat because I was 'too pale', there was another embarrassing incident. I woke up one morning and went through to her bedroom, hoping for a cuddle. There in bed with her was Mr Butler.

"What is Mr Butler doing in your bed?" I exclaimed in surprise. And then suddenly he was not there. Had I been mistaken? I was confused.

"How dare you say such a wicked thing?" cried my mother. "You must apologise to Mr Butler the next time you see him. Now go and get dressed and stay in your room. Do not come out until I tell you, otherwise you will get a slap."

A short time afterwards, when I saw Mr Butler, my mother again insisted I should apologise.

"I'm sorry I said you were in Mummy's bed, Mr Butler."

I do not know who was more embarrassed, him or me.

My stepfather's first few weeks were spent at Pentonville. He was then moved to Ford Open Prison and, with time off for good behaviour, was released after ten weeks. My mother and he agreed to 'start again'. It was a desperate time because they needed to generate income now that the radio business had collapsed. My mother's skill at dressmaking was to save them from penury and eventually bring prosperity. Her special gift was to design, or copy and modify, garments which appealed to a mass market and were affordable. The business had started on the floor of the flat in Luxborough Street. In her document she wrote, *I raised a capital of three hundred pounds.* (She didn't say how.) My mother would make patterns, buy material and, having calculated the costs, build up a portfolio of samples. She started with blouses. Harry's job was to provide business contacts and chauffeur her around.

Mum would present her card (*Joan Kay, Blouse Manufacturer*) and ask if a buyer could look at her samples. They rarely had time to see her. On the other hand if she said, "Joan Kay has sent me", they showed more interest. "Do you know Joan Kay?" she would ask.

"Oh, yes," they would say. "She designs some lovely stuff."

"Yes, she is doing well," my mother would add. "All the shops are asking for her work."

Little by little, sales took off. Within a few months Harry was on the road by himself, selling and taking orders. They took on outworkers but it soon became clear they needed their own workshop and showroom.

One weekend my mother and Harry, together with my sister Penny, then about three years old, set off for the East End. At that time the area around Whitechapel was home to the 'rag trade'. They were hoping to find somewhere affordable to rent but everywhere seemed to be closed. They drove around for a while and eventually parked in front of a dilapidated shopfront on the Commercial Road. It had caught their attention because of a beautiful child's dress on display. Out of curiosity, my mother pushed open the front door. The room was empty. It was not a shop at all. She walked to the back of the house, from where she heard muffled sounds. A woman was machining. She was middle-aged and stout and welcomed my mother with a warm smile. Next to her a man was cutting material for dresses.

"I am glad you came," the woman said.

My mother did not understand. "I'm sorry," she said. "I thought there was someone around because the door was open."

"Don't worry, dear," the lady replied. "The door is always open. There is nothing worth stealing here."

"We have been driving around trying to see if there are any premises to rent, but everywhere is closed."

"Of course they are; it's Rosh Hashanah. Nobody works on Rosh Hashanah. Well, like us, they pretend they don't work. We have to work all the time, you see. We have two lovely boys, praise God, who need feeding, clothing and money for cheder."

"Do you know of any premises to rent?" my mother asked. "I have been working from home, making samples and travelling to get orders."

"Of course," the woman said, getting up. My mother noticed that she was much smaller than expected and had a built-up left shoe. Each step looked like agony as she heaved her bad leg forward with a thrust of her hips. "I'm Ada, and this is my husband, Manny."

Manny was also small, about five foot. He was unshaven, and wore a vest, ragged trousers and a kippah. "Lovely to meet you," he said, smiling broadly. "And so glad you popped by. Ada, put the kettle on."

Harry, who was a giant next to Manny and Ada, introduced himself, beaming. They fetched Penny from the car.

"Oh, what a beautiful little girl!" said Ada, taking Penny by the hand.

Over tea in the little room upstairs, Manny and Ada Shoben explained their plight. They had escaped from Germany in 1938, "with nothing". They had intended to go to the USA, but when the boat stopped in Southampton they could not face the sea voyage and disembarked. Using contacts in the East End they managed to find work, Ada as a seamstress and Manny as a cutter. Things had been hard, however, and they lived a life of penury. Their present plight was desperate. They owed 142 pounds and lived in fear of eviction.

The Kays and Shobens bonded. They chatted away amiably. Time passed quickly.

What a wonderful evening we spent with Ada and Manny on that first meeting, wrote my mother in her document. *They cooked a wonderful dinner of roast chicken, baked potatoes and lochen pudding. We sat up talking until 5am; luckily Penny slept through.*

This chance encounter was to lead to a fruitful partnership. Harry agreed to pay off their debts; Manny and Ada wept with relief. The Shobens provided a shopfront and workshop and took over the manufacture of my mother's designs. Harry continued with the travelling, but with an expanded list of clients. Several nights a week my mother would stay over in the Commercial Road, Ada having redecorated and furnished one of the bedrooms. It became a life of patterns, sewing, cutting, bagels and smoked salmon. Soon they were making lots of money – but just as importantly, they became a sort of family and my mother felt the warmth of the East End. She felt accepted as a clever, chic Jewish girl with a flair for fashion design.

She described her change in lifestyle as follows:

During the week I would stay over at the Shobens' in the Commercial Road, toiling away at patterns and samples. At weekends I was the elegant Jewish lady Joan Kay, famous fashion designer, who wore haute couture dresses, went to the finest restaurants, had the best seats at the theatre, popped across to Paris for the races at Longchamp and played roulette at the casino in Ostend. When Harry announced, "Get ready quickly, we leave for Deauville in two hours" I was always prepared to go, even at a minute's notice. If I ever said, "Oh, I must go out and buy this or that before we leave", Harry would say, "You can buy anything you are short of over there."

Sometimes, during school holidays, I accompanied my mother to the East End. The Shobens had two sons, Barry and Martin, who were both about my age. I got on well with them. We swapped comics and messed around on the piano. I am not sure how my mother, reinvented as a Jewish lady, explained me to the Shobens.

"Don't show your willy to Barry or Martin," she once said.

"Why would I do that?" I said.

"Well, if you are weeing together or something."

I pretended not to hear her.

One day in early September, just before going back to Peterborough, I was with my mother at the Shobens' house, helping her pack boxes and trying to make myself useful. After a while I asked her for some money for lunch at the café along the road. I had been there before on several occasions with my mother, and Mr Green, the proprietor, always gave me a warm welcome.

As my mother was fishing around in her purse for a two-shilling piece she looked up at me and said, "Barry, when you get to the café please wish Mr Green a happy New Year."

"A happy New Year?" I said in surprise. "It's only September."

Looking even more serious and raising her voice, she repeated, "Barry, go to the café and wish Mr Green a happy New Year. Don't argue. I want you to say this to him clearly, sincerely and with a smile, otherwise you won't get any pocket money for going back to school."

I thought my mother was becoming loopy again. However, I had no option but to concur with this strange request and, taking the 'two bob' for lunch, set off for the café. As I entered Mr Green gave me a friendly little wave. Feeling nervous and expecting to be thought a complete idiot, I screwed up my courage and looked him straight in the face.

"A happy New Year, Mr Green."

His eyes widened and his face lit up. Grinning from ear to ear, he opened his arms as if to give me a big hug.

"And a happy New Year to you, my boy."

1952–1953

Happy Families

Penny was a cute little girl. My mother would parade her proudly along Marylebone High Street in pretty dresses with pink smocking. When I came home from school I would take my turn with pram-pushing duties. Every few yards some lady would peer at Penny and say, "Oh, what a lovely baby!"

"What about life in the flat?" I asked Penny many years later when we were both adults. Like me, she remembered the tedium of it all. "Mum and Dad were out all day and tired when they returned in the evening. They didn't read to us or play with us. We were left to our own devices."

Penny bore the brunt of our mother's mood swings. When she was about five years old she witnessed a frightening scene. Mum had been agitated for a few days. Suddenly she was shouting and screaming and throwing ashtrays and plates at Harry. She started to burn five-pound notes. Dad was terrified.

"There was nothing he could do," said Penny. "In those days you couldn't call the police for a domestic scene. On another occasion I remember Dad holding her up on her feet and dragging her around the flat, making her walk in order to keep her awake because she had taken an overdose of sleeping pills."

Mum's outbursts were always unpredictable, occurring for no apparent reason. There was always a torrent of abuse directed at Harry. Things were never her fault. Her ability to hide her illness from people outside the family was remarkable, as was her capacity to manipulate. Even doctors were fooled. Mum was once persuaded to see a Harley Street psychiatrist. After the consultation he spoke to Harry. "I can find nothing wrong with your wife," he said. "You and your daughter seem to be the problem."

On the other hand, Penny remembers many happy times during the early 1950s. Mum could be affectionate. On Saturday evenings Harry regularly went to the dog racing at the White City. Penny and my mother stayed in the flat. "The two of us would watch television and laugh and cuddle. We would eat pomegranate seeds using pins, and maybe have some cake or chocolate. I was never in doubt that my mother loved me, although as I grew older I realised that she was not the person to turn to for advice, particularly on personal matters such as periods and sexuality. With Mum you always had to toe the line. She always had to be right, always knew what was best for me. Forced me to wear clothes I hated and that sort of thing."

"What about Dad?" I asked

"I adored Dad. He protected me when Mum got out of control, telling me that it was not normal behaviour. Every Wednesday evening, when I got a bit older, we would have a date while Mum was with his sister, Aunty Betty. We would go for dinner at the Cumberland Hotel in Marble Arch. The food was delicious and there was a live band. It was marvellous being with him on those occasions. All my anxieties vanished. I loved him so much."

"What about Dad's parents?" I said. "As you know, I never met them. I never existed as far as they were concerned."

"I don't understand why you were excluded. We just didn't mention you. Mum had that way of steering the conversation away when there was any mention of her life before she met Dad. Dad's family were observant Orthodox Jews; not Hasidic, although many of their extended family were. They lived in Dollis Hill in this dreary house. They were quite poor. Dad, Betty and I visited them regularly. Mum rarely came. Dad wasn't religious at all. He had rejected all that sort of stuff. After all, he was a man of the world, a man of the people, an ex-communist. He was not going to be put in a box by some religious sect.

As the business progressed my mother's small team became more efficient. She had bursts of creative energy when, hardly stopping for breath, she would sketch new designs and make up the first sample herself. She was totally absorbed. No one was to disturb her. She existed on tea and cigarettes. Once satisfied with a particular design, the patterns would be passed to Manny and Ada for cutting and machining. Armed with the new season's samples, Harry would do the rounds of old and new customers, taking orders.

Their big break came with a two-tone blouse. This particular design, in poplin, was grey in the upper right and lower left, and white in the upper left and lower right with bishop sleeves and a high neck. One evening when my mother and Harry were watching their tiny, flickering television there was a shriek of delight. Sylvia Peters, the country's most famous presenter, was wearing my mother's 'two-tone'. The orders came tumbling in. Manny and Ada were now working flat out. Within two years business in the Commercial Road was so good that more spacious premises, nearer to the outlets, had to be found.

In early 1952 the operation moved to the West End and occupied two floors of 55 Wells Street, W1. The signs on the windows read *Joan Kay Ltd, Manufacturer, Blouses and Separates*. The machinists were on the second floor. Within a short space of time over fifteen staff were employed. Downstairs was the office and showroom. At the back of the showroom were six or so finishers who would sew on buttons and check the garments. There were two packers and a sketcher who made drawings for fashion magazines. They also employed a salesman who did the rounds of specialist dress or 'madam' shops. Harry was also an excellent salesman but was rarely given credit. In many respects he kept the enterprise together by 'troubleshooting', settling disputes and listening sympathetically to employees' concerns.

The success of Joan Kay Ltd meant that we could at last move out of the gloomy basement flat in Luxborough Street. Our new home was in Carlton Hill, just off Hamilton Terrace in Maida Vale. It was a small maisonette located in a bright, airy estate with an underground car park. On the ground floor there was a kitchen/dining area together with a small sitting room, and above were two bedrooms. No sooner had we moved in than my mother became restless. She was abrupt with the neighbours, who in turn avoided her.

"These are not my sort of people," she said.

"What are your sort of people?" I asked her.

"Don't be cheeky," she said. "They are all English."

"They are all what?" I said in disbelief. "I'm English, for goodness' sake."

She then left the room in a huff. I knew perfectly well what she meant. Carlton Hill was not Jewish enough for her.

It was difficult for my mother to articulate her feelings. Virtually everyone she knew on a day-to-day basis were first-generation refugees from war-torn Europe. They were both charmed and bemused by my mother. I think they all believed she was Jewish. If any of her friends had doubts they kept them to themselves, or, more likely, thought them unimportant. Mum wanted to be 'one of them'. She had escaped from her old world to join theirs. Taking on a new identity and anglicising one's name was a way of life for so many people my mother had met in the rag trade. In this subculture mystery and ambiguity about one's roots were respected, not probed.

Returning to school (by then I was about thirteen), boys were invited to put their names forward for confirmation into the Church of England. There were many candidates and for me it was a natural thing to do. Spiritual matters were stirring within me and being confirmed was a way to channel these emotions.

We had to have parental permission to take confirmation classes.

"I don't know what I am signing, Barry. It's an English thing, isn't it?"

Throughout my childhood and adolescence there were unspoken rules. During term time, eighty miles away in Peterborough, I was Barry Chambers ("Christian, or whatever," my mother would say). As soon as the train conveyed me back to King's Cross for the holidays I became Barry Kay, son of the successful Jewish couple, Joan and Harry Kay. In order to make this work they had to keep me 'low profile' when I was at home in London. I was excluded from social events ("You will be bored, Barry"). Also, all signs of Barry Chambers were erased from the London home. For example, I had several athletics certificates from sports days which I would bring back to London to show my mother.

"These are wonderful, Barry," she would say. "I will put them somewhere safe." But as soon as I went back to school she would destroy them. She was not going to have material in the house with the name Chambers on it.

Once, when I was home for the holidays, my mother said anxiously, "What will we say about Barry's bar mitzvah?"

"Say he had a wonderful bar mitzvah," retorted Harry, "and that Solly Katz did the catering, and then everyone will know we spent real money on it."

We all laughed.

Sometime later, when my mother once more called the neighbours 'English' and I had remonstrated with her as usual, I rushed into the living room to confront Harry. He was idly watching the TV.

"Mum doesn't like it around here," I said sarcastically, "because there are too many English people." I confronted my stepfather. "What about you? Are you English?"

He smiled and got up slowly from his chair and came over to me. He gave me a hug, and I began to cry. Suddenly I was overwhelmed with his warmth, his generosity of spirit. Here was a man I could cling to, here was a rock. Many years later my mother, in her account, wrote:

Harry was a gentle man, tolerant, amusing and worldly-wise. He loved and understood people of all races and creeds. As a Jew he had known suffering, and that was why his heart always went out to those more unfortunate than himself. His friends were many, he always forgave and forgot an unkindness. He was a man of the people and they loved him for this.

After one of these chats, when he was taking me to the station for the train back to school, he gave me advice.

"There is no need for you to bring up Jewish matters with the boys at school. You are a Christian, that's fine. Just remember not to let an unpleasant remark about Jews go unchallenged."

Harry Kay, my dad, was my hero. I loved him and resolved never to betray him.

The train pulled out of King's Cross. As I sunk back into my seat I was joined by some other King's School boys. "Look, it's Po Chambers," one of them said. "Was that your dad with you on the platform? He looks foreign to me."

"No, no," I said quickly. "He's just a friend of my mum's."

1953–1954

Survival

Academically I had performed quite well in the junior school, having won the form prize in Year 3. So it was unpleasant to learn that on entering the senior school I had been placed in a 'B' rather than an 'A' form. Many years later, Roland Jermy explained why.

"You were still barely ten years old when you entered the senior school; some boys were nearly twelve. It seemed sensible, at the time, to spare you the pressures of the A stream."

Nevertheless, I got it into my head that I was just not good enough to be in 1A, an attitude that was to hold me back in the years to come. Anyway, academic prowess was not foremost in my mind during those first few years; surviving each day unharmed was the priority.

John Roberts was a boarder from 1951 to 1959. His mother, an actress, was divorced and worked in London. Like us all he was homesick initially and bullied although things improved as he grew older. He found conditions at the boarding house Dickensian and was outraged by the sadistic nature of the house prefects who, even at fifteen or sixteen years old, were empowered to administer corporal punishment for the slightest misdemeanour. One of the housemasters enjoyed listening with his ear to the dormitory door for anyone talking after lights out. Any guilty party would be required to report to his study at rising bell the following morning in his pyjamas, where the slipper was administered with gusto.

Nevertheless, John Roberts was proud of the KSP ("the best school around"), and eventually became the head boy.

Bill Tibbles, a contemporary, but in the form below, characterised everyday school life as "lack of time, lack of food and fear of corporal punishment". Being one of seven children and brought up in Ramsey, a Fenland town some thirty miles away, he was unprepared for the Pig and Whistle. Bill was thickset, tall and strong for his age, with wavy black hair and a jutting jaw. He had won a county scholarship after his eleven-plus examination but because of the overcrowding at home had had difficulty in getting peace and quiet to study. With little warning he was sent off to be a boarder at the KSP. For him, like all new boys, the first year was the most challenging. Having come from a carefree family life with minimal discipline, this was an unwelcome regimented existence.

"We were constantly on the go," he recalled. "The rush to the bathroom, being in time for assembly, remembering our things. A prefect gave me the slipper once just for returning to the dormitory to collect a book."

Like Bill, I remember that the food was terrible. Porridge, dry toast and weak tea at breakfast; stew with little meat and overcooked vegetables for dinner; and for tea something awful-looking on toast.

A beating on the backside with a slipper was the prerogative of the prefects and they went about the task with enthusiasm. On the other hand it was unusual for a schoolmaster to resort to the slipper or cane, although one incident stands out. A history teacher, Mr Pybus, a tall, thin man with an awkward walk, became incensed by the noise coming from a classroom between lessons. Storming into the room, he thundered that he would exact punishment by slippering every third boy, "starting with the fat one," he added, pointing to a lad called Sendall. Mike Sendall was probably the quietest, most unassuming, best-behaved boy in the school, but his backside was not spared. (He went on to be a distinguished nuclear physicist at Cambridge, and at one time supervised Tim Berners-Lee, inventor of the World Wide Web.)

Notwithstanding, Mr Pybus was a fine teacher with a wicked sense of humour. Once he gave a boy nought out of twenty for his essay, adding, "A marked improvement."

Although initially Bill Tibbles had a difficult time adjusting to life at the Pig, he soon flourished since he possessed the essentials for survival – physical strength and sporting prowess. He was the Northampton county, and all England, boys' champion discus thrower, as well as a talented rugby player. Unfortunately he was also a bully and I was frequently on the receiving end. Although I tried to avoid him our paths kept crossing and at times he came looking for me with his entourage of sycophants. Encouraged by him, 'baiting Po Chambers' become a 'national sport'. I tried to humour him by acting as the court jester but, although I sometimes amused him, he still walloped me. I am sure that Tibbles had his demons like everyone else. Beneath bullying there is often inner anger. Boys resented their families for sending them away but were unable to articulate their frustration. Looking back, many of us were dealing with emotions over which we had little control. We focused on the immediate; on the need to survive, to fill our tummies, to be liked, to be loved by our parents and to get from one day to the next without being beaten by a prefect or teacher.

Boys who were good at sport were respected whatever their shortcomings in other areas. I had started off quite well in athletics and won a few certificates on sports day. Excellence at rugby and cricket were essential for real sporting prestige, although hockey came a close third. In the first form I was competent on the rugby field and remember speeding down the left wing scoring the occasional try. At the start of one term we were told that "as an experiment" there would be, for the first time, an under-twelves team. A member of the English staff (whose name escapes me; I shall call him Mr Smith), who was not usually associated with sport, was put in charge. I was surprised and pleased to be elected the captain. Four fixtures had been arranged.

We lost the first three games, each by a small margin but enough for morale to be low and my leadership to be called into question. Hoping to redeem myself, I gave the team an exaggerated pep talk on the bus to the last event at Oundle School. On arrival it was clear that something was wrong. It was the custom for the visitors' bus to be greeted by the captain of the host team. On this occasion the boy in question was huge. He towered above the tallest in our team. After we had changed and come out onto the pitch we were confronted with an opposition of giants. Mr Smith conferred with the Oundle master. There had obviously been a mistake; the Oundle under-thirteens had been matched against the KSP under-twelves. Undernourished eleven-year-old grammar school lads were pitched against well-fed public school boys at least a year older. It was decided to play on regardless. A ritual slaughter followed. The Oundle boys walked through our pathetic defence, scoring try after try. They were too big to tackle and if they held the ball high up we were too small to jump up and grab it. There was one moment of glory when I managed to grab the ball, run hard, dodge some surprised back player who had not seen any action for the entire match, and reach the try line. The final score was 120–3. It was humiliating.

On the bus back to Peterborough, Mr Smith, rather than admit he had made a ghastly error with his fixture, decided that we had not shown enough guts and team spirit. "You didn't try hard enough," he proclaimed.

On Monday, at the school assembly, the headmaster announced the results of the Saturday fixtures. He did not explain about the unevenness of the contest. Mr Smith had shifted the blame from himself to the team, and the team decided it was my fault. News of the score was received with both gasps of amazement and laughter. Not until the sixth form was I selected for any rugby XV. I was never allowed to forget the 'Oundle bloodbath'.

Being an inmate at the Pig and Whistle was bad enough for any young boy but the introduction of a dysfunctional teacher was to make life even more unbearable. Sometime around 1952 a Mr Benson (not his real name) arrived as assistant housemaster. He was small in stature with a ruddy complexion and a supercilious grin. Every misdemeanour, however trivial, was rewarded with the slipper. For Benson young boys were by definition devious and dishonest. He created a reign of fear, but he did not last long. One day he hit a boy in a fit of rage and was dismissed.

The boarding house was becoming rudderless. Since the departure of Roland Jermy and his benevolent leadership, there had been a procession of well-meaning but ineffectual housemasters, assistant housemasters and matrons. They struggled in dreary surroundings. Madeley House had become more run-down with broken furniture, plumbing which barely coped, peeling plaster and grubby decoration. The staff, for the most part, seemed exhausted. The most they could do was supervise meals, prep and bedtime routines, and try to prevent us from becoming feral.

Avoiding the predatory Mason presented another anxiety. He was the house prefect in charge of the junior dormitory and went about his duties after lights out with a permanent erection under his trademark blue tracksuit. His victims were heard begging him to desist, sometimes angrily, usually pathetically. The housemasters, either through fear or ignorance, turned a blind eye to Mason's nocturnal activities. As far as I was concerned, he never went beyond groping and fondling, although one boy claimed he tried to penetrate him in the fives court but he had screamed and escaped. The dangerous times were after dark when Mason seemed to be lurking around every corner, especially in the toilets and the changing rooms. Some boys, the prettier ones, opted to be 'protected' by him. This had the advantage of immunity from bullying but the disadvantage of having to collaborate with Mason on his favourite activity. Boys used to say that mild homosexual activity around the time one's voice broke was normal. But there was nothing normal about Mason. Rumour has it that he ended up as a convicted paedophile.

My friendship with David Pitman had provided an escape from some of the worst excesses of the bullying but I was still desperate to be liked and accepted by other boys. To be 'one of the gang' it was necessary to participate in several punishable activities, such as illicit smoking and playing pontoon for money, neither of which appealed to me. I was moving towards a wretched choice. It was either the tough oafs or precious Pitman.

One Saturday afternoon Pitman and I escaped into town, but with no particular plan in mind. We popped into the town library and rummaged in the music section. Pitman wanted to look at miniature scores and seemed surprised that I knew nothing about Mahler. We then browsed in some bookshops.

"Do you have any Ezra Pound?" asked Pitman in a superior fashion.

"Edna who?" the bookseller replied.

"I can't believe he didn't know Ezra Pound," said Pitman, and waltzed out of the shop. I trailed behind, embarrassed.

"Let's go to the cathedral," he said. We admired the spectacular West Front. Did I know it was one of the finest examples of early English Gothic? (No, I didn't). Was I aware that the foundation went back to the Anglo-Saxon King Peada? (No, I was not). What did I think of the perpendicular fan vaulting? Did I know that the Spanish nobility still honour the tomb of Catherine of Aragon and bring pomegranates; her symbol? Had I seen the Hedda Stone? And so my education continued. Walking back to school I was asked my views on the forthcoming general election, the miners' strike and the London theatre. By the time we reached Park Road I had been thoroughly talked down to and seemed to have little self-esteem left.

Turning into the school gates we saw Tibbles with a few of his entourage. They were tormenting some small boy, but our arrival distracted them and the victim broke loose and ran away. Annoyed at losing his prey, Tibbles rounded on the two of us. He started by shoving me about with his strong arms, angrily hurling abuse. His hangers-on laughed.

"Why are you friendly with this drip?" said Tibbles, pointing at Pitman. "You'll never be one of us if you hang around with him."

He suddenly grabbed Pitman in a half-nelson, pulled his hair back and thrust his face towards me. "Go, on, give him one," Tibbles taunted me.

For a moment I hesitated, but confused and angry, and seizing the chance to get in with Tibbles and his gang, I punched Pitman hard in the face.

I never got over the shame of that awful incident. I had been made to choose between being 'included' by the gang and my friendship with David Pitman. For a fraction of a second I made a stupid decision, mostly through cowardice. Luckily Pitman did not hold it against me because on other occasions shortly afterwards I stood up for him and took on other boys who tried to bully him. At that time, the early 1950s, the staff took little or no interest in such behaviour. The feeling was that survival in a group of peers was all part of growing up – a 'sink or swim' culture. Unfortunately some boys sank. Without explanation their parents took them away from the school. The result was that nothing was done to curb the tortures that many had to endure.

1954

Spoke Wheeler and Statutory Declaration

When it seemed as if the Pig and Whistle could sink no further in terms of grubbiness and low morale, along came leadership and stability in the form of Kenneth ('Spoke') Wheeler. Mr Wheeler was a slim, upright man of medium height with dark hair and a good sense of humour. He was a former naval officer who had seen active service in the Far East. "For me," he would say, "the war consisted of endless periods of inactivity interrupted by short interludes of terror. During the lulls I was never bored because Keats, Byron, Dickens, Macaulay and other friends kept me company."

On discharge from the navy he went up to Oxford to read history, married Margaret and arrived at the Pig as the new housemaster with his wife and their baby daughter, Pamela. The Wheelers inherited a run-down, decayed Madeley House and immediately set about improving matters by means of a massive DIY operation. Boarded windows were taken down, the rot cut out and the sashes replaced. Broken furniture was repaired, cockroaches were eliminated, walls were scrubbed, shelves constructed and doors rehung. The boldest project was re-landscaping the garden. The front driveway was returned to good order, the almost derelict side lawn was levelled and re-sown, and flower beds were dug and trees pruned. Gangs of boys went about these tasks with varying degrees of enthusiasm.

Silly punishments such as writing lines were abolished and replaced by cleaning or maintenance tasks.

As Mark Hatton, a former KSP boarder, noted, "Ken ran the Pig like a ship." Little by little things improved, even the food. The Wheelers were a formidable team. They were energetic and enthusiastic. Margaret Wheeler, thin, pretty, with long auburn hair, refused to be called 'Matron', although that in fact was what she was. She managed the laundry of fifty boys with her own twin-tub washing machine, and acted as our nurse and mother as well as bringing up her own child. Mrs Wheeler was a kind woman who made a great effort to see that the boys were happy, well fed and well dressed.

Shortly before the Wheelers' arrival at the boarding house Cecil Marriott Harrison was appointed headmaster to succeed Harry Hornsby. The contrast was striking. Whereas Mr Hornsby had been approachable and cheerful, Mr Harrison, at least on first acquaintance, was austere and pious. He was tall and had a saintly bearing. This "scholar, teacher and priest", as his clerical friends described him, was a Cambridge Classics double-first. After teaching posts at Dulwich College and Charterhouse he was appointed headmaster of Felsted School. Unfortunately he had a head-on clash with the governing body and chose to resign. The issue was much to his credit. He had admitted a black boy without consulting the chairman. This was too much for the social prejudices of the 1940s but for Harrison it was a matter of principle and he did not give way.

Cecil Harrison was soon dubbed 'Holy Joe' – he was eventually ordained, spending his retirement as a priest in Yorkshire. It was clear to most boys at the time that there were tensions between the new headmaster and his staff. One of Harrison's first acts was to ban boxing which, although a sensible move, was before its time and went down badly. Boxing was seen as manly and attempts to stop it were greeted with derision. The new head then decreed that the whole school should attend services at the cathedral at least three times a term (we boarders already went once a week), and that boys should kneel for morning prayers at assembly. The school was obliged to purchase hassocks for the purpose.

Notwithstanding, the school flourished under his leadership and university entrance increased. For Cecil Harrison the Classics were the only pure academic pursuits. Languages and literature were tolerated but science was looked down upon. I was bending towards science and so it seemed I was likely to be ignored. Mr Harrison, however, did had a love of the theatre and was a talented actor. I have never seen a person more transformed by a costume and greasepaint. We were often invited to see him perform in a City Drama Group (the 'Masked Theatre'). His Shylock was sinister but his Sir Andrew Aguecheek was delightfully playful. Harrison took over school drama, and that was when I got noticed. I managed to land a few big parts – not least as Titania and Katherine the Shrew.

Inevitably most boys who came under the headmaster's influence found themselves in his confirmation classes. These were held in his study. It was a serious commitment. We learnt the Apostles' Creed, the Ten Commandments, the Lord's Prayer and the catechism. There was continuous encouragement for self-examination and striving for purity. Mr Harrison would fill the room with pipe smoke, slowly exhale and ask, "Have you renounced the Devil and all his works, and all the sinful lusts of the flesh?"

"Yes," we all said, pinching ourselves.

The big day came for the 'laying-on of hands'. The bishop beamed as, in turn, each boy knelt in front of him (we had all been given strict instructions not to wear Brylcreem). Back at school, tea was served for the newly confirmed and their parents. My mother was totally uninterested in the event and asked my grandmother to go along to the reception afterwards. Grandma felt embarrassingly out of place and nervously clutched her teacup. She just managed to talk to the headmaster about the weather. I had never seen her so ill at ease.

The following Sunday was my first Holy Communion. I was taking religion seriously. The headmaster had presented each of us with a tiny booklet called *Before the Altar: The Devout Christian's Manual.* It was my constant companion. I was determined not to be sinful. As I cycled to the cathedral to attend the 8am service I felt spiritual and righteous. I was a fully-fledged member of the Church of England.

Term ended and, as usual, I returned home by train to London. I was relieved not to be going back to Luxborough Street and happily took the Underground to St John's Wood and walked up to Carlton Hill to our new home for the first time. It was not all that different in size from Cheviot Court. But it was new, light and airy and situated on two floors with three bedrooms and a sitting room – more a maisonette than a house.

Shortly after my return Harry announced that he had arranged for the four of us to go on a continental holiday. We would spend a week in Blankenberge, a small seaside town about ten miles north of Ostend. There was great excitement. What would my mother wear? How hot would it be? Was there a race track or a casino nearby?

My mother and Harry had passports; Penny's name was added to my mother's. No provision had been made for my travel document. Pleasant thoughts of a happy family holiday were suddenly in jeopardy.

"Just let him go as Barry Chambers," I overheard my stepfather say.

"Absolutely not," said my mother. "Never, never, never."

"Then we will have to change his name by deed poll or something," said Harry.

"There must be another way. We will go and see a solicitor."

"The first thing a solicitor will need is his birth certificate. Have you kept it?"

"Of course not," screamed my mother. "Do you think I would keep a document which bears his father's name?"

And so the conversation ended.

A day or so later Harry took me to one side and explained that I needed a passport for the trip to Belgium, and to get a passport required my birth certificate which my mother had lost. But I was not to worry because a copy could be obtained at Somerset House.

"Your mother and I are busy at the moment. Off you go to Somerset House and get a copy of your birth certificate. There will be a fee. Here is ten shillings."

So off I went to Somerset House and strode into the reception area. The staff were bemused by a twelve-year-old boy searching for a copy of his birth certificate. Luckily they were friendly and gave me instructions as to what to do. It was quite easy to locate my birth certificate since I knew all the essential details. An attendant took the large ledger to a typist and my 'certified copy' was prepared. So there, in black and white, was the official evidence of my existence. My name was Anthony Barrington Chambers and my father's name was Anthony Chambers. No surprises there. I paid the two-and-sixpence fee and departed.

On my return home I handed the copy of the certificate to Harry, mumbled something about the fee and was told I could keep the change. He was relieved my journey had been successful and pleased I had saved him a chore which he would not have enjoyed.

A few more days passed. As we sat at breakfast, my mother seemed nervous and said abruptly, "Barry, you have to come with Harry and me to sign something."

"To sign what?" I asked.

"Just do as you are told. It's to do with your passport. You still want to come with us to Belgium, I suppose?"

"Why, yes," I said, anxious to sound enthusiastic.

We arranged to meet at 'the business' in Wells Street and from there we walked to Marlborough Street to the offices of Cox, Clutton & Hodgetts, Solicitors. I did not question anything because I thought it quite natural to go to a solicitor's office to get a passport. We sat around in the waiting room and were eventually called into Mr Cox's office.

"Ah, yes," said the elderly gentleman. "The statutory declaration form. I suppose you know why you are here?" He looked at me.

"To get a passport, I suppose," I replied cheekily with a grin.

"Well, yes, in a sense. This formality has to be gone through before you can apply for a passport in your own name."

"In my own name?" I was surprised.

"Precisely. And so, let us proceed. His birth certificate, please," he said to Harry, who then produced it. The solicitor unfolded a light blue sheet of foolscap paper which he studied carefully. He peered at the birth certificate, and again at the other document, and eventually looked at me with a slight frown. "Please say the following after me."

And so, after him, I repeated, "I do solemnly and sincerely declare that I have been known as Anthony Barrington Kay since October 26th 1947, and that I am the same person as described on the attached birth certificate." *Why October 26th 1947?* I thought, and then remembered that that was the day my mother married Harry Kay.

"Sign here," Mr Cox said.

We both appended our signatures at the foot of the light blue paper. I had fulfilled the provisions of the Statutory Declarations Act 1835.

That was that. A few minutes later we were back on the pavement, my name having been officially changed.

The fact that I had never been consulted, never had the procedure or reasons explained ahead of time, had never entered my mother's head. I, in turn, for reasons unclear even as I write, never questioned her judgement. A new name was a fresh start, a reinvention. But there was no question of me using my new official name whilst still at boarding school. That would have to wait until I left there in a few years' time. My mother was pleased with the outcome. A deed poll would have been cumbersome and drawn-out, and involved a court order. The statutory declaration form had been quick and simple. What she did not say, and what I did not realise at the time, was that in my mother's mind I had entered that solicitor's office as Barry Chambers, some sort of Christian, but left as Barry Kay, a nice Jewish boy.

1954

When Did I Last
See My Father?

The holiday in Blankenberge was not a success. It poured with rain every day. My mother and Harry lost most of their holiday money at the casino. The food was stodgy and not much better than that at the Pig and Whistle. Most of the time I had to look after Penny, who had caught a tummy bug and was feeling miserable. I was glad when it was time to go home. On my return to school I invented stories about my fantastic continental holiday and produced a bottle of Vichy mineral water to prove it. I failed to impress.

The question of my change of surname suddenly became an immediate issue. The O Level examinations were looming and at the start of the autumn term we were all given forms to complete in order to register with the examining board. I became anxious and embarrassed and did not fill in the space for my surname. Fortunately, the schoolmaster tasked with compiling the information had some knowledge of my situation and suggested that I have a talk with the headmaster. A few days later I was summoned to Mr Harrison's study for a chat. We sat on either side of his fireplace.

"How long have you been at the school, Barry?"

"Since I was four years old, sir," I replied. "Nine and a half years."

"Four years old. How very young! I am surprised you were accepted. But your parents separated, I believe?"

"Yes, sir," I said awkwardly, looking at the floor.

"And your mother married again shortly afterwards?"

I nodded.

"And now you want to take your stepfather's surname?"

"My parents want me to be called Barry Kay. Barry Chambers embarrasses them. They want people to think that Harry Kay is my real father."

"But you must have a view on this. A change of name is, well, a change of identity."

"I don't think there is any going back, sir. They made me sign a document and I now have a passport with the surname Kay."

Cecil Harrison gritted his teeth and inhaled deeply on his pipe. He blew the smoke out slowly, looking at the ceiling. Eventually he said, "I think I need to have a word with your parents. I will write to them."

A few days later I called my mother on the phone. I used to phone her regularly from a coin box about half a mile from the school, always reversing the charges. She sounded nervous and excited.

"Your headmaster has written to us. What is all this nonsense about your name? You are Barry Kay. You have always been that as far as I am concerned. Why do we have to go and see this man?"

I tried to explain that I had always been Barry Chambers at school, but decided not to persist. I knew a conversation like this could trigger an ugly mood swing in my mother. Eventually she told me that Harry would come and see the headmaster and sort things out.

A week or so later Harry took the train from King's Cross to Peterborough and arrived at the school wearing a smart dark suit and holding a large leather briefcase. He was to speak with the head alone, and I was to wait outside Mr Harrison's study and then accompany Dad back to the station. My stepfather looked uncomfortable in these Anglican, academic surroundings and put on a fake posh accent, more from nervousness than affectation.

After about half an hour or so the two of them emerged full of smiles and handshakes.

"What did you talk about?" I asked Harry as soon as we were out of earshot on the school drive.

"Well, we just sorted things out. There isn't a problem. Here at school you will continue to be called – well, what you have always been called." (Even Harry didn't like saying the name Chambers.) "When you leave school you will be known as Kay and all your documents will be Kay, and that's the name you will use from now on for applications for exams and university and so on."

A taxi drew up at the school gate.

"Oh, that nice headmaster of yours arranged a taxi for me to go to the station so you don't need to come with me. He's a good bloke. Said his best friend was Jewish." Then he roared with laughter and the taxi pulled away.

The confusion and embarrassment associated with my change of name has never really left me. It is true that, at the time, I looked forward to leaving school with a new identity, leaving Barry Chambers and all the teasing behind me; starting a new life. It would even have been fun to pretend I was Jewish from time to time if the situation demanded it. It would have pleased my mother. The reality, however, was quite different because I was rooted in an Anglo-Saxon culture. That was my identity. It was weak of the headmaster not to have stepped in and advised against a name change. He should have anticipated the problems it would cause later in life.

What were these problems? First, it cut me off from my old school. When I left there at the age of seventeen I did not join the Old Boys' Association (the Old Petriburgians). What name would I use? I reasoned I was obliged to sever contact with the institution which had been so important in my life because Barry Chambers was no more. Secondly, I had no convincing answer to the uncomfortable question "What is the origin of the name Kay?" It was after all a simple reduction of an unpronounceable Eastern European name – not very Anglo-Saxon.

Over the next few weeks and months I tried to put these issues to one side. My schoolwork was going from bad to worse because at that point in my life it was more important for me to be accepted by my peers than to perform well in class. As far as the teaching staff were concerned I was becoming another hopeless case – not worth wasting time on! My school reports were pretty dreadful and I think my mother and Harry became quite worried because my poor results were not compatible with a career in medicine.

My mother had always assumed I would be a doctor. This was partly the Jewish mother stereotype of 'my son the doctor', but it was more deep-seated than that. As a child in Peterborough she had noticed that the family doctor was held in awe. Mum once told me that from the time I was a little boy she had hoped that one day I would graduate from medical school. Fortunately, it was a wish we both shared. A career in medicine had appealed to me from an early age, maybe as young as thirteen or fourteen after I had read *Microbe Hunters* by Paul de Kruif. I remember that the real appeal of the book was the excitement of discovery. It was not my intention to practise as a family doctor but I did not tell this to my mother. When I reflected on the future it seemed obvious that my first step would be to get a medical degree; the choice of a speciality could come later.

On the other hand, obtaining a basic science degree in the first instance also had its appeal. Once, after solving some tricky chemistry exercises in preparation for O Levels, and feeling quite pleased with myself, I exclaimed that I would rather like to be a chemist when I grew up. My mother jumped up and, with a look of horror on her face, exclaimed, "What, and sell aspirins behind the counter in Boots?!"

During the Easter holidays of 1955, when I was nearly fifteen, I managed to pluck up the courage to ask my mother about my real father, Tony Chambers. I must have caught her at a good moment because she was unusually calm and answered my questions without getting upset. This was the first time I was told that Tony Chambers was already married and that his wife had appeared "out of the blue" on the doorstep. I had always believed that he and my mother were divorced, although no real reason was given apart from my mother insisting that Tony was a "wicked man". The news of him being a bigamist was quite a revelation and finally explained why our family life in Northampton had ended so suddenly. I asked my mother whether she thought Tony Chambers was still alive.

"Of course he is," she replied. "Go and see him if you want. Get it out of your system."

I was thunderstruck, almost trembling. "But where is he?" I asked.

"Go to Northampton, to The Arcade. Then ask anyone where Tony Chambers is. No more questions, please."

But I had a hundred questions. Who was this woman on the doorstep? Where had she come from? How did she know where we were living? How is it possible to marry twice? Wasn't it a crime? Why didn't he go to prison? What was his explanation?

A few days later I was on the ten o'clock train to Northampton holding a copy of the certificate of Tony's marriage to my mother, and a photo of them on their wedding day which, many years previously, I had stolen from my grandmother's album. The photograph of my mother and Tony seemed to me like one of any other happy couple. They both looked confident. There was no sign of what lay ahead.

On the train journey I tried to recall the few things I remembered about my father from when I was a boy of four, and reflected on the little my mother had told me about him. Before I came along they had made a few friends in their local community and Mum told me she took up riding and went back to dressmaking. Later she worked wiring aircraft panels at the local Express Lift Company, which had been converted to wartime work.

I was also told that Tony was too old to be called up for the army but joined the Home Guard. There is one incident that stands

My mother and father's wedding (August 1936). Unfortunately Tony Chambers omitted to tell Eva he was already married. Grandma, on the right, is looking uneasy. The lady between Eva and Tony is probably a neighbour.

The King's School Boarding House (aka 'The Pig and Whistle') (March 1947). In the front row (centre) are Roland Jermy (the Housemaster) and Lillian Hay (the Matron and my surrogate mother). I am the small boy on the top row (far right). Norman Andrews is on the second row (far right).

A selection of staff from the annual school photograph, February 1948. On the left panel (left to right) are (the lovely) Miss Beaumont, (the stern) Miss Wigner, (the jolly) Mrs Barnes and the school secretary. On the right is Harry Hornsby (the charismatic Headmaster).

Barry, Rushden,
August 1945.

Eva Chambers
(née Pearcey), 1946.

With my mother (February 1944) – a few days before I was left at The King's School Boarding House.

My mother on holiday in Viareggio in July 1947 the year after she married Harry Kay.

Penny outside the
Luxborough Street flat, 1951

Harry Kay (my step-father) with my mother at Selsden Park Hotel.
1954. Mum destroyed most of the photos of Harry Kay after she met
Harry Reuben. This is one of the few that has survived.

A trip to Skegness. Left to right: Cousin Michael, Grandad, Grandma, and Aunty Joan (August 1952).

With my mother at the
Beresford Hotel, Christmas 1954.

My mother and Penny at a wedding
reception somewhere in North London,
November 1953

Barry aged 16.

Harry Reuben and my mother shortly
after they were married in 1963.

Penny with 'Prince' at Norrice Lea shortly before the
'Day of Secrets and Lies', April 1963

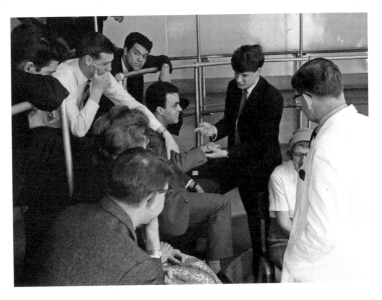

Barry in Edinburgh with fellow Medical Students and the Clinical Instructor a few weeks before qualifying, May 1963.
(Courtesy of Dr John Guy)

Harry Reuben (seated at the piano) with the Jack Jackson Orchestra at the Dorchester Hotel, Park Lane, London. 1936.

out in my mind after all these years. I went with my mother to see Tony on manoeuvres at Hunstanton on the Norfolk coast. We must have driven there, although it is a mystery how they managed to get hold of petrol at the time. Tony was with a group of soldiers manning a large gun. Out to sea was an aeroplane towing an object on a long wire. They said this was a 'target tug' for the soldiers to fire at. Every so often there was an enormous bang. I was terrified they would miss the target and kill the pilot of the plane. To this day I do not understand how they could have practised such dangerous war games.

And then there was the 'pig club'. There was a pigsty at the end of the garden. I remember trying to help my father by attempting to carry the bucket of swill, but it was too heavy for me. One day the pig was butchered and Mum and I cried. Its carcass was hung in the garage. The neighbours who had contributed swill were given their share of the meat.

I remember that Tony was often away from home, either because of his job as an area manager, or with the Home Guard. I was surprised to read what Mum said in her document many years later:

Tony and I were happy at first. We enjoyed musical evenings at home. Both of us could play piano a little. Tony liked folk songs and could pick out a few dance tunes, and I had one or two 'party pieces' I remembered from my piano teacher back in Peterborough.

The Arcade in Northampton was a short walk from the station. I asked a man in the first shop I went into if he knew Tony Chambers. I was directed to a dress shop a few doors along. There he was, standing in the doorway. I recognised him immediately from the photograph. He looked at me in a quizzical way. I handed him the marriage certificate and the photo without saying a word. He looked at them briefly and handed them back.

"So, it's you. Did your mother send you?"

"No," I answered shyly. "I wanted to see you for myself."

"Well, here I am. Let's go and have a cup of coffee." And with that he steered me away from his shop and back along The Arcade to a café.

"Morning, Mr Chambers," said the man behind the counter.

"Morning, Pete. This is a young friend of mine. Give us two coffees, please."

And so we chatted. Tony asked me a few questions about my mother and school. "She made a gentleman of you, then," he said.

I was tongue-tied. I had so many questions but I just could not get them out. He explained he was married again and that there might even be a baby on the way. His current wife knew all about me but did not want to visit his past. It was best not to stir up old troubles. He was friendly but not affectionate. I got the impression that by calling on him in this unexpected way I had broken a pact he and my mother had made when they split up to break all ties and not communicate. I think it may have been one of the conditions for Tony giving her the money to help set up the business in Rushden.

Deep down I had hoped that Tony would be a rich, successful and cultured businessman. What I found was an uninteresting and defensive person with a rough northern accent. He was not the father of my dreams. My questions suddenly seemed irrelevant. I wanted to run away. Feeling uncomfortable and embarrassed, I said I had to get back to London. He went with me to the station. As the train pulled out he thrust a five-pound note at me through the open window and gave me a sort of wink which seemed to say, *don't come back.*

I never saw him again.

Who Was Tony Chambers?

I had always believed that my meeting with Tony Chambers as a teenager had satisfied any further curiosity I had about him. To my disappointment, he had been dull and ordinary. Turning up, unexpectedly, at his place of business had embarrassed him and me. Tony had wanted me to leave. With the passage of time I thought less and less about him. Harry Kay, on the other hand, cared about me. He had become my dad and I loved him. However, for closure, and to tie up a few emotional ends, I wanted a little more basic information about my biological father.

Using genealogy websites such as Ancestry and with the help of the 1911 England Census I learnt that Anthony Chambers was born in 1900 at Bishop Auckland, County Durham. He was the fourth child of Thomas Chambers (born in 1865) and Eleanor Gascoigne Chambers (born in 1869). Tony had two elder brothers (Edward and William), an elder sister (Florence May) and a younger sister (Margaret). Thomas, Edward and William were all coal miners. At the time of the census William was only fourteen years old. In all probability Tony would also have gone down the mines when he reached his fourteenth birthday. His brothers may have been conscripted for World War I, but this is speculation. I remember that my mother mentioned that Tony had served in the last year of the Great War, and I did find an army record of an Anthony Chambers who served as a private (service number 34248) with the West Riding Regiment and was discharged in 1919.

Tony's first marriage, when he was nineteen, was to Florence Appleton, a twenty-year-old spinster living in Auckland St Andrew, Co. Durham. The marriage was solemnised in St Anne's Church. Tony gave his occupation as 'shopkeeper'. His wife's father, William Appleton, was a joiner. So Florence Chambers was presumably the lady who unexpectedly called at our house in Northampton in March 1944. I found no evidence of any issue from this marriage and I have no information on when and why the marriage broke up. By the mid-1930s Tony had moved south to Northamptonshire where he was leading a bachelor life.

We know from my mother's writings that Tony and Eva met through their employment at the Darling Washing Machine Company. They were married on 22nd August 1936 at the Peterborough Register Office. Tony described himself as a widower and gave his age as thirty-five years (one year younger than he actually was). Rather than 'travelling salesman' he gave his occupation as 'hardware area manager'. Thomas Chambers, his father, is referred to as a 'commissionaire' rather than a coal miner. My mother is recorded as being an eighteen-year-old spinster; no rank or profession was given. Ten years later she was also to describe herself as a spinster when she married Harry Kay.

On the 28th August 1948 Tony went through a third wedding ceremony, this time to a Mavis Joan Lea, aged twenty-five years. Tony's age is given as forty-five years (he was in fact forty-eight). Under 'condition' the registrar wrote *the divorced husband of Florence Chambers, formerly Appleton, spinster.* No mention is made, of course, of my mother. Tony's occupation is given as a 'wholesale draper' and his address as 119 Boughton Green Road, Northampton. By this time his father, Thomas Chambers, was 'deceased', whereas the bride's father, Horace Edwin Lea, was a company director. Once again Tony was married in a church – Dallington Memorial Church, Northampton.

I have discovered all I want to know about Tony Chambers. It is interesting that, to a small extent, he was upwardly mobile in that he did not follow his father and brothers down the mines but managed to be self-employed in the clothes business. Why did he withhold from my mother the truth about his marriage to Florence Appleton? Was he leading a double life and seeing Florence all the time he was 'married' to my mother? This seems unlikely because I remember my childhood in Northampton as being fairly stable. The few paragraphs my mother wrote in her document about her early days with Tony were quite affectionate; for example, she recalled them playing the piano together, and their interactions with their neighbours. I still find it incomprehensible that as an infant and young child I lived with my father for nearly five years, but from then on he showed no further interest in me. Surely there must have been some father/son bonding? Why did he reject me? Was it just the shame of the bigamy or was my mother's behaviour, even before the discovery of his previous marriage, becoming impossible? Mum showed signs of bipolar disorder – that is, alternating episodes of mania and depression – when she was pregnant with Penny. Were symptoms of her disease in evidence during the nine years or so she and Tony were married? Were her moods unstable when she was pregnant with me? Is it possible that Tony even encouraged Florence to confront my mother as a method of escape? I shall never know.

With so little information about Tony I have little insight into his character. He married at age nineteen and this union broke up. He married again, bigamously, at the age of thirty-six to a woman eighteen years his junior. After nine years of that marriage he was 'found out', severed contact with my mother and myself and, four years later, married for a third time to a woman twenty-three years his junior. This marriage lasted for twenty-three years until his death in 1973. There may have been children from his first and/or third marriages – I do not know. I could find out but, curiously, I have no inclination to do so.

The final information I have on Tony is from his death certificate dated the 27th March 1973. The cause is given as carcinomatosis secondary to lung cancer. He had been living with his wife, Mavis, in Great Horkesley, Colchester, and his occupation was described as 'ladies' dress manufacturer (retired)'. Tony was cremated at Colchester Cemetery on the 2nd April 1973 and his ashes were scattered there shortly afterwards. There is a standard rose memorial in the garden of remembrance to commemorate him. The location is Bed 73, Rose 9. Someday I intend to visit it, but I do not feel under any obligation. He may have been my biological father but he showed no interest in me. Why should I be sentimental about where his ashes are?

1954

A Kiss is Just a Kiss

Life as a boarder at the KSP became more bearable with the passage
of time. By 1954 I was a fourth-former, my voice had broken and
I was beginning to develop physically. I was no longer the puny
weed constantly being bullied. I could stick up for myself and was
sufficiently streetwise to avoid unnecessary confrontations. I missed
David Pitman, who had left the previous year for another school.
I had lost my best friend and so I just hung around with a gang
who had no academic aspirations. It was a choice between minimal
schoolwork and receiving the displeasure of the schoolmasters, or
being accepted by my peers. With little hesitation I chose the latter
and so embarked on a life of bad behaviour.

The role of our awkward squad was to push the boundaries of
what was, and was not, permissible. Flouting school rules, however
petty, brought unpleasant punishments, usually beatings. Such
misdemeanours included not wearing a school cap or tie, even
when in town. Smoking and playing pontoon for money were more
serious crimes, the penalty for which fell just short of expulsion.
And then there were girls.

Our 'sister school' was the local County Grammar School for
Girls. They had a dreary brown uniform which did not do much for
their often ample figures. Many of them cycled past the boarding
house on their way to school. We were not allowed to talk to
County School girls in the street. Once, when I was about ten, my
Aunty Joan cycled past when I was walking along Park Road. She

screeched on her brakes, almost losing her school hat. We had a short chat.

"Chambers," said Mr Parker at teatime in front of all the boarders, "it is forbidden to talk to County School girls in the street."

"But that was my aunt, sir."

(Howls of laughter.)

Greeting girls with oafish catcalls meant being 'gated' for the weekend. This was a severe penalty. However, it was possible to fraternise with girls away from the prying eyes of the school staff.

Diagonally opposite the boarding house was the large, well-kept public park which provided opportunities for flirting and general showing-off. Several of us would saunter across when we had an hour to spare between the end of lessons and tea. Ginner Gray was usually our confident ringleader. His naughty twinkle stood him in good stead. He would recount his sporting successes with humour. We could not understand why he was so popular with the girls but now, looking back, it was obvious – he made them laugh.

When flirtation progressed to the next step, usually holding hands, a boy and a girl could decide to 'go out'. This unwritten contract would lead to exchanges of 'love letters'. My first girlfriend was Susan Brummage (aged fourteen). Susan was athletic with handsome, almost classical features and a flowing ponytail which whisked backwards and forwards as she sped down the hockey pitch. It was a favourite pastime to watch the County School girls play hockey or netball as their playing fields were nearby. One rainy afternoon I helped Susan put the games kit back in the sports pavilion as she was monitor for that week. Suddenly there was no one around except the two of us sheltering in the pavilion. We stood side by side looking out at the pouring rain, too nervous to turn and look at each other. We were both trembling. She took my hand. I was too shy to look her straight in the eye.

"I do like you, Barry," she said, almost teasingly, and then we kissed. My first unforgettable kiss. What a thrill to feel the heat and the smell of a girl's body for the first time. And there we stood, the two of us amongst the goalposts and the lawnmower. She pressed her wet hockey tunic against my sodden school blazer. I could feel her breasts against my chest. We kissed some more and then she laughed, gently pushed me away and sped off on her bike.

"See you around," she cried.

I walked back to school on air, composing my first love letter. Unfortunately I was ten minutes late for tea and gated for the weekend. I was mortified but managed to negotiate a deal with the head prefect whereby, instead, I got six of the best with a slipper. Prep time was spent writing my six-page letter to Susan. It must have been exceedingly dull. I probably recounted my daily routines, and, of course, how much I had enjoyed kissing her. I suggested going to the cinema on the Saturday evening – the one night we were allowed out.

Letters were delivered by intermediaries. It was a hazardous system and ran the danger of the envelopes being steamed open for a quick peek by the courier. Susan agreed to my suggestion and we 'went Dutch'; a relief because I did not have enough money for two tickets. We saw *Monsieur Hulot's Holiday* with Jacques Tati. Both of us were enjoying the film until I spoilt things by trying to put my hand around her shoulder and pull her towards me. She shrugged me away. I felt very foolish.

We went for a cup of tea after the cinema. After talking about the film for a while I ran out of conversation. Was this the same girl I had written to with such passion and who had filled my head with tender thoughts, I wondered? Susan wanted to tell me about her family, what her brothers and sisters were doing and how her dad had just built a garden shed from some old wood he had found on a building site. She then began to probe me about my family and why I was at the boarding house. I invented a silly story about my mother being a famous actress who had to stay in London. I said my dad was her manager. Then we fell silent again. At last Susan said she had to get back home by ten. I walked with her to the bus stop. We held hands briefly and I kissed her shyly on the cheek.

I sauntered back to the Pig. What had gone wrong? Such confusion. On the one hand there had been the ecstasy of touching and kissing, and on the other the misery of how to fill in the gaps in the conversation. Why had I become so tongue-tied? Susan's small talk about her family bored me and I had no inclination to tell her about day-to-day life at the Pig. But, then, I was the boring one. I was the boy with nothing to say. Or rather, I had plenty to say but it was all bottled up. I could have talked about my home in London, about my crazy mother and being a Christian in Peterborough and a pretend-Jew in London but this was too deeply embarrassing.

1954

Change of Direction

I exaggerate when I say I led a life of mischief and bad behaviour. My difficulty was one of attitude and a reluctance to get down to work and study for exams. I was in with a 'bad' crowd who thought that paying attention in class was the hallmark of a 'swot' and to be despised. Our gang sat at the back of the classroom. We were unruly and irritated those who taught us. It was clear that our 'set', me included, had been given up as a bad job because of our reluctance, or inability, to apply ourselves to schoolwork.

The O Level exams were approaching. We were expected to pass at least six subjects to stay on in the sixth form. I was put down for maths, chemistry, physics, English language, English literature, Latin, French, history and religious education. Part of me wanted to knuckle down and work because the fear of failure was just as painful as alienation from the gang.

One morning, towards the end of the Easter term, I arrived at the chemistry class just as the science master was entering the room. Instead of ignoring me – expecting I would drift to the back of the class to misbehave and cause commotion – he gestured me to one side.

"Chambers, you are a silly ass. You are quite capable of passing the science subjects but you waste your time and mine with your juvenile behaviour. Try working for a change. It's your last chance."

These remarks, so spontaneous and so casual, were a Damascene moment. His intervention was clear and unambiguous. Either I kept my head above water or I drowned. If I sat at the front I would lose face with my oafish classmates. After years of being ignored and bullied by them I was at last being accepted – even liked. This was happiness. But now I was being tugged in another direction: an invitation to 'grow up', to take the first serious step along a career path. What was it to be – breaking wind and giggling at the back of the room or some serious studying? To my surprise I decided to sit in the front row and apply myself to the lesson in hand. It was not easy. I was far behind in chemistry (and all subjects, in fact). There were two weeks of term left, then three weeks of Easter holidays and about six weeks to the exams.

I started to study furiously. When there was free time I escaped to the school library, which had plenty of nooks and crannies where one could hide with a book. Maths was the first problem. The maths master, Les Bambridge, had time only for boys who were both good at his subject and played cricket – he was a former county player. My cricket was below average and my concentration span in maths lessons was poor. However, I knew I had to get through the syllabus. We had good textbooks with plenty of exercises and answers. I worked hard at the 'problems and answers' and got my head around algebra, geometry and trigonometry. I was too frightened to ask for help from Mr Bambridge. I had already been labelled as a fathead.

English language was not actually taught. It was general knowledge with some spelling and grammar. What was there to revise? English literature, on the other hand, was taught by Mr Deer. The set pieces were Pope's *The Rape of the Lock* and *The Rover* by Joseph Conrad.

With our Pope text in front of us Mr Deer proceeded to read the first canto. His voice was monotonous, his face expressionless. He struggled to convey the emotions behind the prose. It was years later that I learnt that in Canto 1, Belinda is supposed to have woken up from a sexy dream. For Mr Deer to have explained this, or even conveyed it, would have been preposterous. No one in the class gave two hoots whether the Baron cut off a lock of Belinda's hair or not. What I do remember is Mr Deer's flat, dreary voice saying:

Here thou, great Anna! whom three realms obey,
Dost sometimes counsel take – and sometimes tea.

"What is that an example of, boy?" He was addressing me.
"Don't know, sir."
"Anticlimax, boy, anticlimax – a bit like you," he said, to general laughter.

The Rover was a difficult read by any standard and I was unsure what questions about it would be asked in an examination. I did not warm to Peyrol; one moment he was a sort of swashbuckler and the next – well, a wet fish. The book buzzed around from biblical allusions to classical myths. I did not get it.

And so to Latin. I had to pass O Level Latin to get into medical school. That was the rule in those days, but looking back it certainly was not necessary. Our Latin master, Mr Vigor, was good fun. He marched up and down the classroom with a ruler as a sword and a dustbin lid as a shield, acting out passages from *Bellum Gallicum*. He was also impatient with anyone who did not quickly master the rules of grammar. I was such a person, but tried my best by marching around the nearby park, reciting irregular verbs to myself. They took a long time to sink in.

French was the saddest of all. I had started off pretty well in the first form and got A-grades in most of my homework. As my passage through the school deteriorated academically so, in turn, did my aptitude for French. Our French master at the time of our O Levels was a Mr Howitt, a burly, thickset man with bushy eyebrows and a permanent frown. His method of teaching was to give us an exercise in translation from our textbook, and then put his feet on the desk and read the *Daily Telegraph*. Boys were discouraged from asking questions and his anger threshold was low. I never heard Mr

Howitt having a conversation in French and often wondered how he would get on ordering a cup of coffee in Boulogne.

History, on the other hand, was a doddle. 'Spoke' Wheeler was clear and concise. I really did care about the Great Reform Bill and the Chartists and could rattle off the causes of the Crimean, Boer and Great Wars. I was not expecting a problem in that subject.

No one took religious education seriously, although everyone had to sit it. Classicists romped through because there were always chunks of Greek to translate. Mere mortals, like myself, relied on Bible stories. We were also taught about the workings of the Episcopalian Church, but not about other religions.

My exams were at the beginning of June. May was hot and glorious and I had just a little time to flirt with my new girlfriend, the buxom Madeline Fisher, another County School girl who lived quite close to the boarding house. Fortunately Maddy was a chatterbox and so my silences were of no consequence because she could not stop talking.

During the second half of May I began to sneeze and had a runny nose and itchy eyes. By the time the exams started, at the beginning of June, my eyes and nose were streaming constantly and I was sneezing in paroxysms and felt tight-chested. Hay fever had come with a vengeance. I got through about three handkerchiefs with each exam paper and felt quite miserable.

At last it was all over and term ended. We were given a postcard on which to write down the subjects we had taken. Results would be posted to us in due course. As usual, Barry Chambers departed from Peterborough North Station and arrived at King's Cross as Barry Kay. It was going to be a long summer holiday since the business was booming and there were no signs that my mother and Harry were planning a vacation.

The exam results slipped from my mind until one day, in the first week of August, my postcard arrived. It read *Maths, Chemistry,*

Physics, and History – PASS. English, English Literature, Latin, French, Religious Education – FAIL.

Four passes out of nine; not good enough to get into the sixth form. I sat at the bottom of the stairs looking miserable. My mother emerged from the bedroom and looked at me.

"What's wrong, Barry?" she said with a frown.

"It's my school exam results. They're not good."

Hoping for sympathy, I got the reverse.

"What?!" she yelled. "Bad exam results?! How are you ever going to become a doctor? And I pay all that money!"

Luckily my mother did not understand much about O Levels and so I managed to placate her by saying they were not all that important after all and, anyway, I would have another chance to sit the subjects I had failed the following term. This was partially true. In fact the school could decide to boot me out at sixteen but since I was now only just fifteen they would either put me in the sixth form and make sure I passed four more O Levels and proceeded to A Levels, or put me back in the fifth form and get rid of me at the end of the year. I would just have to wait for the verdict when I returned for the Christmas term after the holidays.

The Summer of 1954

The first few weeks of the summer holiday of 1954 went slowly. My mother was immersed in business matters. Trade was booming and she had little time for me. Sometimes I hung around the factory in Wells Street talking to the machinists, particularly the pretty ones, or chatted to Harry in his office. My mother complained about Harry's apparent lack of activity and accused him of being a useless business partner. This was unfair because he had a stabilising influence on the company and would mediate with conflicts and disagreements as they arose. However, he felt cooped up and yearned for the old days when he spent most of his time at the race track with his friends.

One day Harry announced he had urgent business somewhere in South London and would be out for most of the day. My mother was annoyed as it was a busy day and she needed all the help she could get, particularly with constant telephone calls from customers.

"But, Joan," said Harry, "I have to go to the Ginsburgs' in Whitechapel Road. They could give us the order of a lifetime. Solly Ginsburg insists I show him your whole range of autumn samples and let him know about delivery times."

"Go! Go! Go!" screamed my mother. "But if you don't get the order of a lifetime, don't bother to come back."

Harry shuffled quickly out of the office.

One of the staff, Mick, was asked to tidy up Harry's paperwork and David Marle, the cutter, was also in the office checking delivery notes. Inside the door was a flickering black-and-white television which was turned on when there was horse racing, which was most afternoons. However busy they were, my mother and Harry always seemed to find time to pick a horse and ring the bookmaker. On the afternoon Harry was doing his 'urgent business' there was a race meeting at Kempton Park. As my mother passed the office to peer at the television to see who had won the 2.30, the camera panned the crowd. Although it was pouring with rain and everyone seemed drenched, there, for a few seconds and as clear as daylight, was Harry Kay placing a bet. Everyone in the office saw it. Mum's jaw dropped. Mick and David looked stunned. Then they all laughed.

"Give Solly Ginsburg's store a ring," Mum said to Mick, "just in case he did get the order of a lifetime and went to Kempton Park to celebrate."

Mick dialled the number and asked to speak to Solly. "Thank you," he said, and put the phone down. "That was the telephonist," he told my mother, grinning. "Solly and his wife are in New York for his daughter's wedding."

Mum rubbed her hands with glee.

Harry's return was eagerly awaited. At last, at about 7pm, he appeared looking wet and sheepish. His hat and raincoat were soaked and his shoes and trouser turn-ups were covered in mud.

"Oh, Harry," said my mother, being uncharacteristically solicitous, "what a busy day you must have had, working so hard. Tell me, did you get the order of a lifetime from Solly Ginsburg?"

Harry looked uncomfortable and replied quietly, "Solly liked the samples very much but couldn't decide. He took ages looking at them, consulted another buyer and finally said that although he loved many of the designs he would have to think about it and get back to us. So I went off and did the usual round of customers."

"And then you fed the ducks in Regent's Park, I expect," said Mum, looking at his muddy shoes and trousers.

Harry winced.

"Never mind," continued Mum. "I expect the order book is full. Let me see it."

After much fumbling in his pockets and briefcase, Harry bleated pathetically, "Perhaps I have mislaid it; perhaps it's still in the car."

"Perhaps you left it at Kempton Park," said Mum triumphantly.

And with that David and Mick, who had stayed behind to watch the fun, burst out laughing. Harry capitulated and was told about his brief television appearance.

Mum had scored a victory, but Harry was let off lightly. She was actually very good about the incident and her sense of humour shone through. After all, she had a great story to tell.

Mum and Harry decided to rent a flat in Brighton for the month of August. They did not want to leave the business for too long, so they came down just at weekends. When we were together as a family we had a reasonable amount of fun depending on my mother's mood. The flat was quite pleasant, with a balcony overlooking the sea. On a typical day I would do the shopping and make breakfast, but we would have lunch and dinner in restaurants. On Saturdays, Penny (now four years old) and I would be dragged along to the races; during the week our parents left us alone in Brighton with an au pair girl. I would wander the streets or walk up and down the East and West Piers.

I became friendly with an elderly sailor who owned a fishing tackle shop in one of the seafront arches. He was small and stout and wore a sailor's cap and a crumpled blue blazer adorned with obscure badges. I was regaled with stories of deep-sea fishing and his time in the merchant navy. His gravelly voice and arthritic hip had shades of Long John Silver. Sometimes he would leave me in charge of the shop whilst he had a liquid lunch at the nearby Yachtsman's Club. He would roll back at about three and immediately fall asleep. There were few customers. Why was I spending so much time with this old codger and not with boys of my own age? Well, I did not know anyone my age in Brighton. I suppose he was a sort of father figure who seemed interested in me and in his gruff way was affectionate.

One weekend Harry telephoned to say that Mum was not well and they would not be coming down to Brighton. I asked what was wrong but got an evasive answer.

"It's her nerves."

"What about her nerves?" I said, and went on to protest that I did not like being in Brighton with nothing to do.

"Maybe you should come back, just yourself. Leave Penny with the au pair. But you will find your mother in a bad way," sighed Harry.

I took the first train back to London and arrived in Carlton Hill about four on a Saturday afternoon. I could hear my mother crying out as I approached the flat. As I entered I saw Harry holding both her wrists as my mother was talking incoherently and trying to strike him. As soon as she saw me she calmed down a bit, but then slumped into a chair and started to sob.

"What's going on? What's the matter?" I demanded.

"She has been like this for over a week. One moment she is agitated and irritable and blames me for everything, the next she is down in the dumps and thinks everyone is against her."

"No, I am not," wailed my mother. "You are the mad one." She glared at Harry. "Your dad is the mad one. Don't you see this, Barry? I am living with a mad person." With that she hurled the ashtray across the room. "Oh, Barry, Barry, what am I to do?! What am I to do?"

I wanted to hug and comfort her but found myself unable to do so. She was a monster in those moods.

"Shall I go to the chemist and try to get something to calm her down?"

"Yes, yes," said Harry. "Good idea."

I rushed to a chemist shop near St John's Wood Underground Station. "My mother is having a nervous breakdown," I said to the pharmacist. "What can I give her?"

He looked alarmed, thought for a moment and told me to wait. He then appeared with a rolled-up piece of newspaper shaped like an ice-cream cone which was filled to the brim with colourless crystals. "Dissolve them in water and tell your mother to drink it all."

"What is it?"

"Potassium bromide."

Feeling puzzled, I walked back home and carried out the pharmacist's instruction. My mother cooperated and swallowed the medicine with a frown. Ten minutes later she was quite drowsy.

The doctor came. He arrived quickly, being familiar with my mother's case. Her drowsiness did not last long. The effect of the bromide wore off quickly and she became uncontrollably violent again. After a great deal of crying and screaming an ambulance was called and my mother was sectioned. I did not go to see her in hospital. It would have been too painful, and anyway, she had become depressed and did not want any visitors. When I returned to school for the autumn term she had still not been discharged.

1954

The Sixth-Former

I was glad to get away and start the new term in Peterborough as a sixth-former. I missed Grandma, Grandad and Aunty Joan and got an early train so I could spend some time with them before reporting at the boarding house. I was greeted with smiles and laughter, and given a delicious lunch. Joan seemed a little thinner, but cheerful. I assumed that, as usual, she had been playing with her food and not eating properly.

"She has this awful cough." Grandma sounded nervous.

"It's nothing," Joan interjected, and then had a rather alarming coughing fit and had to lie down in her room. I told them I would visit when I could but that this would be a busy term.

It was with some apprehension that I walked the mile or two from my grandparents' house to the school. What would be said about my miserable O Level performance? Sure enough, on the first evening of my arrival I was summoned to the housemaster's study.

Spoke Wheeler was dressed in his signature blue blazer and grey flannels, standing erect and confident, always the naval officer. He strolled around the room for a few moments, stopped and turned to me.

"You're a bit of a lazy blighter, aren't you?"

"Yes, sir."

"I mean, four subjects. That's pretty pathetic. What were you doing all year – thinking about girls?"

"No, sir." I blushed. "I am always worried about my mother."

"Mm," said Spoke, who knew there was some truth in that. "You want to be a doctor, I hear?"

"Yes, sir."

"Any particular reason?"

"I want to save lives and prevent misery."

"What tosh! You want to be a medical student, more likely. You've probably been watching those *Doctor in the House* films."

"Well, sir, there may be a little of that," I conceded, blushing again. "But I have always wanted to be a doctor. At home it has always been assumed that that's what I'll be. It is expected of me."

"Expected of you?!" said Spoke dubiously. "You are not from a medical family?"

"No, sir, but that's just how it's always been and, yes, I do want to read medicine. I like biology and chemistry and I am quite prepared for a long haul."

"Do you know the minimum requirements for acceptance into medical school?"

"I think it's at least eight O and three A Levels, sir. One of the O Levels has to be Latin."

"Precisely," said Spoke. "And your Latin mark was a disgrace."

"Yes, sir."

Spoke eyeballed me, frowning. His look was meant to make me feel nervous, which it did.

"Why should we bother with you?" he said after a pause. "You had every opportunity during fifth form to get a decent set of O Levels but you just mucked around, wasting time with undesirables. You sat at the back of the class being disruptive, your schoolwork was a mess. You were late for classes, late for meals, couldn't get up in the mornings and were caught smoking by one of the prefects. You also got found out playing pontoon for money and on numerous occasions were seen talking to County School girls in the street which, as you know, is against school rules."

I looked at the floor. After a second or two I said, "That's all in the past, sir. I really do want to succeed."

"You really do want to succeed," he repeated, with an air of disbelief. "What about A Levels? Which subjects do you have in mind?"

"Chemistry, physics and biology, sir."

"Hmm," said Spoke. Another long pause. Finally he said, "There is good news and bad news." He smiled for the first time. "We discussed your 'case' in some detail at this morning's staff meeting and took into account that you are about nine months younger than the average age for your class. It was decided – after some opposition, I may add – to give you one more chance. The headmaster, with remarkable magnanimity and generosity, has agreed to help you with Latin and will give you one-to-one revision sessions so that you can resit at the end of this term. You are to report to his study every Tuesday evening at ten minutes past six precisely, armed with a clean exercise book and Virgil's *Aeneid*."

I began to feel wobbly at the knees. The head only taught the Classics sixth-formers, who were the crème de la crème. They had all passed Latin O Level standing on their heads. I feared I was in for nothing but humiliation – generosity or no generosity.

"That's most kind of him, sir. I am extremely grateful," I gulped.

"Excellent. And there is more good news. You will be given a free period every afternoon to prepare, by yourself, for the English language and English literature resits. I will be on hand from time to time to help with any questions you may have. But make them brief."

"Yes, sir."

"Biology is not a subject we have cared much about at this school. However, Mr Wilmot-Dear will take a small group of boys to O Level in Year 1 and A Level in Year 2. Thus at the end of this academic year you should have a total of eight O Levels under your belt, providing of course that you don't let us all down."

"Absolutely not, sir. I will do my best."

"Let us hope your best is good enough."

"Yes, sir. And the bad news, sir?"

"Ah, yes, the bad news. You will not be eligible to sit the Oxford or Cambridge entrance exams."

"Not eligible?"

"Oxbridge exams will be in one year's time. You will only be sixteen years old. That's too young. The head would have to plead a special case explaining that you are a person of outstanding intellectual ability, which you are not. It's true that, theoretically, you could stay on for a third year in the sixth form but that would be unwise. You need to get cracking on a medical course, which could take five or six years."

"I don't mind about that, sir. I already know what medical school I want to go to."

"Which is…?"

"Edinburgh, sir. It's the best."

"And so it is. A wise choice and a noble ambition. Furthermore, it's practical because the Scottish universities admit students at seventeen. All you need to do now is work hard. In your case, easier said than done. Right! Dismissed! And, by the way, the *Aeneid* – you are doing Book 6, old chap. I believe it begins *Sic fatur lacrimans* – thus he spoke in tears. Could be quite appropriate for you if things don't go well."

Mercifully my Latin sessions with the head did not turn out so badly. He was patient, and encouraging when I got things right. I made a point of acquiring a translation of the Virgil which I learnt off by heart. It was just a matter of putting the Latin and English together. I made a big attempt to improve my Latin grammar and spent more hours memorising irregular verbs while walking around the park, reciting as I went. At the end of the term I resat the examination with some confidence. To this day I am amazed that Cecil Harrison, head of a school of 450 or so boys, found time to give me individual Latin tuition. I will always be grateful to him for this.

English language and English literature (set pieces *The Pilgrim's Progress* and *Julius Caesar*) were enjoyable. Studying by myself, at my own pace, was a great relief and I did not seem to have much trouble with these subjects the second time round.

The sixth form was my happiest time at the KSP. There were twelve of us or so in the science sixth. Physics was taught superbly by Alan ('Vic') Oliver. Chemistry was also well taught by John Adams, but his style was somewhat laid-back and he missed things out from the syllabus which we only found out about at the last minute.

The person who inspired me in biology and the life sciences was Peter Wilmot-Dear. He had been at the school for only two years or so and, besides teaching biology and chemistry, was an enthusiastic thespian. W-D was small and thin with elfin features. His gestures were theatrical and his communication skills were excellent. Biology lessons were fun. He opened my horizons to evolution, genetics and human physiology, all of which I found intriguing. Most importantly he confirmed that my choice of career was realistic and helped me on my way.

News from home was a little better. My mother came out of her depression after about six weeks and when I went home for half-term she seemed relatively calm – although still with little insight into her condition. After she had calmed down in hospital and the section was lifted she spent the next few weeks in a private nursing home, which she called 'a health farm'.

"I was there just for a rest," she insisted, "to get away from your father, who has been behaving badly."

"In what way?" I asked.

"Well, accusing me of being mad. Can you believe it? He's the mad one. Of course I had to get away until he came to his senses."

Harry, who was in the room hearing all this, rolled his eyes. It was a blessing, however, that things were relatively tranquil and I could return to school without the huge knot in my stomach – a frequent companion when my mother was loopy.

Grandad and Grandma

My grandparents, Gus and Gertrude Pearcey, lived at 314 Walpole Street in a standard 'two-up two-down' near the railway marshalling yards in a run-down area of Peterborough. It was dismal although adequate by working-class standards of the time. The front door was set back from the pavement by a few feet, but never used except by the doctor. Everyone else went up the passage to the back door where, on the left, there was a kitchen/scullery and on the right an ill-lit parlour with a coal range, a table, chairs and a small sideboard. Outside in the yard there was a privy and a coal shed.

Grandma was particularly proud of her front room, which she kept spotless. It was light and airy, although hardly used except for playing the piano. One wall was dominated by a glass cabinet with ornaments and souvenirs from trips to the seaside but, curiously, no family photographs. Upstairs there was a small bedroom overlooking the street for Mum's brother George. Later it was used by Aunty Joan. There was a bedroom opposite for Gus and Gertrude. Off their bedroom was a tiny space, just big enough for a small single bed, where Eva slept until she got married in 1936. The house was lit by gas until the late 1940s and water for washing hair would be drawn from a well in the communal backyard. The only books in the house were the Bible and a small encyclopaedia of family health. The family liked to listen to the 'farm radio' which before the war was powered by a sort of car battery which had to be frequently recharged, which they usually could not afford.

Both my grandparents loved me. I never had a cross word from them. They were proud I was at The King's School and tried to help me when they could. From the time I was a little boy of four until I left school at seventeen they provided continuity. Importantly, their house was a refuge, especially during those dark days between the ages of ten and thirteen when the bullying at the boarding house was at its height. Unlike at the Pig and Whistle, I could expect only kindness there.

I was about eleven or so when I started to visit by myself. I was always a bit ashamed of my grandparents' house because it was in a poor part of the town. As I walked or cycled along to their tiny terrace I would look furtively around to make sure there was no one from school who would recognise me before darting down the passageway and knocking on the back door.

As soon as she saw me Grandma's eyes would light up and, smiling, she would give me a kiss. "Ooh, how you've grown," she remarked, even if it was only a week since I last saw her.

The house smelt of fried potato, the coal fire and Grandad's greasy overalls. Grandad, obviously pleased, would greet me with, "Come in, lad."

My Aunty Joan, Mum's younger sister, six years older than me, would exclaim, "It's Barry! He's come for tea."

Sometimes I brought schoolwork to revise. Grandma frowned when she saw my pile of books. "You'll ruin your eyes," she said with a worried look.

There would be ham, tomatoes and cheese for tea. Grandma would usually make a lemon meringue pie and bake an extra one for me to take back to school. I would share it with other hungry boys; it was quickly devoured. Grandma sliced bread the old-fashioned way, holding the big, square loaf under her armpit. She would smile when she saw me eating up furiously. On the other hand Joan, my aunt, would pick at her food, much to the dismay of her parents. Joan was quite thin with dark hair, brown eyes, a pointed nose and bird-like features.

"Why don't you eat, girl?" Grandma would say.

"I'm not hungry," cried Joan, as she fled from the back parlour.

Later, Joan and I would be allowed to sit in the front room. We would play the piano and sing, usually hymns. I was asked about my schoolwork. Joan corrected my spelling, my French pronunciation and even read over my essays, shrieking with laughter – often much to my embarrassment.

Joan sailed through her school certificate but left school at sixteen and became a shop assistant. Sadly, there was never any question of her staying on and doing higher education. *What a waste!* I thought. At the age of sixty-five Joan was at last able to attend night school, where she passed A Level Latin first time.

George, Mum's older brother by three years, represented another dynamic in this strange household. Whenever I mentioned Uncle George to my mother she would become silent and seemed uneasy. George, in his turn, was more forthright about living with his sister Eva.

"Eva was a bit crazy. We had fights," he told me when I was about thirteen. "There was a lot of shouting, women's stuff, I suppose. She thought she was right about everything. We just didn't get along. Of course the build-up of tension with our mum and dad was sometimes unbearable. I was able to get out of the house and go off with my friends. Eva couldn't; she had to stay there. She probably resented me for it."

George became a coppersmith. He left home in his early twenties to marry Edna, a local girl. They had one child, Michael, about my age. George remained opinionated and gullible.

A very strange thing had happened over time, however. My grandparents stopped speaking to each other directly. For the last twenty-five years of their marriage, they communicated only through a third party. When it was time for tea Grandma would call Joan and me to the table. With him sitting next to her, Grandma would say to Joan, "Tell your dad to pass the salt" or, "Tell him to wash his hands." I often wondered, later, whether Joan's eating problem was a form of manipulation in a subconscious effort to gain some control over Grandma and Grandad's non-communication.

Mum had said in her document that Grandma could have been much kinder to Grandad when she spoke to him. The problem, my mother believed, erroneously, was solely poverty – *If we only had money everything would work out all right.* The main reason for Grandma's treatment of Grandad, which I only understood when I was an adult, was probably Joan herself, or rather her conception. She was fifteen years younger than my mother. Grandma was forty-six when she had her. The pregnancy was not intended. It was 1933 during the great economic depression, or 'slump'. The timing could not have been worse. Grandad had been laid off and the family was on the dole. From then on, according to my mother, Grandma would not let Grandad near her. All forms of intimacy and direct communication ceased. But worse than that, Grandma had somehow got it into her head that her husband had done a wicked thing by getting her pregnant. He would have to pay a price.

My mother grew up always trying to please Grandma. That meant going along with her mother's cruel assessment of her husband. In her document Mum recalls a scene from when she was a child:

"Why are we so poor?" Eva would ask innocently.

"It's your father," was the unexpected answer. "He is bone idle and a good-for-nothing. He squanders money on cigarettes and beer while I struggle to put food on the table and pay the rent."

However puzzled my mother was by this explanation, she was to hear it many times and grew up believing it to be true even though it was grossly unfair. Grandad was just an ordinary, kind, hard-working, responsible family man who occasionally had a pint of beer in his working men's club and smoked a few Woodbines. "There was also a class difference," my mother would say to me, snobbishly. "Your grandmother married beneath herself. After all, she had been a secretary to a businessman before she met your grandad."

Grandad was born Hubert Augustus Pearcey in 1889 and spoke with a Yorkshire accent. His family originally came from Wiltshire but moved to Keighley when he was a small boy to find work in the wool mills. Trained as an engineer, he had difficulty at first finding employment. One of his four brothers, Sidney, emigrated to the United States in 1900 and Grandad went to join him. But he could not settle there and after two years returned to England and got a job in Peckham. It was there, through a matrimonial agency (not uncommon at the time), that he met and married Gertrude Delves, my grandmother. War was imminent but he did not join up as he was only five foot three. Grandad heard about vacancies at Peter Brotherhood's in Peterborough. The job paid more than he was getting in London and the firm helped with housing. During the war Brotherhood's stopped making turbines and changed to armaments. Grandad worked there for forty years. "All he got in the end," Aunty Joan said, "was a barometer."

Grandad had a fine tenor voice. It was said that fellow passengers had paid to hear him sing on his passages to and from the US. On summer evenings I heard him in the distance coming back from his allotment. *Take a Pair of Sparkling Eyes* would ring out along Walpole Street, but immediately he turned into the passageway he stopped abruptly. Grandma would say to me, "Tell your grandad to stop that horrible noise."

"But, Grandma, he has got a lovely voice!" I would protest.

"The neighbours will start complaining." She sounded angry.

Grandad placed the lettuce, carrots, broad beans, potatoes and onions he had grown in the kitchen sink. No response came from Grandma except possibly a word to Joan about there being "too many slugs". Grandad, oblivious, got back on his bike and went off to his club or to play bowls in the recreation ground. I could hear *Keep Right On to the End of the Road* in the distance.

Seven years previously, when my mother and I had unexpectedly arrived on their doorstep after Tony Chambers' wife dramatically appeared at our house in Northampton, it was Grandad who took me in hand, trying to distract me with his unlikely tales. Pulling me onto his knee and between chesty coughs, he began, "When I was in t' jungle there were lions and tigers. But I 'ad me sword, see." He then brandished the poker.

"Tell your grandad to put down the poker," Grandma said immediately.

"When I was in t' jungle," he continued in his booming voice, and clutching his pipe like a pistol, "I 'ad me sword – and me gun." Actually Grandad was not allowed to smoke his pipe in the house, but he liked to use it as a prop for his stories.

Grandma admonished him with a frown.

"Around one corner comes a tiger." This time more softly, his eyes bulging with simulated fright. "But I've got me sword, so it's off with his 'ead. Then a monkey jumps on me and I wrestled 'im and knocked him for six. But then I fell in the river. Along comes a crocodile. Tries to eat me, but I 'ave me gun, see…" And so the stories went on with one miraculous escape after another.

Grandma was an austere, anxious person who 'knew her place'. But she was basically kind. To her professional people were gods. Once I heard her boasting to the neighbours that, "The doctor called today and he accepted a cup of tea from me."

My mother was highly protective of Grandma. She would do anything for her, and tried to get her down to London. Grandma, for her part, was uneasy if forced out of her narrow comfort zone. After much persuasion she would eventually come, but she hated going out to restaurants or the theatre or meeting strange people.

Throughout the 1950s when the business took off and my parents became relatively wealthy, Mum showered Grandma with gifts. She arranged weekly deliveries of groceries. No longer, my mother reasoned, would her parents' household be burdened with the expense of everyday items.

"Eva," my grandmother would say, "this is too extravagant, too expensive. What will the neighbours say if they see we have a whole leg of ham, a bottle of sherry and bananas galore? Ooh, I can't accept this. It's far too much. Far too much." Eventually, after much protesting, and much to the relief of Grandad and Joan, Grandma would give in and accept the largesse.

One day a television was delivered unexpectedly to the house. This set Grandma trembling with fear. "I don't want that thing in the house."

"I have been instructed to install it," said the aggrieved owner of the local radio and TV shop, "and to put an aerial on the roof."

"Put a what?" said Grandma. "Instructed by whom?"

The man looked down at his piece of paper. "By a Mrs Joan Kay in London."

"It's Eva again," wailed Grandma.

By now this exchange had attracted the attention of Grandma's neighbours. "A television, is it?" they said excitedly. "How wonderful! Can we come and see it?"

Grandma did not protest for long. Deep down she was as curious as the rest of them. The TV was installed and everyone gathered around the flickering black-and-white screen in amazement.

Shortly afterwards there was a banging on the front door. "Whoever can that be?" Grandma asked.

"I'll go," said Joan. She reappeared, white as a sheet, clutching a small brown envelope. "It's a telegram," she said, handing it to Grandma.

The room was silent. Grandma's hand was trembling again. Telegrams only brought bad news. Everyone knew that.

Grandma tore open the envelope and scanned the contents. With a sigh of relief she said, "It's only Eva. She says she's coming to Peterborough tomorrow and can I meet her at the station. Why doesn't she write letters like everyone else? That must have cost her" – Grandma counted up the words in the telegram – "five shillings and sixpence. A stamp would have cost twopence."

Grandma was only feigning surprise for the sake of the neighbours. Mum, who visited Peterborough two or three times a year, always heralded her arrival with a telegram. It was easier than writing a letter. In the 1950s the journey from King's Cross to Peterborough took about an hour and a half. My mother would travel first class and enjoy a leisurely lunch. She would be dressed both to shock and to provoke envy in the provinces. That usually meant a straight, narrow, close-fitting, calf-length skirt, producing the 'wiggle' look. There would be a broad belt to show off her figure and she would be wearing gloves and a hat, and top her outfit off with a swing coat and an expensive handbag.

"Oh, Eva," Grandma would say on meeting her off the train. "What a get-up! Come along quickly and we can just catch that bus."

"A bus?!" protested my mother. "A taxi, surely?"

"No, no, a bus," insisted Grandma, knowing that this way there would be more people to admire her daughter from London.

Arriving home, Mum would distribute presents – a frock for Grandma, a sweater for Joan, cigarettes for Grandad. Grandma pretended to be overwhelmed. "Oh, Eva! So much, so much!" she would exclaim. "All this extravagance. Where does the money come from?"

"Business is good, very good," said my mother.

In the parlour of 314 Walpole Street there was no sign of Joan Kay, the Jewish girl with her Yiddish phrases. She was back to being Eva Pearcey, the child with a Peterborough accent. She was desperate to show her mother how successful she was, showing off about the money she was earning.

In the following years there were more extravagancies. A telephone and a new bathroom and kitchen were installed. Eventually Mum bought the house itself so they no longer had to worry about the rent. There were never any thanks. Somehow Grandma could not show gratitude.

Grandad in the meantime sat back, observed and kept his opinions to himself. He showed little sign of resentment at his loveless marriage and just carried on with his routines. Off he would go on his bike at seven in the morning for the twenty-minute ride to Peter Brotherhood's. Back he would cycle home at twelve o'clock for his 'dinner hour'. Tea was always at five. In the summer evenings he could get out of the house. Winters, on the other hand, went on forever. He would hide behind a newspaper, or *Tit-Bits* magazine, which was passed around the neighbours in the backyard. He did not have any close friends but was always polite and deferential, raising his cloth cap to ladies.

The only time I saw my grandad distressed was when Joan was ill. Her chronic cough was the first sign of tuberculosis. Years of picking at her food had taken their toll. Both my grandparents were beside themselves with worry, understandably because of the dreadful reputation TB had at that time. Joan was sent to Thorpe Hall, a Georgian house outside Peterborough which had been converted into a sanatorium. Luckily she responded well to the new 'wonder drug', streptomycin, which had cured Penny's meningitis a year or so earlier. After a while she became resistant to the medication. But other anti-tuberculosis drugs came along and she survived into her seventies.

Grandad retired in 1950. He would come by the school in the summer to watch us play cricket. I was always pleased to see him, although embarrassed by his shabby clothing, cloth cap and smell of engine oil. I would give him a hug and sit on the crossbar of his bike as he commented on the bowling and batting. Mentioning him in my letters home from school got no response from my mother.

When Grandad died I was at university. My mother never told me about the funeral until after the event ("No point in coming all that way," she said). Grandma died in the early 1970s when I was doing post-graduate studies in America. Again my mother did not inform me until weeks later, and then only in a perfunctory way. I never had a chance to say goodbye to my grandparents, never mourned them properly, but often think about them. They played an important part in my formative years. They loved and cherished me. I wanted them to keep on being proud of me.

1954

Roland and Lillian Jermy

When Roland Jermy and Lillian Hay had had enough of being housemaster and matron of the Pig and decided to get married, I still made a point of calling on them regularly at the flat they had rented in Lincoln Road about a mile from the school. Lillian had done her best to fill the gap left by my mother when she dropped me at the boarding house when I was only four years old. In those early years it was Lillian I turned to for comfort. I had to accept that my mother would pop in and out of my life at irregular intervals and when it suited her. I was quite a cute little chap, but after a while I think she got bored with me and there was always the problem of who would look after me during the school holidays. My grandparents could not cope in their small terraced house. Like any small child I needed constant supervision. In Rushden I was in Mum's way – in the way of her dress business, in the way of her affairs with the American servicemen and in the way of the Jewish life she was beginning to embrace.

The Jermys, on the other hand, were always delighted to see me, and encouraged me to visit as often as I wished.

"Come away," Lillian would say in her soft Scottish lilt when I rang their doorbell. "We have missed you. Where have you been? How was the school holiday? Tell us what you have been doing."

Roland would chuckle and show me his latest project and get me involved. Perhaps he was carving wood or restoring a piece of furniture or immersed in a drawing, watercolour or oil painting.

Meantime I was asked about my activities since my last visit. This was always difficult and a cue for fabrication. After all, I had not been doing much of interest except hanging around the flat in London whilst Mum and Harry were working at the business. I was too embarrassed to tell the Jermys about the endless rows and my mother's flaky behaviour, so I just invented stories about going to plays, concerts and restaurants.

Roland and Lillian were non-judgemental. They knew enough about my background to realise it had left scars. Lillian, after all, had had an unhappy first marriage herself, although I never knew the details, and never asked. Peterborough, sitting on the edge of the Fens with its nondescript town centre and countryside scarred with ugly brickworks, must have been a far cry from Montrose where Lillian was raised. Photos of her childhood, taken when she was seven or eight, show a determined young lady standing confidently with her four elder siblings. Her father, the Reverend James Hay, was an enthusiastic photographer and he seems to have captured their idyllic family holidays with tennis, riding and walking in the hills of Aberdeenshire.

Comparing Lillian Hay to my mother always seemed faintly ridiculous and yet they were, in essence, my 'two mothers'. Lillian was predictable and gave of herself entirely, not expecting anything in return. Mum was a show-off, boasting about her trips to Deauville or the fancy clothes she had in her wardrobe.

Roland was devoted to Lillian. He was full of fun and always active. He had an external degree from London University and taught English. Apart from that I knew little about him or his background. He showed little emotion. If a question was in the slightest way personal he would sidestep it with a laugh. I never saw him as a surrogate father, just as Lillian's loyal husband.

Sitting in Lincoln Road by an open log fire one cold autumn afternoon, I asked Mr Jermy if he had been happy as housemaster at the boarding house. It was a slightly bold question because, as he and Lillian had decided to get married, it was naturally time for them to leave and find their own home. I was really trying to get more information surrounding my arrival at the school, curious to get more details.

"No time to feel unhappy, old boy," he replied, laughing quietly. "Goodness me, no. Well, when you first arrived that day with your mother the war was still on. And it was worse after the war. Feeding all of you and keeping you clothed and warm were our priorities."

"But we did have some good times," I said. "Do you remember the mulberry tree?"

"Oh, yes, sitting around it picnicking on those hot summer afternoons when you were all small boys. We got hold of some silkworms and you put them in jam jars and fed them mulberry leaves."

"And you gave us those tiny vegetable plots and we tried to grow radishes, lettuces and carrots. Of course we were always so hungry. How did you manage to feed us with all those shortages?"

"We just had to manage, old chap." (More chuckling.) "Couldn't have done it without Lillian, of course. There was enough spuds and bread, but everything else, particularly meat, was always difficult to obtain." Then he remembered the roof, and all those buckets placed on the top landing when it rained heavily, and the antiquated boiler which ate coke but did not give out much heat.

Whilst Lillian was out of the room making the tea I said to him, "It must have been odd having me, a four-year-old, to cope with."

The chuckling continued as he searched for an answer.

"Wasn't it?" I persisted.

"Lillian was the one who looked after you. You were a good little boy, at least at first." (More laughter.)

"How do you mean?"

"Well, when your mother first brought you, you were naturally upset. Took quite a long time for you to settle down."

"Do you remember my mother and the circumstances which brought me to the KSP?"

Roland's expression changed and for a moment he looked quite serious. "Well, you had come from a broken home. Can't remember the details, so many boys had similar stories. As for your mother," he said, brightening up, "she was a striking lady; pretty, lovely clothes. Some of the boys thought she was a film star, or an actress. Of course many of the staff were surprised that you got accepted."

"I sometimes felt I was just dumped there; you know, abandoned."

Roland looked at me with full eye contact; something he rarely did. "One day, when you are older, you will get a more balanced view of your predicament and how it was managed. Your mother's options were limited. If I recall correctly there was no question of you staying with your grandparents. They had enough on their plate. Your mother had to look to your future. She was very anxious that you got a good education. Taking you with her to Rushden when she set up her business there was not an option. Having a young child in tow would have been – well, very difficult."

"More likely she just didn't want me around," I said rather sulkily.

Lillian, who had been listening to this conversation from the kitchen, entered the room carrying the tea tray. Smiling at me, she said, "Barry, never doubt that your mother loved you. Over the years she and I had many conversations on the phone. It was agony for her to leave you at the boarding house at such a young age. Your mum missed you desperately; not having you with her made her feel guilty and sad. You may have felt abandoned but it was for the good. It really was."

1955

My Cousin Michael

When I arrived back at school at the beginning of the spring term of 1955 I was feeling quite confident. I had a respectable number of O Levels and there were no exams to worry about in the foreseeable future. A Levels were eighteen months away; far enough away to put them out of my mind. Mock A Levels at the end of the coming summer term could be ignored.

Most of my friends – Ginner Gray, Chips Rafferty, Ian Arbuckle and David Pitman – had left the school. Bill Tibbles had stopped bullying me and, as we shared a common interest in athletics, we almost became friends, although I was always wary of him. Since my voice had broken and I was becoming hirsute, I was no longer attractive to the sex pest Brian Mason. He was free to abuse the new batch of ten- and eleven-year-olds, which he did with impunity right under the noses of the housemaster and their assistants.

My mother was going through a relatively calm period. We had stopped writing letters to each other. Instead I regularly telephoned her from a call box near the school. I tried to enthuse her about my schoolwork and how I had caught up with the various exams required for university entrance. She was mildly interested, saying that since she paid the school fees, passing exams was the least I could do. As usual I reminded her that she did not pay school fees as there were none; she paid a nominal amount for my board. She said I was splitting hairs and insisted it was a financial burden (which I knew it was not). I told her I had visited Grandma and Grandad, which she was always pleased to hear, and also that I had been seeing more of her brother Uncle George and his family. Mum was not interested in George. Again I tried to find out why she was so negative about him but she quickly changed the subject.

"When are you coming home for Easter?" Mum said.

"Oh, sometime in early April, I think."

"This year your dad, Penny and I will be going to the Cuplins' for Pesach; we will have a Seder meal. It's best if you are not around, although I will give you some money to go out with your friends."

"I haven't got any friends in London," I replied

"Well, find some, or stay in Peterborough with Grandma. And another thing – if you are here, or at the business, when the Cuplins are around you must say that you already had your bar mitzvah in Peterborough."

"Had my bar mitzvah in Peterborough – what are you talking about? I was confirmed into the Church of England last year; you were supposed to be there to support me. You were the only parent who didn't come."

"Say you had your bar mitzvah in Peterborough," Mum repeated. "Anyway, I am too busy to talk now", and she put down the telephone.

I walked back to the school, angry and almost in tears. How could my mother go to such lengths to perpetuate the lie that she was Jewish? Why was she involving me in this absurd deception? Why did she not have the courage to tell the truth for once about her background? I still wanted to be loved by my mother, to be accepted in her life. Maybe this was the price I had to pay. Maybe Barry Chambers should leave The King's School in Peterborough and go as Barry Kay to a local grammar in London and get up to speed with being Jewish. Maybe then my mother would love me.

Deep in these thoughts, I entered the school gates and, looking up, saw Phyllis Harrison, the headmaster's wife, cycling towards me.

"Ah, Barry," she said, braking suddenly. "Cecil was so pleased you got Latin under your belt. All set for medical school now, what?

Jolly good! Just keep working as hard as you did last term and, hey presto, all will be well. But don't forget the theatre. I did love you as Katherine in *The Shrew*, but you are too old for gels' parts now. Next term we have a wonderful treat in store. We are going to do that charming operetta *The Pride of the Regiment* by Walter Leigh (lovely man, Walter; in the same regiment as Cecil, sadly killed at Tobruk). Anyway, it will be such fun and I have a special part in mind for you. More of this later. Must rush."

Phyllis Harrison had a deep, booming voice and was usually dressed in tweeds. Full of energy, she involved herself in all aspects of the school as well as being a local Justice of the Peace. We all knew that during the war she had worked on something 'hush-hush' but it was only years later that we learnt she was one of the codebreaking team at Bletchley Park, although she would never talk about it. Phyllis took a special interest in me, even when I was wilful. I was regularly cast in school plays and my acting skills were passable. The Harrisons had a soft spot for those interested in the theatre. I believe this helped me in subtle ways during my time at the KSP and perhaps explains why I was not given up for lost.

But, again, it was confusing. Was this what I was? A sensible, scholarly Anglican on his way to qualifying in a profession, and at the same time trying to broaden his education with music and drama? Perhaps, but what right had I to such aspirations? Would I not be a fish out of water; someone who could not explain his background? An imposter perhaps, the product of a crazy mother and a dodgy Jewish stepfather whom nobody talked about. Was I running the risk of entering a world where I would be put down at every twist and turn, a world ruled by connections and the old school tie? Where did I belong? Perhaps it was with Grandma, Grandad and Aunty Joan. Maybe they were my people and I should be more like them.

One Saturday afternoon during free time I decided to cycle to Walpole Street. I would be just in time for tea. When I arrived

Grandad greeted me in the backyard. He was mending his bike. "Michael's here," he said.

I entered through the back kitchen, gave Grandma a kiss, and there was my cousin, Michael Pearcey, rocking in Grandad's chair and grinning like a Cheshire cat.

"All dolled up in your posh school uniform, I see," he said.

"We have to wear it," I said, "even out of school."

"Even that daft cap?"

"Even the cap."

"Come on," said Michael. "Let's go round to my mum and dad's. It's boring here."

"But I've just arrived and haven't seen Grandma and Grandad for ages."

"OK, but come around afterwards when you can and we'll have some fun." He got up, brushing past me. "Bye, Grandma," he called out, and was off on his bike.

"Off already," said Grandma. "I don't know what to make of that boy. Always rushing around and getting up to mischief."

Over the years I had had little interaction with Uncle George and Aunty Edna, and was always wary of their son Michael. They lived in a prefab in Dogsthorpe, a suburb of Peterborough. Like Grandad, Uncle George had trained as an engineer, but by the 1950s he was driving lorries (but for whom, and hauling what, I was never told). George was affable, small and wiry. We used to talk about the 1930s and Mosley's Blackshirts. He said that when Mosley came to Peterborough on one of his rallies he got a bit swept away by his rhetoric, but regretted it. He was now a patriot, and 'to prove it' he had a medal from his time in the Home Guard. I thought of Harry and his hatred of fascists, and how he had fought against them when they marched into the East End.

George's favourite topic was the internal combustion engine. He seemed surprised at my lack of knowledge of motor cars. "How do gears work? What is a carburettor? What is a distributor?"

I did not know.

"Don't they teach you anything useful at your school?"

Aunty Edna was kind and motherly and was always happy to see me when I popped round for tea. Like her husband she was slim. I asked her about my mother and why she and George did not make a point of seeing her when she came to Peterborough, but I got a non-committal answer and felt I had 'touched a nerve'. I never did find out what the problem was. Perhaps they did not want to talk about Tony Chambers and Harry Kay. Perhaps it embarrassed them. I think they got on well with Tony and were shocked when they heard he was already married. Maybe they were trying to protect me by keeping quiet about the past.

Michael was their only child. He was a year older than me and went to the local secondary modern school because he had not passed his eleven-plus. Confident and surly, Michael was wilful. In his opinion my school was 'stuck-up' and deprived me of life's real experiences. He was pugnacious, a street fighter, lewd about girls, and 'talked big'. Although only fifteen (he looked older), he boasted that he was served beer at the local pub, having some kind of understanding with the landlord who allowed him to buy a drink as long as he sat quietly in the snug away from the regular clientele and did not cause trouble.

After a quick tea with Grandma I cycled across to Dogsthorpe to catch up with my cousin. George and Edna greeted me and Michael explained to them that we were going out for a bike ride together.

"Ever been to a pub?" Michael said as we were pedalling along.

"Lots of times," I lied.

"All right, we'll go to The George."

The George! I had heard that some of the school staff went there. I started to feel nervous.

When we arrived Michael told me we should leave our bikes in the car park. He then took me in via a side entrance and we sat in a quiet corner away from the locals. Before we entered the pub Michael had made me hide my school blazer, tie and cap in the bag on my bike. After a while he appeared with two pints of beer and said we had to drink them up quickly as the landlord was in a bad mood and was worried he would lose his licence if anyone saw him serving underage customers.

"Well, go on. Sup up," said Michael, seeing me staring at the pint.

We clinked glasses and Michael downed about half of his in three or four gulps. I sipped half a mouthful. It was my first real taste of bitter ale. I did not like it. Michael kept telling me to drink up, nervously looking in the direction of the bar. I took a deep breath and downed a few more mouthfuls.

"That's more like it," said Michael, who by this time had almost finished his pint.

I drank some more but was beginning to feel dizzy. Michael kept urging me to finish the glass. At that moment the landlord came rushing across. "'Ere, 'op it, you two. Customers are complaining. I'll get into trouble."

Michael got up and went to the door. I staggered behind him, feeling peculiar and a bit sick. We crossed the car park to retrieve our bikes. Just as we were about to cycle away a car pulled up and a man and a woman got out. They turned and looked at me in surprise.

"Chambers, what are you doing here?"

It was Spoke Wheeler and his wife, Margaret.

I arrived back at the Pig in fear and trembling. Would Spoke know I had been drinking beer in the pub? Luckily, I had met him in the car park, not inside. But he probably noticed I was a bit wobbly when I cycled away.

After supper I was summoned to his room.

"What were you doing in the car park of The George public house?"

"It was like this, sir." By now my story was well rehearsed. "I went out for a cycle ride with my cousin Michael. We had been biking for miles and we were both thirsty. We knocked at the back door of the pub for a glass of water."

"A glass of water!"

"Well, he did say we could have some lemonade if we preferred."

"So a glass of lemonade made you stagger across the road?" he said. He was very angry.

"No, sir, we were just feeling hot, and that's why I took off my jacket, tie and cap."

"Boys have been expelled for entering a public house, let alone drinking in one! This may be expulsion for you, Chambers. I shall discuss this with the headmaster."

1955

More Mischief

For three days I lived in the shadow of expulsion. I poured out the story to my mother on the telephone. She exploded in fury, blaming everything on Michael. Eventually she managed to speak to Cecil Harrison, pleading for him to be lenient and pointing out that I had been led astray by her 'wicked' nephew. She even telephoned the pub. The landlord denied all knowledge of selling beer to underage boys. Eventually the headmaster and Spoke Wheeler were won around and to my great relief the matter was quietly dropped.

Thus my second experience with alcohol had also got me in trouble. Drinking beer was not what it was cracked up to be. Girls were far more interesting. A point of view shared with my new friend, Gray Jolliffe.

Gray, who eventually became a distinguished cartoonist, was in the year above me. He hosted regular parties at his house, an impressive twelve-bedroom Georgian mansion set on the edge of the Minster Precincts with a front door opening onto a view of the magnificent West Front of the cathedral. Gray was full of mischief. He was handsome and irresistible to most girls. With jokes and anecdotes he had everyone in stitches. He also had delightful parents and I would often drop by and chat to his mother in her spacious kitchen as she busied herself on their ancient Aga. *How unlike my mother*, I used to think at the time. Gray's mother listened, gave advice and encouragement, rarely talked about herself and, like Gray, sprinkled her conversation with laughter. She did get a bit annoyed about the parties. Gray's parents were often away at weekends.

"I don't know what you get up to," she would exclaim with a twinkle, "but don't get up to it in our bedroom. There are eleven other rooms to choose from."

Another friend was Michael ('Mac') McDermott. Mac was quiet and just tagged along, agreeing to whatever scheme was suggested to him. He and Gray were both seventeen, a year and so older than me, and had passed their driving tests first time. I was too young to have a licence. Gray's father owned a magnificent AC 2-Litre saloon with swerving, sensuous curves and a top speed of eighty miles per hour.

One Sunday afternoon Gray drove Mac and me in the AC to a disused American World War II aerodrome about twenty miles from Peterborough. He would then drive up the runway slowly, carefully inspecting the surface for potholes or debris. When he reached the end, which was just over a mile, he turned around and drove back as fast as the car would go. It was exhilarating.

"OK, Barry," said Gray. "You have a go."

I had never driven a car before.

"There's nothing to it," he said as he showed me how the gears and the clutch worked. I got the hang of it fairly quickly and slowly drove back to the end of the runway, practising the gear changes and braking all the time.

"Don't kangaroo," said Gray every time I did a jerky gear change.

We got back to the end of the runway. I was now feeling more confident.

"Right." Gray grinned. "Do what I did. Go as fast as you can. Keep to the centre of the runway and keep your foot down hard on the accelerator."

And so I set forth; twenty miles per hour, then thirty, then forty, then fifty. But this was much as I dared.

"Faster, faster," said Gray.

I managed sixty, then sixty-five. Unfortunately I kept my eye on the speedometer for too long and was veering to the left of the runway.

"Keep to the centre! Keep to the centre!" yelled Gray, pushing the steering wheel clockwise in an attempt to rectify things.

I panicked and slammed on the brakes. The car skidded and went round in two circles with a loud screeching sound before stopping, facing the other way.

"What did you do that for?" said Gray, grinning. Realising I had had enough excitement, he got out of the passenger seat, gave the car a cursory inspection to check that no damage was done, and took over the driving.

"Watch this," he said, and drove a little off the runway in the direction of the old control tower. In front of us was a small mound, or hump. Gray drove towards it at about twenty miles per hour. The car floated momentarily in the air before gently landing on the other side, cushioned by its magnificent suspension.

Meantime, Mac, who had been in the back of the car during all of this, said he felt queasy. He got out and sat on the scrubby grass for a while before we called it a day and drove back to Peterborough. He was envious of the AC and its performance.

"Let's do this again next week. I will bring my mother's new Ford Popular."

"OK," said Gray. "How about a race?"

"You bet," said Mac.

Somehow Mac had got it into his head that the Ford Pop (as everyone called it) could 'do eighty'. It was the most basic car on the market, sometimes requiring a handle to start it. Mac's mum was a proud owner and only reluctantly allowed him to borrow it from time to time. ("You must drive slowly, be careful. Don't do anything silly," she always said.)

The following Sunday, Gray and I set off for the aerodrome in the AC with Mac chugging along behind in the Ford Pop. Of course the Ford did not stand a chance against the AC, since apart from anything else its top speed was only sixty and its acceleration was pretty pathetic.

"That car is a bath on wheels with a sewing-machine engine," taunted Gray.

I saw Mac go white with anger. With grim jealousy he watched as Gray repeated the hump trick. Again the AC sailed like a bird as it left the ramp and floated for almost a second before gently landing on the tarmac.

Mac, not to be outdone, jumped into the Ford Pop and drove straight to the ramp, possibly even a little faster than Gray had done in the AC. The way up was as gracious – the landing marred by an enormous crunch. The Ford recovered, but lopsidedly, and moved away with an ugly scraping noise. The mudguards were buckled and the suspension was probably broken. Mac was in despair. We tried to straighten the mudguards, but to no avail. The Ford Pop managed to hobble back to Peterborough, but Mac's driving career was suspended until further notice.

1955

Christmas Already

Gray Jolliffe published several funny and successful books of cartoons. The most famous is *Wicked Willie* but my favourite is *Christmas Already* (subtitled *The First Jewish Christmas Book for Nearly 2,000 Years*) because of its charming irreverence – Jewish jokes on the Nativity and Father Christmas. Importantly, it resonated with the contradictions I endured each Yuletide.

During the 1950s, when the business was doing well, the problem of Christmas was solved simply by opting out. Mum and Harry had been told about the Beresford Hotel on the South Coast near Bexhill-on-Sea. It was a retreat for those wishing to avoid the annual Christian festival.

The hotel was sumptuous. In the foyer stood a large Christmas tree studded with coloured lights. At the appropriate time the manager would dress up as Santa Claus, with his staff acting as reindeer pulling a sledge piled high with presents. This was the secular Christmas; no mention of Jesus, the Nativity, wise men or shepherds. Diners sat in the spacious ballroom as a palm court orchestra played. There was dancing and cabaret-style entertainment. Men wore dinner jackets and the ladies sparkled in their jewels and sequins. A little bit of Hollywood came to Sussex.

We spent Christmas at the Beresford several years running. During the few days leading up to our departure we were always anxious about my mother's mood. Would she be relaxed and charming or, more likely, tense and angry – or worse, violent and unpredictable? Joan

Kay Ltd was exceptionally busy at that time of year with demanding retailers, spring samples to be produced, and cards and presents to be arranged for important customers. Also, my mother had her family in Peterborough on her mind. How would she manage to see them, and what gifts to buy? Her wardrobe was another source of anxiety as she felt obliged to compete with the Jewish ladies at the hotel. Mum took her frustration out on Harry who, unfortunately, always looked as if he was idle although he was sitting quietly in the office going through the paperwork, checking the accounts and listening to staff problems. He received no credit for this. My mother would just call him a lazy pig, or words to that effect.

Still, there was always the hope that once we had set off for Sussex my mother would remain calm and, if she did, Harry, Penny and I would heave a sigh of relief. More often than not her anger bubbled over for the whole journey and on arrival she had a face like thunder as she strode into the hotel. If we were lucky she would reunite with a guest from a previous year. This prompted her mood to change abruptly for the better and she became gay and charming.

"This is my son," Mum would say proudly as I stood there in my smart suit from Harrods' 'younger man' department. "He's going to be a doctor."

Looking at me inquisitively, and probably thinking, *This boy doesn't look Jewish*, Mum's new acquaintance would just say, "How wonderful" as she kept chatting to my mother about 'business'. A large number of guests were in the rag trade so it was usually easy for Mum and Harry to strike up conversations.

So, if my mother did calm down, we had a pleasant Christmas. The food was delicious (paradise compared to the Pig) and I usually overate and had a tummy ache. There were no boys of my age and no opportunities to make friends. I hung out mostly with members of the band who were friendly to me. I asked them about their instruments and how to read dance band music, and what life was like as a professional musician. They liked to chat to this boy so full of curiosity, and taught me a great deal about a side of life I knew little about.

I also gossiped with the maids. One was called Caitlin. She was aged about sixteen and doing a holiday job. I tried to kiss her but she laughed and pushed me away, saying I was too young. It did not matter because we became friends and she told me all about Ireland and her family in Skibbereen. When I was older, she said, I must come to Ireland and visit her. We would sail to Sherkin Island and walk together along the cliffs, and maybe I could kiss her then. She said it did not really feel like Christmas here at the hotel because, unlike home, there were no carols or Bible readings.

"I think there are a lot of Jewish people here." Then, embarrassed, she said, "You're not Jewish yourself, are you?"

"Of course not," I replied abruptly, and told her about Harry being my stepfather and how back at school I would revert to being Barry Chambers.

"You poor darling," she said. "Maybe I will give you a wee kiss after all." And she gave me a peck on the cheek before hurrying off to do her work.

That Christmas at school had been particularly moving for me. My voice, now broken, had settled and I was enjoying singing the bass part of my favourite carols. I'd had my usual romantic concepts of the approaching festival, and again there had been the let-down on returning to London for the holidays. There was no sign of Jesus in the Kay household. As usual we drove off to Bexhill-on-Sea. I casually told my mother I intended to go to midnight Mass on Christmas Eve. Harry looked alarmed, thinking I had converted to Catholicism.

"Do what you like," said my mother, "but don't involve us and keep it to yourself."

I found out from the concierge that there was an Anglican church about two miles away which held a midnight service. But once I was in my dinner jacket and we had sat down to eat on Christmas Eve and were listening to the dance band, the thought of trudging two miles there and back to a church at midnight was not appealing.

A few minutes into the meal when the band had 'taken ten' there was a commotion at the entrance to the dining room. The hotel manager had been dealing with a problem in the kitchen and the new assistant manager was left in charge. A church choir, about twenty of them, dressed in surplices and cassocks and led by the local vicar, had arrived unexpectedly, asking to sing carols to the guests and to pass around collection boxes. The assistant manager, a young Italian, thought that there was no harm in this (it was Christmas after all) and invited them into the dining room, announcing that a choir had turned up to sing Christmas carols, and weren't we lucky!

Acute embarrassment seized the room. This was the sort of thing the guests had come to get away from. I, on the other hand, was delighted. Our family was sitting fairly far back and so I got up and stole gently to an unoccupied table at the front near to the choir. It was obvious to everyone in the room that I was the only one enjoying the carols, and indeed the choir sang quite nicely. The vicar, however, was not happy with the glum faces and suggested that the guests should join in *Good King Wenceslas*. I happily sang along, again the only one joining in. The vicar, disappointed with the cool reception, decided to call it a night and members of his flock passed quickly around the tables rattling tin boxes. Most guests were reluctant to give anything, and half the women had walked out with the excuse of going to the ladies' room. The choir left and the manager returned, immediately realising the mistake his assistant had made. He gave a sort of apology as the band struck up and normality resumed.

Meanwhile, back at our table, my mother looked furious.

"What's wrong with carols on Christmas Eve?" I said sheepishly, knowing the answer full well, of course.

Mum fell silent and started chain-smoking. Harry said I had been tactless, and did I not know that many people here did not believe in Jesus? I kept up my righteous, stupid stance. Mum became more and more despondent. The next year we went to a different hotel.

1956

The End of Barry Chambers

In the first term of my final year I felt quite grown-up. I had more confidence, although I was worried about A Levels which were looming. I had not done well in the summer term mock exams and had made little time for revision during the holidays.

Spoke Wheeler tackled me on my return for the autumn term. "You will have to do better than that. You managed to fail all three subjects in the mocks. Pull yourself together; it's your last chance. Have you applied for Edinburgh yet?"

My stomach went into a knot. "I don't know how to apply," I said pathetically.

"You just write away for the application form, you chump. The school secretary has kindly obtained the address." He handed me a card on which was written: *Admissions, The Medical School, Teviot Place, University of Edinburgh.*

I looked at the address and my heart began pounding. Was it really time to apply for university? But I had failed all my mocks. What would the school say when they were asked to write a reference?

I wrote away for the application form, which arrived a few days before the end of term. It was to be completed and returned by the end of January; there was plenty of time. I took it home during the Christmas holidays and tried to involve my mother and Harry in answering some of the questions. One was, *Are there any Medical Professionals in your family?*

"I'll just write 'no' for that," I said.

"Don't be silly," interjected Harry. "Say your mother was a nurse."

"That's absurd," yelled my mother. "Do you want him to start his medical career by lying?"

"Who's to know?" said Harry, looking puzzled.

When I returned to school after the New Year I asked Spoke Wheeler to look over the form, which I had filled in lightly in pencil. He read it carefully and said, "The most important question is, *Why do you want to become a Doctor?* Your answer is far too sentimental. Try again."

I had written a lot of drivel about wanting to save lives and cure cancer. My next attempt was more mature and I emphasised job satisfaction and security, a caring profession, opportunities to do research, and teamwork. Spoke approved of my final version and the application form was duly sent off.

Sometime in February I received a letter from Edinburgh University inviting me to attend for an interview. I was elated. I cycled around to tell Mr and Mrs Jermy. Lillian's face lit up. The thought of 'Little Barry' being a medical student in her native Scotland seemed to thrill her as much as it did me. She offered to write to her brother who lived Haddington, near Edinburgh, to ask him to put me up and to see that I got to the interview on time.

And so it was that on a sunny, cold and windy day in March, during the Easter holidays, I set off for Edinburgh. Grandma came with me to the station. Looking nervous as usual, she gave me sandwiches and a lemon meringue pie. She smiled and wished me good luck. I had never been farther north than Grantham. This was an adventure.

The journey seemed endless. I ate the sandwiches and wondered what to do with the lemon meringue pie. I had no utensil to eat it with. There was no alternative but to leave it on the luggage rack.

Mr James Hay, Lillian's brother, met me at Waverley Station. He was a small, serious man.

"We must walk to St Andrew Square and take the bus to Haddington," he said. "It will take about forty-five minutes."

We walked along Princes Street. I looked up in amazement at the castle towering over the city. Mr Hay pointed out Jenners with its smart women's clothes in the windows, and I thought how much my mother would like to shop there. George Street was imposing but the grey granite buildings were gloomy. We caught the bus and eventually arrived in Haddington. By this time it had started to rain. The sky was grey, the buildings were grey – everything was grey.

The Hays lived in a spick-and-span bungalow. They welcomed me warmly. We talked about Roland and Lillian and life in Peterborough. After supper Mr Hay and I played chess until about ten o'clock. I tried not to think about the interview. I did not know what to expect. I had had no preparation and was nervous.

Mr Hay was an accountant who worked for a firm in George Street. It was important that he got the eight o'clock bus back into Edinburgh so he could get to his office by nine. Since I was returning to Peterborough that afternoon I said my goodbye and thank-you and was given clear instructions on how to get to the Medical School.

The New Quadrangle in Teviot Place was entered via a black arch. I reported to the office and was directed to a seat in a corridor where there were two other candidates who looked considerably older than me. When I was finally ushered in I was confronted by three quiet gentlemen who spoke with gentle Scottish accents. I must have looked very young because the first thing they did was ascertain that I would be seventeen by the time term started that October.

The interview went surprisingly well. My application form was discussed in detail. Why had I chosen Edinburgh? What branch of medicine particularly interested me?

Back at school two weeks later I got a letter of acceptance conditional on passing three A Levels. I was over the moon, but at the same time anxious that something might go wrong with the exams. There were only four months to go. Would I make it?

A different feeling of apprehension also took hold. If I passed I would leave The King's School and the boarding house forever. The Pig had been my real home since the age of four. Despite the changes in staff it had represented continuity and reliability, qualities I had not enjoyed at home with my mother and Harry. Part of me wanted to step out into the world, although the thought of leaving these familiar surroundings filled me with unease. Life at the boarding house was now rather pleasant. Bullying had stopped. Sixth-formers were being treated as students rather than schoolboys. Restrictions were relaxed. I was a prefect and could come and go more or less as I pleased. I had had some success on the athletics field, having been the junior long-jump champion at the county games. This gave me considerable credibility amongst my peers.

There were other distractions, of course. A certain status came with having a girlfriend – usually a County School girl or one of the beauties from Westwood House, a private girls' school on the other side of town. A highlight of sixth-form life was an invitation for boys to attend Scottish country dancing lessons at the County School. It was there that I met Judy Pledger, a jolly girl who wanted to train as a midwife. On Sunday afternoons I would take the bus to her home in Werrington. There in their front room we would listen to Eartha Kitt songs for hours on end whilst her parents kept a discreet distance in another part of the house. At four o'clock precisely, Mrs Pledger would emerge with an enormous tray of tea, sandwiches and cakes, the quantity and quality of which surpassed even Grandma's considerable offerings.

Mr and Mrs Pledger were kind and took a genuine interest in my ambition to become a doctor. Although it was fun to kiss and cuddle with Judy, I was more stimulated by my conversations with her parents. They were both wise and caring. What a contrast to my mother and Harry. The Pledgers gently questioned my reasons for wanting to study medicine and gave advice without being patronising. Years later when I married and had daughters of my own, I used to think of the Pledgers and how they involved themselves wisely with their girls' suitors.

The spurt of revision before the exams went well. After it was all over I thought I had not done badly, but was not certain. On the last day the headmaster asked all leavers to congregate in the school hall for his traditional 'end of school' advice. We all knew what was coming but were respectful and tried not to snigger.

Looking serious and waving his pipe, Mr Harrison said solemnly, "If you are ever under the influence of alcohol, never be in possession of a woman, a revolver or a motor car." We were now ready for the wide world!

The leavers' service was held at the cathedral on the last day of term. I was in a bit of a daze and emotional. The service was always the same and the whole school attended. Each leaver was called out by name, invited to come forward and presented with a Bible. When my turn came the headmaster said, "Barry Chambers" but in my Bible he had tactfully inscribed, *Barry Kay*. We then recited the school oath in which we promised *always to uphold the good name of The King's School, Peterborough*. Most moving of all, the choristers quietly sang the Nunc Dimittis: *Lord, now lettest thou thy servant depart in peace according to thy word...*

At the end of the service the teaching staff stood in a row to shake hands with the leavers and wish them luck. I was in a daze and had difficulty accepting the finality of the moment. I even protested, saying that I was not really leaving and that I had probably failed one or more of my A Levels. Most of the masters grinned.

But it was the end, not just of my schooldays, but of Barry Chambers. I had changed my name – there was no going back. The moment I stepped out of the cathedral I was Barry Kay. At home my mother had erased all signs of Barry Chambers long ago. My passport, my university entrance, my A Level and O Level documents were all in the name of Kay. People from school would still think of me as Barry Chambers, but for those I would meet in the future I would be Barry Kay. Barry Chambers was no more.

1956

A Pigite No Longer

In the summer of 1956 I had just turned seventeen. I was swept along by a feeling of freedom. Freedom at last from The King's School Boarding House – my home, for over thirteen years. There was a caveat, of course. I had to pass my A Levels. If I failed there were two options, neither of which was attractive. I could return to the KSP to resit – this would have been humiliating – or I could go to a 'crammer'. That would have meant living at home. I would just have to sweat it out for the next few weeks until the results came and hope for the best. I tried to be positive. I convinced myself I would pass all three subjects. Before going up to Edinburgh I was going to have the holiday of a lifetime.

I intended to hitch-hike on the continent and see as many sights as possible. It was the era of hitch-hiking. The whole world, especially Europe, had become accessible to anyone prepared to stand by the edge of the road and thumb a lift. Many of my friends at school intended to do this. They had pored over maps and planned routes. It was generally agreed that it was best to travel alone because car drivers did not like taking more than one passenger. I was eager to try it. It would be a great adventure.

First I had to earn some money. Cadging from my mother and Harry was not good for my self-esteem, and anyway it would bring too many conditions, such as cleaning the house and running errands. The foreign travel allowance in those days was only twenty pounds, although the checks at customs were not stringent. For me it was still a lot of money. I would have to spend the first few weeks of the holidays trying to earn some.

When I got back home to London I relayed my plans to my mother and Harry. They mentioned they also were planning a trip to France, driving to Juan-les-Pins in the south. "You are better off hitch-hiking with your friends," said my mother. (I didn't tell her I was going alone.) Anyway, there was no opposition. The thought of getting me out of the way for most of the holidays appealed to them. They agreed to contribute ten pounds, unconditionally. Things were looking up.

I had heard from a boy at school that the Lyons' Corner House main shop in Marble Arch, where the confectionery was made, was taking on students for the summer. I made my way there as soon as I could and filled in the application form. I was hired immediately at four pounds, twelve shillings and sixpence a week. The world of manual labour was a new experience, but I liked the camaraderie. I worked in a maze of underground passages, emerging only occasionally into the sunlight to deliver items to the main shop. The tasks were monotonous, consisting mainly of hauling trays of buns and cakes from the cellars to the shop, washing up various receptacles and putting labels on tins. Eating or even touching any of the cakes or buns meant instant dismissal.

Virtually every employee was Irish. The women called me 'their little darling'. The foreman, Patrick O'Shanassy, took me under his wing.

"Now, Anthony—" he would begin.

"But I am not Anthony, I am called Barry."

"It's Anthony I have got down on me list and so Anthony it will be. And why are you not using your name, Anthony? Don't you know that if you ever lose anything all you have to do is pray to St Anthony and he'll find it for you? He's the patron saint of lost things. He may come in handy one day, you never know."

We sat on boxes during our tea breaks. My new comrades told me stories about Ireland and leprechauns. They seemed to like me.

I told them what I was going to do with the money I earned. They were somewhat bemused since they all sent their wages back to their families in Ireland. Why didn't I give the money to my parents, they asked? "It's just a one-off adventure," I told them.

I would always find an excuse to talk to the lovely Molly Donovan. She was in her mid twenties with long auburn hair and worked behind the counter in wedding cakes.

"Have you got a girlfriend, me little darling?" she said.

"Not at present," I replied, blushing.

"Well, I'll be your girlfriend and you can take me to the swankiest restaurant in town, you being a posh boy and all."

"I'll save up."

"I'll be too old by then." She laughed and, looking around furtively, planted a quick kiss on my cheek.

My time at Lyons' went by quickly. In three weeks I had saved twelve pounds. My exam results still had not come through.

A few days later Gray Jolliffe phoned me at home to say he was coming to London with two girls. He knew that our house in Carlton Hill was empty because I had told him that my parents and Penny had gone on holiday to Juan-les-Pins and would be away for a month.

"Who are the girls?" I said.

"Well, there's Janie, who I am going out with, and your old friend Maddy."

I remembered Janie, slim and curvaceous, always hanging around Gray's neck, and Madeline Griffin, a sort of girlfriend of mine with whom I had had an on-and-off relationship. She was easy to get on with although she did not stop talking.

"Well, I suppose it's all right," I said, "but there is a housekeeper who comes in each day."

"Pay her off," said Gray, "and tell her not to come in until we leave."

"I could, I suppose." My mother had left some money and told me to give Mrs Lee her wages each day. So I gave her a week's cash and told her not to come while we were there. And so the four of us, plus Mac McDermott who was at a loose end, took up residence in Carlton Hill.

The question of sex, and how far we would go, was high on the agenda. Mac was shy with girls and not interested in physical encounters, saying he preferred to admire pretty girls from a distance and bide his time for when the right one came along. Gray, on the other hand, had turned nineteen, almost two years older than me. From the moans and groans that frequently came from the bedroom (he had been allocated my parents' room) it was clear that he and Janie were past the petting stage. Every time he emerged he would greet me with a mischievous grin and ask how I was getting on. Had I done it with Maddy yet?

Now, it was not that I did not find Maddy attractive; just the reverse. She was buxom and curvaceous with a pert little nose, brown eyes and auburn hair. Furthermore, she made it clear that she was up for more than just fondling and petting. I, for my part, was, as usual, confused. On the one hand I was being given an opportunity on a plate, but on the other hand I was apprehensive. Although I probably did not realise it, I was torn between losing face with Gray and simply wondering if I was really ready for this 'loss of innocence'. Added to this was the obvious fear of a possible pregnancy. This was too awful even to contemplate.

In any event, Maddy had made it clear that nothing was going to happen unless I armed myself with a Durex or 'rubber', as condoms were referred to in those days. I was sent on a mission to purchase some. It was a disaster. I was paralysed by fear and embarrassment every time I went into a chemist shop. I came back empty-handed. Maddy did not take it too badly. I think that, like me, she was also relieved. We were too young, just not ready.

The five of us still had a good time driving around London in the Joan Kay Ltd business van, seeing the sights. After about a week they all left. The results of the A Level exams had still not come through.

*

I killed time preparing for my big adventure. I bought a duffel bag, khaki trousers, a fold-up waterproof, a beret, a tin mug and plate and, most importantly, a Michelin guide to France with all the youth hostels marked. I also purchased a large map of France and spent hours planning my route. I was particularly excited about seeing the Mediterranean Sea as it conjured up images of *Quinquireme of Nineveh* from *Cargoes* and other Romantic poems we had learned at school. However, it was important to stay clear of Juan-les-Pins. To have to tag along with my mother, showing off to her friends and doing the round of casinos, filled me with dread. *I don't need them any more*, I thought.

Sitting on the stairs, a few days after my friends had gone back to Peterborough, I heard a dull tap as an item of mail was popped through the letter box. There on the floor was a postcard with my name and address staring up at me. All I had to do was turn it over. I trembled for a moment, too frightened to see the results. Eventually I turned the card over. By *Physics*, *Chemistry* and *Biology* had been written, *Pass*. All subjects passed!

Relief oozed out of every pore. Emotions ran high. First came disbelief, then excitement and, at last, the unequivocal fact that I had left The King's School, Peterborough for good. Never again would I be called Barry Chambers. I was going to Edinburgh University as Barry Kay, a medical student.

But first, *la belle France*.

Summer of 1956

La Belle France

I crossed the Channel from Dover to Boulogne. My plan was to stay in youth hostels, although I had been warned they were often full in the summer. I had thirty pounds (forty thousand francs in old money). It had to last. I kept counting it nervously.

I got a bunk in the local youth hostel. It was full of young French, German, Dutch and Danish men. I was the only English person there.

"Where are you heading?" a Danish boy sitting opposite me asked.

"To the sunshine… the South of France, hopefully. After that will depend on how much money I have left."

"If you stay in the south until the beginning of September you can get a job grape-picking. It pays well and they give you a bed and meals. The only problem is the mosquitoes." He laughed, then introduced himself. "My name is Morgons. Are you going to the south via Paris?"

"Yes, I don't think I could give Paris a miss. My name is Barry."

"Well, Barry, stick with us tomorrow and try your luck at 'autostop'."

Morgons was about twenty years old, tall, broad-shouldered and with thick blond hair. He told me he was a student of theology at Aarhus University and, as a child, had witnessed atrocities perpetrated by the Germans. The local pastor had taught him not to hate and had encouraged him to join the church. He was part of the new youth of Europe: full of hope; forgiving, but not forgetting, the past.

We had a simple meal of tomato salad, cheese and pâté. I had my first taste of garlic. Someone plucked a guitar and with the help of some wine I drifted into a daze. I was in France. There were adventures ahead. This was life.

The next day, with Morgons' help and advice, I got a lift to Rouen with an English vicar driving a 1932 Rolls-Royce Phantom.

"God bless the country," he said. "Everywhere we are reminded to defend the afflicted."

"Defend the afflicted?!" I replied.

"Don't you see? *Défence d'afficher.*"

Suddenly I did not feel too bad about failing O Level French.

The reverend shared his lunch and supper and let me sleep in his car. I had not spent a single franc the whole day.

The next morning I was on my way to Paris. There was a sea of people rushing in all directions, laughing, shouting and gesticulating. Open-air cafés spilt out onto the road. Drivers hooted their horn at the slightest inconvenience, but no one paid attention. There was a pervading smell of baked bread, rotting fruit, car exhaust, cheese, urine, perfume, garlic, Gitanes and Gauloises. It intoxicated me, and it got more pungent as I descended into the Métro. Here were added body odours mingled with the rubbery smells from the trains.

The only youth hostel in Paris was full. The hotels in the centre were too expensive. I began to despair. Eventually I was given the address of a bed and breakfast in the Malakoff area, about an hour's walk away. I made friends with a serious German called Hermann. He was eighteen years old from Mainz, short and stocky with a crew cut.

"Autostop in Germany very easy," he said as we were walking along. "Wonderful autobahns. Not here in France. They do not like Germans. Who can blame them? But it is not our generation's fault. Eighty per cent of Cologne kaput with bombing. My father, brother, both killed. But let's not talk about the war."

The bed and breakfast was also full, but we were offered mattresses in a corridor.

The next day Hermann and I 'did' Paris – the Louvre, Notre-Dame, L'Orangerie, the Eiffel Tower and Sacré-Cœur. In the evenings we wandered around Montmartre and stared in disbelief at the brazenness of the prostitutes in the Place Pigalle.

Hermann opened up and told me about himself and his family. They were from a small village near Bad Godesberg on the bank of the Rhine, a few miles from Bonn and Cologne. As well-off farmers they did not feel privations until late in the war. His father, although in his late forties, had been suddenly drafted into the Wehrmacht in 1944. After a few months he was reported missing, presumed killed on the Eastern Front. Hermann's elder brother, Carl, joined the Hitler Youth. In March 1944 when barely fourteen he was forced to join a fighting unit trying to halt the Americans when they crossed the Ludendorff Bridge at Remagen, south of where they lived.

"Carl was just a boy," said Hermann. "He didn't know what he was fighting for. My mother was never told how he was killed. Such a waste. But, my friend, you British also did terrible, unnecessary things. All those bombs, night after night. Cologne and Bonn nearly destroyed. And Dresden!"

I pondered on what he said. It had never dawned on me that there might be two sides to the story. I had thought that the German people deserved everything they got; now I was not so sure.

It was good to have a companion whilst sightseeing but I preferred to be alone when travelling. By now I had spent thirteen thousand francs, about a third of my money. More panic. Should I proceed to my goal, the Côte d'Azur? What if I ran out of cash, or lost it, or it got stolen?

Bravely I pressed on to the south. I arrived in Lyon in the pouring rain and departed the next morning in glorious sunshine. I was able to keep going on bread, cheese and fruit.

A commercial traveller gave me a lift in his new Citroën DS, which 'took off like a bird'. He took me to a fine restaurant and I had my first taste of *cuisses de grenouille*. Would I like to go with him to visit *les femmes*, he asked?

"No thanks," I replied. But he let me sleep in his car and so again I saved money.

The next day a Swiss lady gave me a lift on the back of her scooter. As we raced along I clung on to her in a rather intimate way. By late afternoon I was in Avignon, almost the South of France. I became aware of the noise of cicadas and the fragrance of pine, olive and jasmine. Everything was new and exciting again. I soon found the youth hostel – the best yet – and I ate and slept well. I was down to about fourteen thousand francs.

I explored the Pont d'Avignon and wondered if Mr Howitt, my old French master, would have been impressed that I had made it to the place of the song he had made us learn. Seasoned hitch-hikers had told me in Paris that the place to make for on the Mediterranean was La Ciotat. It had the best youth hostel in France. The price for full board, including breakfast and dinner, was quite reasonable.

I got a lift to Aubange, then a bus to La Ciotat. As the bus turned a corner on the brow of the hill on the road running down to the village I caught my first view of the Mediterranean. It took my breath away: that calm turquoise sea shimmering in the bright sunshine. Unfortunately the *Auberge* was *complet*. I wandered down to the beach and ate some bread and cheese - left over from lunch. The evening was warm and balmy. The thought of sleeping on the beach did not worry me. It turned out to be an uncomfortable night, however. Sand got in everywhere. I climbed into a nearby rowing boat and tried to stretch out but it was impossible, so it was back to the beach again, to the pebbles this time, with my duffel bag as a pillow.

The next day I got a place at the youth hostel. It was teeming with young people of all nationalities. I soon got into a gang and, feeling happy and able to relax at last, drifted from the hostel to the beach for a few days of glorious sun, sea and sand. We had splendid dinners at a long table which overflowed with aubergines, courgettes, fruit, cheeses, bread and wine. Sometimes there was chicken, or a meat casserole, and always soup served from a huge tureen. Time passed quickly.

After five or six days I realised that I was running dangerously short of money. Would I have enough to get back to London? Once more I started to panic. Finally I was obliged to confess to the *patron* that I was challenged financially. He graciously said I could pay him when I got back to London. What a relief! But I still only had eleven thousand francs. This would not cover youth hostel costs and food for more than four days. I was running the risk of finding myself destitute in France. What was I to do?

There was nothing for it. I had to go to Juan-les-Pins and get bailed out by Mum and Harry. It was only about two hundred kilometres away. I would just breeze in, borrow twenty pounds worth of francs and leave immediately.

I said goodbye to my new-found friends in La Ciotat and was back on the road early the next morning. A car soon stopped and took me to Toulon, then another to Fréjus, and by lunchtime I was in Juan-les-Pins. My parents had told me the name of the hotel they were staying at. I soon found it. *I expect they will be pleased to see me*, I thought.

The contrast between rural France, with its post-war run-down villages, and well-heeled Juan-les-Pins was striking. Style and luxury were everywhere – in the hotels, the clothes, the shops and the cars. Expensive yachts bobbed up and down in the bay. Bronzed holidaymakers, mostly English (and looking slightly smug), strolled lazily along the promenade.

At my parents' hotel the doorman blocked my way. "*Qu'est-ce que vous voulez?*" he said.

"*Je cherche mes parents, Monsieur et Madame Kay.*"

He seemed surprised, sneered at me and, after a pause, said, "*Ils sont probablement sur la plage.*" He pointed to the beach.

The hotel was by the seafront. As I got closer I saw rows of brightly coloured umbrellas. It was the hotel's private beach. People lounging on lilos stared at me. I stared back, and there was muttering behind my back. Where were Mum, Harry and Penny?

I walked down to the water's edge and there, coming towards me wearing a bright blue bikini, was my mother. She was ambling along, looking up at the sun and smiling.

"Hello, Mum," I said breezily.

She lowered her head and stared at me in disbelief as if having difficulty in recognising her own son. "Barry, what are you doing here?"

"Just passing," I said.

She did not seem pleased to see me. "You look awful," she said with a scowl. "Your hair is like a scarecrow's. Your clothes are filthy. I don't think you have washed yourself for weeks. And as for that duffel bag with the tin mug hanging down – you might as well be a tramp. You can't meet my friends looking like that!" Pointing to a bench on the esplanade, she said, "Go and sit there and don't move until your father comes." With that she turned round and walked briskly away.

Some welcome! I thought. But I did what I was told. I needed the money.

Presently Harry appeared, looking jovial and saying what a pleasant surprise it was to see me. He asked about my trip and I described some of my adventures.

"Your mother says I have to 'smuggle' you into the hotel by the back entrance, and that you are to have a bath."

"OK by me," I said.

I was whisked up to my parents' room and luxuriated in the bath. A few minutes later there was a knock on the bathroom door.

"What size chest and waist are you?" demanded my mother. The door was not locked. Mum opened it and stormed in with a tape measure. I jumped up and grabbed a towel to cover my lower half. Quick as flash, my mother measured me and was out of the door. I was told to stay put.

About an hour later I was handed a new pair of shorts, a pair of long trousers and two rather loud shirts.

"Where is your swimming costume?" asked my mother.

I produced it from my duffel bag, which I had hidden on the top of a wardrobe as it was clearly embarrassing her.

"Your costume is just about passable," she conceded. "Now take him to a barber," she told Harry.

By late afternoon I had been washed, scrubbed, hair cut short and kitted out in new clothes. Mum looked at me, paused, and then gave a huge smile. "Oh, how lovely to see you, Barry. How was your trip down? Tell me all about it."

Meanwhile Penny, who had been out with a friend and her mother, appeared and whooped with delight to see me. "How long are you staying?"

There was a silence. Mum and Harry looked at me, waiting for an answer.

I felt like saying, *If you give me twenty pounds worth of francs I will go right now*, but thought better of it. "Well," I finally responded, "let's say a couple of nights and then I will head off back to London."

"There is a spare bed in Penny's room," said Harry.

And so it was settled. I was to have a short period of luxury without having to worry about money. That evening we had a relaxed family meal in the hotel restaurant. Mum was in good form. Everyone laughed as I told stories of my hitch-hiking. The next day we lazed on the beach and swam and played in the sea (it was unpolluted in those days). Most of the London rag trade seemed to have gravitated to Juan-les-Pins.

"Say hello to Hetty," said my mother proudly.

"Hello, darling," said Hetty Arbiter. "Just flown in, have you?"

"No, I came down with my friend in his Jaguar. He had to press on to Monaco where his dad has a yacht. They are off to Venice. He asked me to join them but I get terrible seasickness so I thought I would stop off with Mum and Dad for a while. He will collect me on the way back."

Mum beamed, delighted I was playing her game so well.

Towards the end of the afternoon I noticed that my mother was getting a little restless. Suddenly she announced that she was going with Harry to the casino in Cannes that evening, and that I was to look after Penny, then only eight years old. So, after dinner they set off in the Ford Zephyr, saying they would probably be back late.

About two in the morning I was woken up by a commotion coming from their bedroom. Mum was crying. Dad was shouting, "Two hundred pounds! Two hundred pounds! How could you have been so stupid?"

"Don't you dare call me stupid," came the response. "It's all your fault for taking me there in the first place."

"We have hardly enough money to get back to London," Harry wailed.

At this point the night porter knocked on the door asking the two of them to be quiet as guests were complaining.

The arguing continued. Finally I got back to sleep. Breakfast the next morning was a dismal affair. Mum stayed in her room. Harry was tense. Penny was crying; she knew something was wrong. I reminded Dad that I was leaving that day and told him I was low on cash and needed money to make it back to London.

Harry, usually calm and not prone to intemperate outbursts, exclaimed loudly, "Your mother has managed to lose all our holiday money at the casino. We have a hotel bill to pay and somehow we have to get back home. Don't ask me for money. In fact, how much have *you* got left?"

"About twelve pounds' worth of francs," I said.

"Right, hand them over. We have got to get out of here."

Luckily Harry had paid the hotel a deposit and managed to persuade the manager to accept a cheque for the balance. I handed over my francs, we packed hurriedly and by midday the four of us were on the road heading north. My parents' holiday had been cut short by a week because of the casino incident. Mum continued to blame Harry. She chain-smoked most of the way back to Calais. We had two overnight stays: one in a grubby hotel in Lyon, and one in a slightly better hotel outside Paris (although I had to sleep in the car to save money).

Before we left Calais I told Dad about the bill I had to pay for my stay at the youth hostel in La Ciotat.

"Did you give them your address?" he asked.

"No," I replied.

"Then you have nothing to worry about."

"It's a matter of principle, and I promised."

Dad looked bemused, but finally he handed over the money and I went to the nearest *Bureau de Poste* and sent off a money order. We only had ten shillings between us when we finally arrived back in London.

My 'holiday of a lifetime' had started so well. I had felt free and grown-up, ready for life. Stupidly, I had not budgeted wisely. Mum's reckless gambling had spoilt the holiday for Harry and Penny. Little did I realise that this was just a forewarning of what was to become a much more serious problem.

1956

Liminality

When I stepped out onto the cathedral close in Peterborough after the school leaving service in July 1956 I was elated by the prospect of freedom. I was going out into the world at last and, if I got the necessary A Level passes, I would be a medical student on the road to a noble profession, to respect and admiration. I did not need The King's School any longer. I was not even sure I needed my parents – apart, of course, from them providing subsistence and a house to stay in during the holidays.

With the summer over I whiled away the time between returning from France and starting university. Unexpectedly, instead of a pleasant anticipation of university life and what life had in store for me, I had a vague sense of anxiety. I was not going back to school. I should feel elated. Why wasn't I?

Finally, at the beginning of October I was on my way to Scotland. My grandmother had insisted on seeing me, even if only for a few moments, when the *Scotsman* stopped at Peterborough.

"Keep warm," she said anxiously, and again thrust a lemon meringue pie at me. "It's awfully cold in those parts."

I arrived in Edinburgh, this time having managed to eat the whole pie, and set off for 184 Dalkeith Road, the digs I had been allocated by the student accommodation office. My landlady, Mrs McBride, was in her early fifties. Always dressed in her 'pinny', she had a shuffling gait and a quiet Scottish voice. She seemed happy to have so many young men under her care. A few weeks earlier

Mrs McBride had been Miss Rose. She did not act much like a newly-wed. Mr McBride sat in the back parlour and was hardly ever seen or heard. If his wife had divided loyalties between the new batch of students and her husband, she concealed them. We were well looked after with breakfast at eight, supper at six and tea and sandwiches at half past nine. The food was generally excellent and the house spotless. My roommate, Chris Ingram, was a pleasant dental student. We became friends. In the room next door was Matt Haczkiewicz, a chubby and emotional Pole of whom I also grew fond. Before the war his father had been a professor of medicine at Krakow University. When the Germans invaded in 1939 the family had fled through Romania and were then interned by the British in Egypt. They finally ended up in the Midlands where his father was head of a TB sanatorium. Matt found studying difficult although, paradoxically, he was rarely seen without a textbook in his hand, but he was jovial and kind, with a love of the theatre and grand opera.

Other comrades at '184' were a cadet policeman, an agricultural student who played Little Richard records at full blast late into the evening, and a history undergraduate called Dave who rolled cigarettes and taught me to smoke, a habit I found hard to give up. We all rubbed along together pretty well.

The first year (called 1st MB) was a doddle. It was physics, chemistry, zoology and botany – little different from the A Level subjects I had done at school. So, academically, I was not challenged. This turned out to be a mixed blessing. On the one hand I had plenty of time on my hands to pursue activities outside of the curriculum; on the other I would often wake up with no clear plan of where I was going.

I had entered a liminal space. The familiar, i.e. the boarding house, was now behind me, but the future was unknown. Leaving school had stripped me of status and I was left with an ambiguity – excitement about the future with its uncertainties intermingled with yearning for the Pig and its reliabilities. It was my rite of passage.

Once, before leaving school, we had been taken on a day trip to London to see *Hamlet* at the Old Vic. On our return Cecil Harrison had taken me to one side and said, "No doubt you remember Polonius's advice to Laertes on going up to university?"

"Some of it," I replied shakily.

"Choose your friends wisely, get the correct balance between work and play, *Neither a borrower nor a lender be*, and, above all, *to thine own self be true*."

I thought about this short conversation during those first few months in Edinburgh. *To thine own self be true.* What did that mean?

This transition period would also have affected my fellow students to a greater or lesser extent but for them, I suspected, it was the wrench from home life and the wisdom bestowed by parents which they missed, consciously or unconsciously. For me, home life had contributed little or nothing to my preparation for adulthood and university life. To be fair, neither of my parents had been to university so they were not in a position to advise. After all, at my age Harry had been a bookie's runner.

There were fifteen of us in the sixth form at school, but in Edinburgh there were 130 students in the first-year class. The teaching staff were remote. Striking up a one-to-one relationship with a university lecturer was virtually impossible, and attempts to do so were frowned on by fellow students who regarded this as some form of 'creepiness' aimed at trying to get special attention. I might not have appreciated it at the time but my need for guidance from an older man was far greater than I realised. Only seventeen, no longer a boy but not yet a man.

I tried to recreate aspects of school life. I joined the Dramatic Society ('Dram Soc') and the university choir, and played rugby (I was put in the 4th XV). My classmates were largely Scottish and, although there were exceptions, they were for the most part a pretty serious lot. To my surprise, many lived at home with their parents. For them 'the varsity' was a seamless extension of school. Some students lived in halls of residence but I had been too late in applying for a place in one. In one sense I was envious of this form of collegiality although, again ambiguously, I also yearned for solitude, perhaps in a bedsit or a small flat where I would be free to come and go as I liked, have guests, maybe find a girlfriend.

"Finding a girlfriend is easy," said one of my new friends at our digs. "Just go to the Union Palais on a Saturday night, but make sure you have plenty to drink first!"

In those days manliness in a medical student was judged by the number of pints of beer he could consume without falling over. In the Men's Union, a somewhat misogynistic students' club, a ritual would play itself out every Saturday night. Young ladies, who at other times were unwelcome on the premises, would ascend in their finery for the weekly dance held on the spacious upper floor. For the first two hours hardly any men were present, so the girls would either chat amongst themselves or dance with each other. Meanwhile, in the large bar on the ground floor, male students would wind themselves up for the inevitable confrontation with the opposite sex. A mass choir formed around the bar and lewd songs were sung at full belt to a piano accompaniment. Pints of beer would sway back and forth, reminiscent of the student prince in *Old Heidelberg*. At ten sharp the bar would close. Gritting their teeth, young bucks would ascend the stairs to face the 'enemy'. Those who made it to the top floor were often completely drunk and in their attempt to dance would fall about the floor in a wretched state whilst the ladies looked on in despair. *There must be more to student life than this*, I thought. *There must be better ways of finding a soulmate.*

I found the answer in the students' common room in the Old Quad, an elegant Robert Adam room with a vaulted ceiling and classical columns. This was the heart of the arts faculty; medical students were rarely seen there. For me it was a palace of blissful time-wasting, an oasis amid the tedium of studying. It was to become my second home. I would hang out there for hours, sometimes days on end, chatting with fellow thespians from the Dram Soc, music students, would-be writers and poets. We discussed politics, books we had read, parties we had been to, blossoming love affairs and how to survive on our modest student income. This was to be my university life, at least for the first few years. The hours passed like seconds, although from time to time I would be seized with panic about my idleness and the impending exams. And so I would repair to a quiet spot to revise.

I now called myself Barrington Kay. It had a stylish ring. The Dram Soc was putting on *Much Ado About Nothing*. I was cast in the small part of Balthasar, the attendant to Don Pedro. I sang a song – *Sigh no more, ladies, sigh no more...* – which was savagely lampooned at the party after the last night's production. I was star-struck. Virtually all the cast were mature students or postgraduates. Some would go on to be professional actors. The director, Rick Stevens, became a BBC drama producer; Piers Haggard, who directed other productions I acted in, was to become a household name.

I had a crush on the wardrobe lady, Dorothy Stormonth. Three years older than me and bemused by my attentions, she was friendly but mostly kept me at arm's length. The week after the production there was a party at her parents' house in the New Town. I had never encountered such elegant Scottish grandeur. Her father was a top lawyer (a Writer to the Signet or 'WS'). None of her family regarded me as a serious suitor; rather as Dorothy's little lapdog.

The first few weeks, and indeed the first months and years of my student life, were turbulent. My rite of passage was painful because of confusion as to who I was. If I was a serious medical student on the way to curing diseases, then why was I not appropriately studious? If I was some kind of troubadour, what was I doing studying medicine at one of the ancient universities? If I was a Christian, why did I spend so much time thinking about girls?

Initially I had been relieved to shed the name Chambers (a new life, a new name, I reasoned), but I soon came to regret it and anger against my parents, particularly my mother, was always just below the surface. I broke off all ties with school, except for correspondence with a few of the masters who understood and respected my situation. I did not join the Old Petriburgians' Association and for years and years lost touch with friends such as Ginner Gray, John Uzzell and Ian Arbuckle. I was too ashamed of my change of name, my reinvention.

To add to my chagrin I found that Chambers was a perfectly fine and respected name in Edinburgh. Chambers Street, named after William Chambers, a former Lord Provost of Edinburgh, was dominated by university and museum buildings. The name Kay, on the other hand, which I had been so keen to embrace because of its apparent blandness (anything to get away from 'Po Chambers') was easy to explain north of the border. I could say I had Scottish ancestors, since it was an abbreviation of MacKay or McKay. There were many Kays in Scotland. It was more problematic in England, where Kay and Kaye were commonly associated with immigrants, particularly those, like Harry's parents the Kruschinskys, who had fled from the pogroms of Eastern Europe. Would people think I was Jewish? Surely not, but how could I tell them my name was really Chambers?

The end of term came far too quickly and I travelled back to London full of tales of student life. My mother was unimpressed. She thought I would be 'walking the wards'. I told her that this was a long way off and that there would be years of basic science and theory before we saw patients. I bought Christmas cards for my new friends, including a particularly kitsch one for Dorothy. No sooner had I written the messages and addresses than I came down with a bad dose of influenza which laid me low almost until the New Year. I had pleaded with Harry to get stamps and post the cards and to make sure they arrived by Christmas.

"Of course," he said.

"Have you done it?" I asked him later.

"Of course," he repeated.

After I had recovered and was more or less back to my old self Mum and Harry decided to take me to Selsdon Park Hotel for a New Year treat. We set off in the car. I sat in the front because I was still feeling queasy. We stopped at a garage for petrol. Whilst Harry went to pay I idly opened the glove compartment. There were the Christmas cards, unstamped. I overreacted and railed against my stepfather. My mother took my side. An argument ensued. We never got to Selsdon Park.

Eventually I gave my dad the benefit of the doubt. He probably just forgot, and anyway Christmas cards did not mean much to him. What was all the fuss about, he would have thought? For me, at that age, sending cards was a mark of friendship. If you did not send a card this could be interpreted as a slight, a sign that you did not care. What nonsense! The Scots were more interested in New Year than Christmas.

Dad and I made it up. I told him I was taking an interest in politics. This pleased him. He told me about his own youth and the time he joined the Communist Party, and the marches to the East End of London by Mosley's odious Blackshirts.

"Did you really want a totalitarian government? Did you want to get rid of the royal family?"

"Our brand of communism wasn't so radical… although we didn't like democracy as we saw it in the 1930s. I am not a communist now; nor should anyone be after the denunciation of Stalin a few months ago. I am still a socialist and hate inequality. As for the royal family, well, they are an irrelevance."

"There's a man called Muggeridge," I said. "I have been reading about him in the papers. He's been criticising the monarchy. I think they are out to get him."

"Now, Malcolm Muggeridge is very interesting," said Harry. "I have been following his career for several years. All he is saying is that the monarchy is a royal soap opera. We puff up royalty too much. They are just ordinary people."

On my return to Scotland everyone was talking about the rectorial elections due to take place in a few weeks' time. Electing a rector is a quaint tradition of the ancient Scottish universities. The head of the university is the vice chancellor. The rector, on the other hand, is a sort of figurehead who is elected every three years by the students. He does not have much power but he is expected to represent student interests.

To my surprise Malcolm Muggeridge was one of the candidates. He was sponsored by the students' magazine. I decided to join them. Unfortunately the popularity of James Robertson Justice, the medical students' choice, was in sharp contrast to the general animosity felt towards Muggeridge because of his perceived attack on the Queen through an article he had written in an American magazine.

The Muggeridge camp encouraged me to canvass the medical students. I phoned Harry and told him all about it. He too was excited, especially as I told him I would probably meet Muggeridge when he came to Edinburgh on a visit. I heard my mother in the background saying, "Invite him for dinner. Invite him for dinner." *How ridiculous*, I thought.

James Robertson Justice, who had played Sir Lancelot Spratt in *Doctor in the House* (a larger-than-life surgeon, charismatic, demanding, witty, brilliant, caustic, worshipped by the nurses and feared by medical students and junior staff), was idolised by medical students at the time. The film was a box office success and most of my classmates, me included, enjoyed it immensely. In real life James Robertson Justice had many of Sir Lancelot's qualities, and what is more, or so he said, he was a Scot.

My first taste of canvassing was a disaster. With naivety bordering on the insane I made a placard out of cardboard and a piece of wood on which I wrote *Muggeridge for Rector*, and stood on the steps of the Men's Union at lunchtime. As fellow students piled in for their midday meal they gasped in amazement at my audacity. A crowd formed around me, initially laughing and then shouting, "James

Robertson Justice! James Robertson Justice! James Robertson Justice! Muggeridge out! Muggeridge out! Muggeridge out!"

Then someone cried, "God save the Queen!"

Others joined in. Suddenly everyone was yelling, "God save the Queen!"

"He's misunderstood," I tried to say over the noise. "He didn't criticise the Queen. He only said—" Then a tall rugby player grabbed my placard and smashed it to the ground. We scuffled on the stone steps. I managed to break loose, and ran.

It was a narrow escape. I kept a low profile for the next few weeks and confined my canvassing to 'intellectual discussions' amongst my Dram Soc friends in the students' common room, waiting for the day when Muggeridge would travel to Edinburgh and I would meet the great man in person.

A few weeks later I, and other Muggeridge supporters, met him at Waverley Station. He was leaning out of a first-class carriage as the train pulled in, holding a cigarette with a silver holder in one hand and a glass of whisky in the other. He was tanned, with silver hair and a broad smile. When he alighted we saw he was immaculately dressed. Each article of clothing down to his shoes conveyed elegance. The Scots looked scruffy in comparison. I pushed forward to introduce myself.

"I am Barrington Kay, a medical student," I said proudly.

"Delighted," he said, smiling, but then frowned as he realised that the crowd of noisy demonstrators in the background were not his supporters, but adversaries. "Dear boy," he said, handing me his suitcase, "please look after it and see it gets to my room in the hotel."

Anxious to please, I said he could rely on me and explained that there was a direct entrance to the North British Hotel from the station and this way he could avoid the demonstrators. Meanwhile in the hotel lobby several journalists and cameramen were assembling, waiting for the press conference.

"Let's go and meet this motley lot of old hacks," Muggeridge whispered in my ear conspiratorially.

His supporters joined him and we sat down at the long table at the front. Making himself comfortable, Muggeridge sat back in his chair, arms stretched out like a priest addressing his congregation, and, waving his cigarette in its holder, announced that he would begin by making a short statement. Cameras flashed as he pulled a small piece of paper from his inside pocket.

"I was delighted to be invited to Edinburgh by my young friends here—" he began.

"Mr Muggeridge," shouted someone from the back, "does England really need a Queen?"

He frowned at being interrupted so abruptly. "Yes, the monarchical institution in England is immensely valuable and the present incumbent is a delightful exponent of it."

Reporters shouted questions from all directions.

"Didn't you say that the Queen is a rather simple person?"

"Why did you call the monarchy a soap opera?"

"Are you a communist?"

And so on…

Realising the press conference was not going the way he wanted, Muggeridge decided to bring the proceedings to a close, gave his apologies and made a swift exit.

At the dinner in the evening Muggeridge held forth on his not inconsiderable achievements – editor of *Punch*, globetrotting interviewer, documentary maker and war correspondent. He declined the wine, asking instead for a bottle of whisky which he kept at his side for the duration of the meal, occasionally pouring a generous glassful. He flirted outrageously with one of the lady students in the group. She was awestruck but after a while he got bored with her and, turning his attention to me, asked what I was reading.

Caught unawares, I told him, "A P. G. Wodehouse book."

"How splendid!" he said, his eyes lighting up. "Are you a fan?"

"I have read most of his books," I confessed. "I love all his characters. I think I prefer Psmith to Bertie Wooster."

"The P is silent!" roared our guest with laughter.

"It's a pity Wodehouse turned out to be a traitor," I said.

"Nonsense!" said Muggeridge. "You are referring to those broadcasts he made from Berlin during the war. He was just naive. He was tricked into making them. I have read them all. They are harmless. He was stupid but he is not a traitor."

With that he gave an almighty yawn and excused himself. He had an article to write with a deadline. We wished him goodnight and said we would see him off at the station the next morning. He filled another tumbler full of whisky and headed for the lift.

The next morning the 'committee' met at Waverley Station. He shook us all warmly by the hand and went aboard the train. He let down his carriage window and leaned out. "So nice to have met you, dear boy," he said to me.

"You must come to dinner with us in London," I blurted out.

"Delighted, delighted." He beamed. The train pulled out of the station.

As he disappeared into the distance the absurdity of Malcolm Muggeridge coming all the way out to Hampstead Garden Suburb to be entertained by my mother and stepfather struck home, and I burnt inside with embarrassment.

As the rectorial campaign increased in vehemence, so the enthusiasm of the Malcolm Muggeridge campaign dwindled. We had had our press coverage, our point had been made, but the opposition was too strong. In the end James Robertson Justice won by a landslide. Muggeridge got less than three per cent of the votes cast (see footnote). The rector's term of office was three years. With spectacular lack of imagination, Edinburgh students elected James Robertson Justice again from 1963 to 1965, the only rector to have served a second term of office.

When I got back to Edinburgh for my second term of the first year I was anxious to explain to Dorothy Stormonth that I had been laid up with flu over the holidays, and had been too unwell to write, even a Christmas card. We went out for a coffee.

"So sorry you had such a miserable break," she said. "But we need to have a serious talk. I don't want to string you along; you are too young for me. I feel like a baby-snatcher."

"But in a few years' time that will not make any difference," I protested.

"In a few years' time you will have forgotten all about me and I will probably be married to a Scottish lawyer."

"What's wrong with an English doctor with a successful practice in Harley Street?" I joked.

"But there is another problem," she said, looking away nervously.

"Which is?"

"Daddy thinks you are Jewish."

Footnote

In the 1960s Malcolm Muggeridge unexpectedly converted to Christianity. He denounced meat-eating, drugs, sex and violence, and was contemptuous of the Beatles. In 1966 Edinburgh students, presumably in a wave of piety, invited him for a second time to be a candidate and he was duly elected. This time the student magazine played a different role. The editor, Anna Coote, goaded Muggeridge to support the call for contraceptive pills to be made available at the university health centre. He used a sermon in St Giles' Cathedral in January 1968 to denounce the 'permissive society' and dramatically resigned his office, the first rector ever to do so.

1962

The Two Harrys

During my university days Mum and Harry Kay's relationship deteriorated. My mother's mental illness was always just below the surface, although at the time, and because of the stigma attached, we were all in denial, preferring to call her behaviour 'hysteria' or 'nerves'. When I came home from university during the vacations there would invariably be scenes of violence. For example, without provocation my mother would physically attack Harry, kicking him and lashing out with her fists. Whilst screaming and shouting, she would accuse him of laziness and disloyalty and say vile things about him and his family. Harry would usually bear it all stoically and do his best to calm her down. Occasionally he would leave the house in desperation although, with the anxiety of not knowing what she might do in his absence, he would soon return. Calling a doctor or an ambulance was out of the question. It was not only the shame of having a 'mad' person in the family, but the hope that her outbursts would run their course and she would calm down – which was the usual pattern, although it sometimes took days or weeks.

Back at medical school, I tried to understand more about my mother's condition by consulting psychiatry books in the library. I had not done the mental health course and had difficulty understanding all the technical terms. It was clear there was little understanding of her illness in the 1950s and 1960s. The term 'bipolar illness' had not been introduced and mood-stabilising drugs such as lithium had not been discovered. I read about 'manic-depressive insanity' but reasoned that my mother could not be insane. I was misled by the fact that between 'attacks' she acted more or less normally for days and sometimes months. Looking back I now understand that psychiatrists were largely ignorant about the various patterns of this illness and did not appreciate that every case of bipolar illness is different.

I was more than halfway through my medical studies, just managing to keep up with the syllabus despite the attractions of student life and the distractions and apprehensions of what was happening back at home, when there occurred a dramatic turn of events. For a number of reasons, I kept changing my accommodation. I had tried living in 'digs', but either I did not like the landladies or they did not like me – usually both. I lived from time to time in university halls of residence but it was too restrictive, too much like the boarding house. Sharing a flat with other students was an attractive proposition but I would often fall out with my flatmates, either over girls, or money, or bad behaviour (usually mine). Because of my continually changing address I was not easily contactable by my parents. I asked them to write to the Men's Union as a 'poste restante'. This worked pretty well as I would pass by most days to check my mail.

One warm morning in June 1961 our student year gathered in the quadrangle of the Medical School as we were just about to sit our pharmacology papers, an important 'professional examination'. Suddenly a servitor, in full university uniform, appeared on the steps of the faculty of medicine offices saying in a loud voice, "Anthony B. Kay? Is Anthony B. Kay here?"

Some helpful fellow student pointed him in my direction. He walked up to me.

"Sorry to trouble you, sir, but you are wanted on the telephone, in the faculty office."

"On the telephone?" I said in amazement. "But who would want to call me there?"

"I suspect it's from your home, sir." He sounded sympathetic.

Seized with panic and wondering whatever could have happened, I followed the servitor up the stairs. A lady with a kind smile handed me the telephone receiver.

"Hello?" I said.

"It's Dad here," said the agitated voice on the other end of the phone. "You must come home immediately."

I feared that someone had died, or that there had been an accident or illness, or my mother had done something particularly crazy. "What's the matter? What has happened?"

"Your mother has run off with a slimy, rotten bastard." I had never heard Harry so angry or defeated. "He is a rogue, a professional gambler. He has abducted your mother. You must come home right now and help me. You have to confront him. Tell him, and your mother, that what they are doing is wrong." He then broke down sobbing.

"Dad, I am just about to sit an important exam. If I don't do it, I may have to repeat a year, or worse."

"Well, do the exam, then come right home," he pleaded.

The exam I was about to sit was, in fact, the last one of the term. I was reasonably well prepared and had been looking forward to letting my hair down that evening with my pals in the Golf Tavern, and afterwards at a party my current girlfriend's flat. I put this out of my mind; I was too distressed. I needed to get into the examination room, try to concentrate, and return to London as quickly as possible.

I was lucky. The questions were straightforward and the ones I had prepared for. I did not give my best answers in the circumstances but did well enough for a pass.

I decided to fly back to London because the train would get me in too late. I desperately wanted to know what was going on. I felt confident I could bring my mother to her senses and sort things out. I rushed back to my flat, packed a few things and caught an airport bus to Turnhouse for a mid-afternoon flight. Harry was going to meet me at Heathrow. During the flight I thought long and hard about my mother and stepfather's relationship but found it difficult to be objective. I loved them both, but it was clear that for some time their marriage had been destructive. I found myself being revisited by those childhood yearnings for a stable, happy family. The thought of everything breaking up was unbearable. I was worried about Penny. What would happen to her if Mum and Harry split up? Fortunately, at the time, she was away at boarding school and would be spared the present anguish. She was not due home for another few weeks.

My flight landed and I got through the arrivals hall quickly. There was Dad, haggard and unshaven. He gave me a big hug and a tearful account of what had happened.

"For some time," he said, "your mother has been coming home late, saying she had been playing cards at a club in Mayfair."

The fact that Mum was a seasoned gambler and loved going to casinos and playing cards meant this came as no surprise.

"She met this man called Harry Reuben. He's awful, a professional poker player. He's just taken her away with those cruel eyes. It's abduction. I know where they are," he exclaimed. "They are at a flat in Swiss Cottage. We are going there right away and you are to grab your mother, take her out of there and bring her back home."

I should have laughed at the absurdity of his plan, but I was becoming highly emotional myself and felt deeply for my dad's anguish. Maybe he was right. Mum was just doing something on impulse. As soon as she saw me she would come to her senses and return home.

As we drew near Swiss Cottage I became more agitated. Dad had persuaded me that this Harry Reuben was a wicked seducer and my mother was his victim. I was determined to confront them both.

"Hit him if necessary!" shouted Harry Kay as I sprang out of the car and headed for the block of flats.

I bounded up the stairs, by now in a blaze of indignation and fury, resolved to defend my mother's honour. I rang the bell and to my surprise she answered the door.

"It's Barry!" Mum exclaimed with wide-eyed disbelief. "Why aren't you in Edinburgh studying to be a doctor?"

Standing behind her was a man of medium height wearing a dark suit and tie. He had large lips and wore spectacles with thick lenses. This must be Harry Reuben.

"You are coming with me!" I said, as I grabbed my mother's arm and pulled her to the door.

"Stop him! Stop him, Harry," she wailed as I wrenched her forward.

Harry Reuben caught me by the back of my collar and tried to pull me away. I lashed out with my fist, hitting him fair and square on his cheek.

"You snotty-nosed kid!" he shouted, rubbing his face.

"Stop it! Stop it!" my mother wailed. She collapsed, weeping, to the floor.

Suddenly I was crying as well.

Mum got up slowly and went to sit in a chair. "This is my son," she said. "Harry Kay must have dragged him away from his studies and put him up to this."

Harry Reuben looked at me, nursing his bruised cheek. "Hello, son," he said, with an unconvincing smile.

"Don't call me 'son'," I replied acidly. "You are not my father."

"Calm down, calm down, boy. We can sort this out."

"What is my mother doing here? What are you up to?"

"Your mother is a grown woman in her forties," he said.

"Don't remind me of my age," interjected my mother.

"She knows what's best for her and can make her own decisions."

"Listen, Barry," said my mother, almost calmly. "I can't go on living with your dad. You know how it is. We are always fighting. There is nothing but unhappiness in that house. I can't stand it any more. In any event, I am in love with him." She gestured to Harry Reuben, who by then was gently stroking her back.

"How can I study with all this going on?" I said angrily. "And what about Penny? She will be horrified that the family is breaking up. Can't you think of anyone but yourself?"

"Is Harry Kay waiting outside?" said my mother.

"He's hoping you will come home with me."

"Tell him to go away," she said. "Tell him the three of us here will have a long talk and then you can meet up with him later."

"Yes, have a drink first," said Harry Reuben, who had moved in the direction of a brandy bottle. "It will calm your nerves."

I looked at the glass, badly wanting something to control my anxiety but feeling that accepting a drink might look like some sort of acquiescence. Nevertheless I grabbed it, gulped it down, and set off to tell Harry that we were going to parley and that I would report back to him.

My emotions were in a turmoil. I dreaded Mum's moods and aggressive behaviour towards my stepfather. On the other hand, I could not bear to think of the family splitting up. What would happen to Harry Kay? What would happen to Penny? What would happen to the business? I was also feeling angry at Harry Kay for putting me up to this, dragging me down from Edinburgh during exam time, not fighting his own battles – how pathetic, how weak, and how undignified! This was not the way for a husband to handle infidelity. Looking back, I wonder why, at the age of twenty-one and as a medical student well on the way to qualifying, I felt so vulnerable, so confused. Crushed and rudderless, I found myself begging my mother not to take the line of action she planned – or at least for her to agree to wait until I finished my course before breaking-up the family.

For the next few hours Harry Reuben, Mum and I talked exhaustively and emotionally about the future. It became clear that my mother's mind was set and that eventually she would leave Harry Kay. I still hoped that by delaying things her affair with Harry Reuben would turn out to be a temporary infatuation which would pass. I said I would probably drop out of medical school if she did not patch things up with Harry Kay because I would be too upset and unable to concentrate. This argument was persuasive, and so it was agreed that my mother would return to Norrice Lea until

I completed my studies in two years' time. Also, by then Penny would be a little older and, hopefully, better able to cope.

Deep down I did not believe my mother would keep her side of the bargain. I was to be proved correct.

1963

Final Years at Edinburgh

Today, a medical student will have contact with patients during the first few weeks of the curriculum. Clinical problems will be presented by a skilled teacher in such a way that even the neophyte will understand the principles of diagnosis and treatment. This invariably inspires the student for the long journey ahead. In the 1960s, in contrast, clinical medicine was taught in the traditional way. Before walking the wards many hurdles had to be jumped, in particular passing examinations in anatomy, physiology, biochemistry, pharmacology, pathology and bacteriology. We would cram for these and regurgitate our knowledge on the day, only to forget what we had learnt shortly afterwards. That was the way we prepared for a career that would span thirty or forty years.

Having jumped these hurdles, little could match the thrill of being assigned to a 'clinique', as Edinburgh quaintly called the lists of students apportioned to the various medical and surgical firms. Unfortunately the allocation was a lottery. Some cliniques were inspiring, others not so. If one was lucky enough to be attached to Professor Sir Derrick Dunlop's ward then one sat at the feet of arguably the greatest teacher of his generation.

Sir Derrick was tall, slim and elegant, always immaculately dressed in his pinstripe suit and silver-coloured tie. He held generations of students in thrall with his love of language, rolling out eloquent phrases and adjectival clauses. He had exceptional clinical skills and was a superlative teacher. Already, by the time I was attached to his ward, he had become a household name to all who graduated and practised in Edinburgh.

What marvellous good fortune to be on the Dunlop attachment and, every day between eleven and one o'clock, to receive his wisdom. But there was a problem. I had great difficulty getting up before midday. The reasons: sex, drugs and classical music.

I was a relatively late starter by 1960s standards, being nineteen when I lost my virginity. The time and place it happened was familiar – a Saturday night, in a student flat, after a party. On the night it happened I was with a gentle, pretty girl, about a year older than me – a music student called Sylvia. We were smooching to Miles Davis. I happened to have my hand on her bottom and was gently pressing her towards me. "Be patient," she said, taking my hand away, and then murmured between kisses, "Wait until everyone has gone home. Then we will do it." I could not believe my ears. This was it – at last, after years of refusals when attempting to go 'the whole way'.

Sylvia shared the flat with two other girls and had indicated where her room was. But the party dragged on and on. Midnight came and several people were still talking, drinking and dancing. Sylvia was laughing with another man in the far corner of the room, pretending she did not know me, but every so often would give me a sly smile and a wink as if to say, *Hang on. It won't be long now.* Meanwhile my excitement grew to the point that my knees were shaking. Performance anxiety struck. Maybe I would be a 'flop'. Another drink might help, so I poured myself some more Spanish red wine, the standard student's tipple at the time at only six shillings a bottle. One o'clock came, and then two. As soon as the last guest departed Sylvia bundled me into her room but was then obliged to help her flatmates clear up. It seemed like an age until she returned. She smiled at me and slowly undressed. She had done this before.

As I feared, my performance lasted approximately 1.7 seconds.

"It's your first time, isn't it?" said Sylvia.

"Yes," I croaked in embarrassment, with my head in the pillow.

"Don't worry, it will be OK."

And indeed it was, because fifteen minutes later it lasted a whole five seconds. By the morning my record was three minutes.

Sylvia was a brilliant pianist. She had won the Tovey Prize at the Reid School of Music. Occasionally I could persuade her to play Brahms or Beethoven for me, although she made it clear she would rather make love, especially as I was now getting the hang of it. We would lie in bed in the morning. It was either Sylvia or Sir Derrick Dunlop. A difficult choice. I would leap up at about a quarter to eleven, throw on my clothes, kiss Sylvia and rush across The Meadows to the Royal Infirmary and bound up to the wards. The sister in charge would give me a frosty look as I joined my colleagues by the bedside. Sir Derrick, observing my usual late appearance, would comment, "Ah, Mr Kay, ready for knowledge at last."

And indeed Sir Derrick did gently test the knowledge of latecomers. But unlike so many of the grand, often pompous consultants in Edinburgh at the time, he did it teasingly, never hurtfully – and there was always a lesson to be learnt.

"Mr Kay, come and meet Mr Crombie," he said, gently guiding me to a patient sitting up in bed.

"How do you do, Mr Crombie."

"Mr Crombie was admitted last night with severe pain in his upper abdomen," said Sir Derrick. "It radiated down to the groin area. Understandably Mr Crombie *wanted* a painkiller, but when we first saw him were his *wants* and his *needs* necessarily the same?"

This sounded like a trick question and I started to blush because I was not sure what 'the prof' was driving at. My classmates were sniggering, enjoying my discomfiture. At that moment the ward sister whispered something to Sir Derrick about another patient, which gave enough time for a nice registrar close by to murmur in my ear, "He *wanted* a painkiller, but he *needed* a diagnosis first."

The penny dropped.

"Well," said Sir Derrick, turning to me again, "what did Mr Crombie need?"

"He *needed* a diagnosis, sir, and he *needed* one quickly because he *wanted* a painkiller."

Everyone laughed.

"Very good, Mr Kay. And the point of my question…?"

"Don't treat until you have a diagnosis, sir."

"Quite so. Excellent. It's easy to write out a prescription, but it is harder to take a careful history and a thorough physical examination and arrange for the relevant laboratory tests. But having done this you are in a wiser position to advise and institute the correct treatment. This is a simple concept but one which is so easily overlooked when time is pressing and you are tempted to satisfy a patient's *wants* rather than his *needs*."

It was a lesson that stayed with me for life.

And now to drugs. For me this was not a serious problem, although for a while in my undergraduate career it did have a detrimental effect. The fault was not all mine; the university health centre had a lot to answer for. It must be a universal truth that most students, at some time in their progress through college, have problems with studying. It takes many forms – difficulty in concentrating, tiredness, boredom or information overload. Not having enough hours to study and difficulty staying awake when cramming for exams are common problems.

Today students can readily obtain – though illegally – amphetamine stimulants such as Dexedrine or Adderall. They are in common use and the side effects (trouble sleeping, nervousness, hallucinations etc.) are well known. In the 1950s and early 1960s GPs would commonly prescribe amphetamines not only to tired students, but to lorry drivers and housewives. Their use also extended to weight control and alleviating depression. As students in Edinburgh we knew that the university health service would readily prescribe Dexedrine for those who wanted to study a few hours longer. I was no exception. One tablet produced a feeling of well-being – a river of positive thoughts would flow. It would keep me awake until three or four o'clock in the morning, and I would then sleep in until midday. Unfortunately I could hardly recall a thing of what I had been studying the night before.

Luckily my association with Dexedrine did not last long. For me the main side effect was exhaustion. But I tried it enough times to sleep in and miss many lectures. In 1962 GPs, promptly and wisely, stopped prescribing this group of drugs, except in exceptional circumstances. The drugs I was left with for my last two years of medical school were caffeine, nicotine and alcohol.

My love of classical music went back to my schooldays. By the time I got to Edinburgh my trumpet-playing was good enough to get me into the students' orchestra, and I was singing regularly in the university choir and the Charities Opera, an annual production during rag week. I was amassing a sizeable collection of long-playing records, and through Sylvia had many friends in the Music Department. For a while I had 'perfect pitch', or if it was not I seemed to be able to sing any note spot on. The university chaplain, who knew me quite well, asked if I would like to train a small choir he had formed. I found myself immersed in music and performance. I organised and conducted several concerts: Purcell's *King Arthur*, Vivaldi's *Gloria* and the Lalande *Te Deum*. I was on the committee of the University Society for several years and its president in my penultimate year. The professor of music, a delightful man called Sydney Newman, was highly supportive even though I had practically no formal musical training. Sometimes I would meet him in the local pub and he would tell me about his own life as a student. These interactions would pay dividends later in an unexpected way.

The trouble was, however, that these activities took up an enormous amount of time and interfered with my studies. Everything seemed 'touch and go' as far as exams were concerned. I usually managed to scrape through, but only just.

All other clinical assignments were a let-down after Sir Derrick Dunlop's ward. The problem as I saw it was the lack of opportunity for one-to-one contact with patients. Unlike in the London teaching hospitals, 'clerking' of new patients was done by junior doctors; medical students were observers. In those days we had long vacations so there was plenty of opportunity to do 'electives'. It was on these electives, outside of Edinburgh, that I learned the skills of taking a thorough medical history and careful clinical examination. I was attached to the Whittington Hospital in London, the Copenhagen University Hospital Gentofte and, in the last summer before graduating, I spent eight weeks in a state hospital in Utica, New York. It was in the USA that, although only a student, I had to admit every patient. I took a physical and mental history of over a hundred patients under the watchful eye of a great teacher and friend, Professor Rudy Freund, who had been a professor of medicine in Berlin before being hounded out by the Nazis. As I entered final year I had a new-found confidence. Perhaps I would make it to the finishing line.

As far as the future was concerned one thing kept preying on my mind – did I want to spend the rest of my career diagnosing and treating patients? I wanted to know more about the *cause* of disease. But which diseases, and would I be good enough to do research considering all the time I had wasted as an undergraduate having fun?

Returning to London from the USA in October 1962 to start my final year I was still concerned about my mother and Harry Kay. Things seemed to have calmed down a bit but the undercurrent of tension and anxiety remained.

My clinic attachment in the first term was at the chest unit located at the City Hospital, some way from the centre and about a forty-five-minute bus ride. I was disappointed at first. I would just see tuberculosis, chronic bronchitis and emphysema, which seemed somewhat unglamorous compared to cardiology and neurology. I could not have been more mistaken. Firstly, I came into contact with two of the most remarkable doctors I was ever to meet in my career. One was the boss, Professor (later Sir) John Crofton. He was a small man with a military voice and bearing who attracted loyalty and respect. An inspired leader, he built a team which arguably made the greatest contribution to the treatment of tuberculosis by introducing 'drug combination therapy'. His second in command, Dr Andrew Douglas, was an outstanding physician and teacher. He had a fine, small, round head, prematurely bald, and a ready smile. His warmth and humanity rubbed off on those privileged to interact with him. Always on the go, almost running from one task to the next, he taught by example. Dr Douglas was often referred to as the best doctor in town.

One evening when the firm was on call a girl of about twenty was admitted with acute severe asthma (status asthmaticus, as we called it then). She was desperately ill but the registrar who was teaching us was confident that she would respond to steroids.

"They all do," he said. "People don't die of asthma."

During the night she did die. I could not believe it. She was so young and had a condition which we were all told was easily treatable. I was visibly upset. Dr Douglas had been called in during the night but it was too late. Her breathing tubes had just shut down, clogged with mucus as the post-mortem showed.

"But this is not meant to happen," I said to Dr Douglas, almost in tears.

"Aye, lad," he said in his calm Fife accent. "It shouldn't, but it does. It is rare to die of asthma but a few do. I have seen it before. They go downhill quickly. We don't understand the triggers."

"I thought it was mainly due to allergy," I said.

"Often it is, but allergy seems unlikely with this young lady. Something else is going on, or it's a strange form of allergy – something we don't understand. Perhaps the immune system is at fault. Remember that we know less than we think about mechanisms, about causes. There has to be more research. Research, lad. Research. It's the only way forward. I wish I had done some myself but it did not turn out that way. Once you get deeply involved with patient care, well, you are consumed; there is little time to sit back and think."

These words and this sad case had a deep impression on me. I read as much as I could about allergy and asthma, but found the literature confusing. There was little on the causes. Maybe it was an area I could get involved in. But I had not been a diligent student. Only the brightest went on to do research.

I turned for advice to the professor of bacteriology, who had always been friendly to me. He was not encouraging.

"If you want to do research and climb the academic ladder you need a PhD," he said. "When you get your basic medical qualification in a few months' time it will be just an 'ordinary' degree. You won't be accepted for a PhD without an honours degree. Why didn't you do an honours year in a basic science back in your third year before starting clinical medicine? But you were probably too lazy or playing too hard."

True, of course, but I was not going to admit it. Nevertheless, I wondered, was it too late? Could I possibly do an honours year or equivalent after my 'house jobs'? Could I stand going back to being a student again? I made further enquiries with the heads of pathology and pharmacology. Could I do an honours year, followed by a PhD? Again, no encouragement. Their intake for each year was limited; they only took the brightest.

Unexpectedly, one evening at a party, I had a casual conversation with a young veterinarian called Richard LePage. What he told me about his career intrigued me.

"When I did my vet training in Edinburgh I got interested in sleeping sickness in cattle. So after I qualified I looked around for opportunities for research. I had heard on the grapevine about the new Cambridge School of Immunology under Professor Robin Coombs. They had developed new ways of thinking about a range of diseases based on immunological principles. It is a fantastically vibrant group with lots of cross-fertilisation. For instance, there are people there with a background in allergy, transplantation, tropical diseases, transfusion medicine and renal disease."

"Interesting," I replied. "How did you get accepted?"

"Well, like you I hadn't done an honours degree. So Robin Coombs said, 'Do the honours year here in Cambridge' (they call it a Part II Tripos) 'and if you get a first or upper second you can proceed to a PhD.' And so I went back to being an undergraduate for a year; in college by eleven o'clock and all that. I enjoyed every minute of it. And I got a first."

"Well, do you think there is any chance they would accept me? I mean, to do what you did and be a student again?"

"No harm in trying. Coombs likes to have a mix of undergraduates, research students, medics and vets. Just write to him and simply state your interest in allergy and asthma and say you would like to do the Part II Tripos with the intention of proceeding to a PhD."

"I will do exactly that," I said. "Thank you very much."

"A pleasure," said Richard. "Here is my phone number if you require further help." And, looking at his watch, he said it was time for him to turn in.

It was getting late for me too. It had been a long day. What I needed was a good night's sleep. I wandered over to the drinks table for one last beer before leaving.

As I stood there I felt a hand stroking the back of my neck. I turned around. It was Sylvia.

"It's been a long time," she said, smiling. "You don't come to see me any more."

"Sylvia," I gasped. "How lovely to see you. I am so sorry that we sort of drifted apart. I… well… You know – so much studying and finals and things, I just don't seem to have the time to, well, um, socialise."

"So, you've been celibate?" she said with a grin.

"Well, yes," I lied.

"Do you want to be celibate tonight?"

"I don't think so."

Lying in bed the next morning, listening to Sylvia play some Mendelsohn études, I suddenly burst out laughing.

"What's so funny?" she said.

"I *needed* an early night but I *wanted* to make love. Sir Derrick Dunlop says it's important to understand the difference."

1963

The Day of Secrets and Lies

In 1963 the family had lived in Norrice Lea, a house in Hampstead Garden Suburb, for about nine years. My mother loved it, at least at first. She stuffed the living room with expensive antiques and sentimental Victorian paintings. Unfortunately there were a succession of burglaries; the police advised Harry Kay to get a dog. A boxer was acquired, whom we called Prince. Prince was well behaved and had a great bark. There were no more unwelcome intruders.

For the first few years after the move Joan Kay Ltd continued to prosper. Mum's designs were a hit with retailers and the order books were full. More staff were taken on and there was plenty of money around. But all this came at a price. My mother had always reacted adversely to stress, particularly the deadlines imposed for producing the spring and autumn ranges of samples. Although she never worked late, as in the old days, it was remarkable that she managed to get up and out each morning and put in a full day. Mum hardly ever cooked. They would eat out each evening at one of the many restaurants near Wells Street. During the week my mother and Harry were thrust into each other's company. They drove to work, ran the business, ate in restaurants and then travelled home together. They also fought, sometimes violently.

After a few years the relationship began to deteriorate. Mum took less interest in the business and started to spend evenings in London's newly opened casinos. It was there that she had met Harry

Reuben. He was her perfect 'man of the world'. Harry was known everywhere and would take my mother to fashionable gambling clubs such as Crockfords, the 21 Club, Aspinall's and Churchill's. It was a paradise for her, the pinnacle of style and high living. Mum was always elegantly turned out for these events.

She liked to wear silky gowns, often black, sometimes cinched in at the waist to show off her fine shoulders and bust. Her skirts were sometimes swirling, sometimes pencilled, depending on the fashion of the moment. She took considerable time and care over her make-up, making an exaggerated pout (like a kiss) when putting on lipstick. Her eyebrows were plucked and defined, and her eyelashes mascaraed. Then there were her jewels – a favourite was a clustered necklace with earrings to match. Her shoes and handbag would be expensive accessories chosen for the outfit.

Harry Reuben always had a wad of notes in his back pocket which he readily dished out to my mother to squander on the roulette tables. She was thrilled when she glimpsed celebrities, even if they were crooks ("I saw the Kray twins once"). In this new life she would rub shoulders with peers and petty criminals whilst consuming champagne and caviar.

In the Easter holidays of my final year I learnt I had an interview for Cambridge. I came down to London, principally to prepare for this, but also to observe home life at first hand and decide whether my mother had kept her promise of keeping the family together until I qualified. It soon became clear that she remained besotted with Harry Reuben. By way of guilt she would chide Harry Kay, accusing him of misdemeanours and indiscretions for which she had no evidence. Mum was consistently agitated. She began to sleep in until late in the morning and did not seem to care about her work anymore. Unfortunately, without her the business would collapse.

One afternoon, after Dad had gone out, I found my mother sitting in the kitchen, smoking with her head down, gently weeping.

"He is my consolation, my rock. I can't live without him. I am so in love with Harry. You must understand this, Barry."

Obviously she was not talking about Harry Kay.

"Your dad says Harry is a professional gambler," she blurted out angrily. "That's a lie. Yes, he does play poker from time to time, but it's just his way of relaxing. Actually, his family is in the timber business."

I was unconvinced. Later I was to learn that as well as being a serious poker player, Harry Reuben was also an unlicensed bookie who took illegal telephone bets, earning large sums of money, all in cash. He also owned a poker and kalooki club in Swiss Cottage called the Lyndhurst. Clients would play there until the small hours. Large amounts of cash from 'table money' was locked in the safe and never declared to the taxman.

However, there was a different side to Harry Reuben, one that with the passage of time was to endear him to me. Before the war he had been a dance band pianist playing with the Jack Jackson Orchestra at the Dorchester Hotel in Park Lane. Harry had had a classical musical training, although when I first knew him he had not played the piano for many years. Nevertheless, he had not lost his touch and could still 'tickle the ivories' with skill. Harry was a widower whose wife, Stella, had died of cancer a few years earlier. They had no children. He had made generous donations to the Royal College of Surgeons and was given an honour for his philanthropy by the famous surgeon, Arthur Dickson Wright, who had looked after Stella throughout her illness. The two of them had become friends and regularly went to the races together.

Whilst I saw the inevitability of Mum leaving one Harry for another, I was not prepared for the dramatic and cruel way in which she went about planning the 'endgame'.

I had told her that my interview in Cambridge would take place in a week's time.

"I don't understand all this Cambridge thing. I thought you were going to be a doctor and have a nice practice in Harley Street. Why do you want to go back to being a student again?"

"Mum, I will be a doctor and look after patients, but I also want to do research and that requires further training."

"Is there any money in it?" she said. "Anyway, what day is your interview?"

"Next Tuesday, in six days' time."

"Penny will be back from school tomorrow. Perhaps you can take her with you."

"I would rather not," I said. "I need time by myself to think."

No more was said at that point. Penny came back from school, pleased to be back home. "Where is Prince?" she said.

Harry Kay had taken Prince for a walk. When he returned and hugged Penny they turned their attention to the dog. It was clear that something was wrong. Prince did not jump up and greet Penny in his usual way.

"He's sluggish," said Dad. "I don't know why."

I offered to take him round to the vet. Prince was definitely not his old self as he sat quietly in the back seat of Mum's car.

The vet examined him. "He's got a big mass in his abdominal wall. Almost certainly a sarcoma. Boxers are prone to them. It's a problem with the breed – here, feel for yourself."

And, right enough, there was a big, hard lump in his belly.

"What can be done?"

"Not much. Probably best if he is put down."

"But that's terrible. They will be so upset at home, especially my sister."

"There is one thing," said the vet, pondering for a while. "A bit of a long shot but probably worth a try. A Dr Cater in Cambridge has a radiotherapy apparatus for animals. He is doing some research into cancer in dogs. He works in the Pathology Department there."

"But that is a coincidence," I said. "I am going to Cambridge next week, to the Department of Pathology actually, for an interview."

"Well, take Prince with you. I will telephone Dr Cater first and explain the situation."

I got back home and told them all the sad news. Penny and Harry were upset. Mum did not seem to care much. "Better to put him down," she said coldly.

"No. Give him a chance at least."

Penny and Dad agreed. We decided that Penny should after all come with me to Cambridge to help with Prince.

I was unprepared for what happened next. Before we left my mother had been on edge all day, obviously working up to something. Finally she took me to one side and dropped her bombshell. We were in the sitting room. Harry and my sister were out. Mum was shaking and drawing deeply on her cigarette.

"What's the matter?" I said.

"You must promise me that you will not breathe a word to Harry Kay or Penny about what I have planned," she said suddenly. "And you will do as I ask without any questions."

What now? I thought. "Well, that's a bit difficult if I don't know what you are going to ask me to do," I replied.

"I can't go on living here with Harry Kay. Surely you understand that?"

Of course I did, but I was still upset by the prospect of the family splitting up, as I had been two years previously when I had the dramatic confrontation with Harry Reuben.

"So what are you intending to do?" I asked, not expecting a well-thought-out answer.

Mum's eyes were fixed. Taut with self-justification, cigarette hand defiant, she made her announcement. "When you come back from Cambridge tomorrow I will have left this house forever, together with its contents. The removal van comes at 10.30."

"What?!" I gasped. "What about Dad? What about Penny? What about the dog?"

"You are to bring Penny to my new flat in St John's Wood." She handed me an address. "On the train back, tell her I have split up with her father and that she is to come to her new home. We are never going back to Norrice Lea."

"And Dad?"

"He will just have to find out for himself when he gets back."

"And Prince?"

"Do what you like with him; I'm not bothered."

"I can't do this, Mum. I just can't," I blurted out.

"You can, and you will," she replied.

I had a dilemma. If I told Harry Kay all this my mother would assume I had taken his side. There would be an eruption and I would not be able to concentrate on my interview. On the other hand, common sense told me that something like this was bound to happen eventually. Perhaps a clean break was the best way after all, rather than dragging things out for weeks and months. Presumably my mother had taken out a lease on a flat. With whose money, I wondered? Probably Harry Reuben's. Or was it Harry Reuben's flat? Mum would go and live in it anyway. If all Penny's clothes and the furniture were removed from Norrice Lea she would have little option but to go with Mum to the flat. I was trapped and felt it was probably better to go along with the plan. Harry Kay would feel betrayed and our relationship would be irrevocably altered. I had to handle all this and a critical interview on the same day. The fate of Prince was also in the balance.

The train rattled along the Cambridge line. Penny was happy and excited and was looking forward to her day out. Prince sat quietly on the floor of the carriage. I was getting more and more nervous about the interview. There was little time to compose myself. Breaking the news to Penny and facing Harry Kay were foremost on my mind.

We took a taxi to the Department of Pathology in Tennis Court Road. It was agreed that Penny would peel off and go exploring by herself. She was to meet me back at the department at 3.30.

Dr Cater was waiting for me in the reception area. He was a small, friendly, moustached man who wore a neat white coat. I handed Prince, with his lead, over to him.

"You must understand that my work is still somewhat experimental," he said. "But I will do my best. There is no rush to collect him; he will be given a sedative. I should be finished by about four. You have an interview here, I believe?"

"Yes, it's at two."

"Well, use our library on the first floor if you need to prepare."

The interview turned out to be friendly, but brief. There was only myself and the head of department, Professor Greaves. I had expected to see Robin Coombs as well, but it was explained that this was an interview for the Part II course, not a PhD. Greaves himself was a distinguished man who had pioneered the freeze-drying of plasma, a critical development during the war. He was holding my brief CV and two letters, one from Professor Newman and the other from Sir John Crofton.

"It's unusual for the professor of music to give a recommendation for a candidate for immunological pathology. But I am sure it is not unknown, and in Cambridge we like to develop the Renaissance man," he said with a broad smile. "Why do you want to go back to being an undergraduate after six years of medicine? Haven't you had enough of student life?" Again he smiled.

My answer was not difficult. I told him about my wish to work on causes and mechanisms, and my new-found interest in asthma and allergy. I also told him about my conversation with Richard LePage.

"Well, he is doing well. It is a pleasure to have Richard here. We are trying to keep some places open for, well, mature students. If we accept you, what college do you have in mind?"

I had not thought about this. There were many colleges in Cambridge and I thought I would be lucky to get into any of them. The only one that sprang to mind was Jesus College. Thurston Dart, the early music exponent, was a fellow there. So I said, "Jesus", the only reason being that I had several of Dart's recordings.

"Splendid," said the prof. "All seems to be in order. Your referees are most supportive and your motives convincing. You will hear from us in due course." With that he got up, shook my hand and showed me out.

Feeling that things had gone reasonably well I went to the library to wait for Penny to return. I wandered down to the entrance at the time arranged. Penny was already there. "How is Prince?" she said.

"I'm not sure. Stay there and I will go and find out."

I found Dr Cater's room in the basement; Prince was lying unconscious on the floor.

"He will soon come around but will be groggy for a while. He is a sick dog," said Dr Cater. "I am pretty sure the cancer has spread."

Prince slowly regained consciousness. He looked at me woefully. I carried him up the stairs with difficulty because he was quite a weight. The receptionist had kindly ordered a taxi. We got back to the station and on the train to London. Prince was allowed to sleep it off in the guard's van.

The train set off. Penny and I were alone in the carriage. I drew a deep breath.

"Penny," I said. "There's no easy way to tell you this but when we get to London I have to take you to a flat in St John's Wood. Mum has left Dad for good. Whilst we were in Cambridge a removal van cleared everything out of Norrice Lea, including all your stuff. You are to live in a new home."

Penny looked at me in disbelief, then let out a wail of anguish. "She couldn't! She couldn't have!" Then she collapsed in floods of tears.

"She has, I'm afraid." I tried to comfort her but was now tearful myself. Penny was inconsolable. What could I say to ease her pain? "Perhaps it's best they split up," I said.

"Not this way," she blurted out. "I know she has got a new man. I met him once. He is horrible. Is he to be my new father?" And with that she let out more anguished cries.

At this point the guard poked his head around the door of our carriage. "That dog of yours in my van..." he said. "He doesn't look

too good to me. He's been sick all over the floor. I'm not going to
clear it up." He looked at Penny. "What's up with her?"

"She's a bit upset." I stood up. "I'll see to the dog."

Prince was in a bad way, still vomiting. I cleared up the mess
as well as I could with my handkerchief, wrung the sick out of the
window and went to the toilet to wash my hands.

We arrived at King's Cross. I had borrowed Mum's car and we
struggled to put Prince in the back. I drove to St John's Wood.
Penny, next to me, sat silent and sobbing.

We got to the flat and rang the bell. Mum opened the door.
"I'm not going to live here," Penny shouted in her face.

"You're going to do what you are told," my mother said, eyes blazing.

Penny lashed out with her hands. They scuffled, but Mum was
much stronger. She gripped Penny by the wrists and pulled her into
the flat. For a while Penny sat on a sofa, sobbing. I tried to comfort
her. Mum attempted to give her a cuddle but she was rebuffed.
There was really nothing to say. Mum had left Harry Kay for Harry
Reuben. It was no surprise but the way she had gone about it was
selfish and cruel. Mum never questioned her own bad behaviour
but continued to blame Harry Kay, accusing him of ridiculous
misdemeanours which Penny and I both knew were untrue.

Concerned about Dad, and about Prince lying in the back of
the car, I decided to return to Norrice Lea as soon as possible. I was
dreading what I would find. As far as I could see there was not a
huge amount of the Norrice Lea stuff in Mum's new flat, but she had
mentioned something about all the valuable items going into store.

When I got there Dad was sitting on the stairs, head between
his hands, weeping. He looked up at me. "Traitor," he said.

"What could I do?" I was weeping myself now.

I looked around – at the entrance hall, at the sitting room and
in the dining room. Everything had gone; the house was stripped
except for my room which had not been touched. She had left a bed
for Harry and one or two chairs.

He had returned to the house in the late afternoon. The removal men were in the hallway carrying out the last few boxes. He looked at them in disbelief. "What are you doing?" he shouted.

"Sorry, mate," said the foreman. "Just getting on with our job." And with that he pushed past Harry, loaded up and drove off with his two assistants.

Harry kept wandering about the house in a daze. There was no explanation, no note or letter from my mother. His own clothes and a few essential items had been left. My mother must have supervised the house-clearing but left early to ensure she did not have to confront him. In the master bedroom papers and documents were scattered over the floor. She had thrown clothes she did not want any more in a heap for Harry to clear out.

Sitting there with his head in his hands, Harry was a pathetic sight. I had never seen him so beaten. But suddenly he sat up with a jerk and looked frightened.

"You have to help me," he said, and springing to his feet, told me to come with him upstairs.

"What is it?" I asked, puzzled.

"Up there in the loft." And he pulled down the spring-up ladder.

Unfortunately Harry was too big to squeeze through the gap. He told me to climb up the ladder. I had never been in the loft. I did not think anybody else had since the family moved in. Luckily there was a light.

"What can you see up there?" Harry shouted from below.

"Nothing," I said, "except four large, old typewriters."

"Good," replied my stepfather. "We have got to get them down."

"Get them down?! They look very heavy."

"It doesn't matter," he responded with agitation. "We have got to get them down and dispose of them, tonight."

"Dispose of them tonight?" I said with incredulity.

With great difficulty we got the typewriters down the ladder and the stairs and into Dad's spacious black Jaguar. Nineteen-forties Remington typewriters weigh about forty pounds each.

"OK, where shall we dump them?" said Harry, now a little calmer as we drove off. "It has to be somewhere miles from here. Any suggestions?"

"Can you tell me what all this is about?" I said.

"Please do not ask me. Be a good son and help me. All I will say is that your mother could easily embarrass me if the typewriters remain in the house."

Easily embarrass him?! What did that mean? They fell off a lorry? Some dodgy insurance claim? Some unfinished business from his radio shop days? I decided not to ask any questions.

"Try the river," I said. "Somewhere in the Hammersmith, Barnes area."

It was about 10.30pm when we crossed Hammersmith Bridge, parked the car and walked a little way along the towpath. Fortunately there was no one around. The water came right up to the edge. It took the two of us to carry each typewriter and to hurl them one by one into the water. We couldn't chuck them very far. They were far too heavy. In fact the water barely covered them.

"They won't be seen," said Harry.

"Yes, they will," I replied. "The Thames is tidal at this point. They will be high and dry in the morning."

This didn't seem to bother my stepfather. He just said, "Let's go."

Back at the house, Prince was in a bad way. He had not touched his food or water.

"I can't cope with a sick dog alone, said Dad, "and you have got to get back to Edinburgh. He looks so sick and in pain. Whatever you did to him in Cambridge has made him very ill. Take him back to the vet tomorrow, Barry. Ask for him to be put down. I shall miss him. I loved that dog, but there are more important things to deal with."

"I'm sorry too," I said. "I did my best."

The next day I took Prince to the vet. He was put down. I prepared to leave for Edinburgh. Term had already started.

"What are you going to do?" I said gently to Harry.

"What can I do?" he replied bitterly. "I have no family, no home and no job."

2018

Penny and I Discuss our Childhood

One day when having tea with my sister Penny in her elegant house in North London, I asked her if she remembered the document we found in our mother's flat after she died.

Penny's happy face changed. "It was a sort of story, wasn't it? Her story…" She faltered. "I didn't want it. You took it, I remember."

"Yes. Well, it prompted me to write my own story; you know, memoirs of childhood and all that."

"Why, Barry, that's wonderful!" Penny replied.

"And, if it's OK with you, I would like your help to fill in some of the gaps, and to learn how you felt about life with Mum and Harry Kay when you were young."

"Of course I will help," she said. "You may have to take me out for dinner a few times."

"Cheap at the price," I responded.

She sat back in her big chair, luxurious in her cream cashmere sweater. Penny looked so young these days, her hair lighter, waved softly, the springy black curls inherited from her father quite changed. She was smiling, reflecting now, and to my relief, happy to chat about our childhood.

"Isn't it strange that here we are now in our seventies and yet there is so much about our time with Mum and Dad that we have never discussed?"

If, for me, life had its low moments, it had often been worse for Penny. Our age difference, almost nine years, and the fact that I was away at boarding school, and then at university, had affected our relationship in those early years. We had to wait until our mother died before having an adult discussion about our childhood. Before this we had never touched on subjects such as my origins, Tony Chambers or Jewishness. When our mother was alive these were taboo. She had made us afraid and embarrassed to talk about these matters.

I was fortunate enough to have had an excellent grammar school education, even though I was bundled away to boarding school at the age of four and had to cope with suddenly being wrenched away from my mother and father. I remained at the boarding house and it provided important continuity. Penny, on the other hand, went from one unsuitable school to another. The choices may have seemed right at the time, but the truth was her education had been a muddle.

Harry Kay had gone to a grammar school, at least until he was aged fifteen, and had some knowledge base in his attempts to plan Penny's secondary schooling. Mum, on the other hand, whilst intelligent, was not wise. She had had only a rudimentary education and believed that getting a child into a good school was simply a matter of money.

Penny was a delightful child despite all the parental disharmony – pretty, charming, full of fun. She danced and sang ("a bit of a Shirley Temple," we used to say). It was not surprising that my mother, with Harry Kay's encouragement, enrolled Penny at the age of six in the Aida Foster Theatre School.

"Did Mum and Dad want you to go on the stage?" I asked her.

"They might have had that in the back of their minds," she said. "But an important reason was that Aunty Betty" (Dad's sister) "was a secretary there. Betty thought it would suit me well. We were living in Norrice Lea by then so it wasn't far to travel. Also, lots of Jewish girls went. Aida Foster's was quite a big name in the 1950s and I was reasonably happy there."

She told me that the routine of the school was dancing and drama in the morning and ordinary school lessons in the afternoon.

Unfortunately, serious problems, which affected Penny's career on the stage, became apparent quite early on.

"I was doing reasonably well at drama but I just couldn't learn the lines. I tried and tried, but it was hopeless. I started off quite well with ballet but I grew too tall and developed 'flat feet'. My ordinary schoolwork was terrible. I was hopeless at maths – some sort of mental block, I just glazed over. Once or twice Dad tried to help with arithmetic but I just didn't get it. He gave up in frustration. None of the teachers seemed particularly bothered about my general education. I didn't pass the eleven-plus exam and so by the time I left Aida Foster's when I was twelve Mum and Dad hadn't a clue where to send me next. Also, it was a bad time at home. Mum's outbursts were getting more frequent and Dad was often at his wits' end."

The senior school eventually chosen was Tortington Park in Sussex. Penny was friendly with a local girl called Sharon who was a pupil there. It was a Catholic school with a small quota of Jewish girls. Sharon told Penny that life at boarding school was exciting with midnight feasts, loyal friends and mild mischievous behaviour. Our parents were pleased that Penny liked the idea of boarding school. The entrance requirements were not stringent; they would take virtually any girl who was well mannered and whose parents could afford the not inconsiderable fees. Mum and Dad hoped boarding school would improve Penny's general schoolwork. Furthermore, she would have a friend there, Sharon. Penny was fond of her and would quickly settle in. With little difficulty, just a cursory interview, she was accepted and started that September.

Her time at Tortington Park was, "Utterly miserable, especially in the first year." Sharon may have been Penny's friend in London but when they got to school she became "a monster". The two of them were put in a room together. "From the first night she bullied me," said Penny. "It wasn't just teasing, it was cruel and spiteful. She generally undermined me, accusing me of keeping her awake. I was desperately lonely and homesick. It was one of the unhappiest times of my life."

The school itself had an all-female staff and was formal. There were strict rules about the school uniform. The fact that Penny had not passed the eleven-plus did not seem to matter. She remained hopeless at maths, and indeed at most subjects. Nobody really cared. The school tried to be academic and some girls went on to university, but the main emphasis was on 'moral instruction'.

"The girls were mostly horsey, county types with plums in their mouths," she said. "It was like a prison. We were not allowed to have food parcels or to phone home. Reading material had to come from the school library. There were no novels, or magazines or comics. Weekly letters home were 'checked' by a member of staff. There were only two visiting weekends per term."

Penny found solace in food, eating the copious quantities of sandwiches provided. By the time she left Tortington Park, Penny, now fourteen, had developed a serious weight problem.

"Mum addressed my weight issue in her usual way – she took unsound advice and demanded immediate results. I was sent to a quack dietician in Harley Street and given a cocktail of pills including amphetamines and a diuretic. I was also put on a no-carbohydrate diet supplemented with proteins and citrus fruits. My breath smelled of acetone. I had buzzing in my head and could not sleep. Finally I became addicted to amphetamines and remained so until the age of thirty. My weight yo-yoed. Dad was also becoming overweight. We both found solace in food. It was a difficult time.

"So I was taken away from Tortington Park because I was so unhappy. Where was I to go next? Mum and Dad chose Queen's House, a girls' independent day school in St John's Wood. It was another disaster. I was the fat newcomer and bullied. My hair was yanked and my bra pulled off. The only friend I made was a girl called Tina. The first thing she asked me was, 'Are you a virgin?' I was horrified. She told me she was sleeping with her uncle and how marvellous it was. I was given the details about what they got up to. Academically, I was completely at sea. I left Queen's House after two years and was then sent to a crammer to get O Levels, but that didn't work out either."

"But, Penny," I said. "Surely it wasn't all bad. You got into the London College of Fashion and, like Mum, you became a respected women's fashion designer."

"True," she conceded, "and to be fair Mum had a lot to do with getting me accepted at the college. She probably used the same tactics as she did when she got you into that boarding school as a little boy."

We both laughed.

"But at the time I was still full of anger against her and Dad, because of the Jewish issue."

"The Jewish issue?" I repeated, puzzled.

Penny's frown told me she had touched on a painful subject. "I have never told you this story. It was probably the worst thing that ever happened to me. I always thought that I was Jewish. Dad was obviously Jewish and, naturally, I thought that Mum was too. After all, our friends were Jewish and we were in the rag trade. Mum had all these Yiddish expressions and insisted I went to synagogue every Saturday. The house, as you know, was opposite a synagogue and it was a solid Jewish neighbourhood.

"One day, shortly after I left Tortington Park, I was chatting to Mum in her bedroom. Aunty Joan from Peterborough had just left after one of her visits and I was puzzled that she sometimes mentioned 'her church'. Mum had taken me to Peterborough from time to time to stay with her parents. So I asked her quite casually why Grandma and Grandad in Peterborough were so different from Bubbe and Zayde, Dad's parents.

"Mum became silent and started smoking nervously, sitting on the bed. 'I am not Jewish,' she said at last.

"'Not Jewish?!' I couldn't believe it.

"Mum then told me about her Peterborough family and her early life, and about you and her first husband. I was thunderstruck. My mother was not Jewish; therefore I was not Jewish. I felt terrible – horrendous. But mostly I was ashamed, as if it was my fault. My identity had been suddenly ripped away. I had been deceiving my friends all these years. So I kept it all bottled up and didn't tell anyone. I was too embarrassed to share this awful secret. The shame turned to anger, not so much against Mum but against Dad for not telling me; for not discussing it. I felt my world had come to an end."

"How awful," I said, and then fell silent. We were talking about events which had happened almost sixty years ago as if they had occurred yesterday. From her grave, our mother was making us angry again. I told Penny about my own experiences and how Mum would often try to get me to pretend that I was Jewish in order to conceal her early life and real identity. When I started to explain about Barry Chambers and Barry Kay and my different identities at home and at school, Penny looked alarmed.

"Barry," she said, "although it was clear, after that dreadful conversation with Mum, that you were not Jewish, I had always thought until then that Harry Kay was your real father. That was the first time I had heard of Tony Chambers; the first time I knew that you are only my half-brother. Do you remember in about 1962 when I was a bridesmaid at Aunty Joan's wedding in that Methodist chapel in Peterborough? I couldn't tell my friends about it. I hid the photos. I thought my friends would 'find me out'. Actually, it was the same when you got married in Edinburgh. All my friends assumed you were Jewish. I couldn't share the experience of your church wedding with anyone."

"I am sorry, Penny, but I also felt strange and embarrassed when you married Gerry in the synagogue. I gave you away. Remember? I had to walk down the aisle wearing a kippah. *Everyone will think I am Jewish.* I was horribly embarrassed." After a pause I said, "Do you think Mum's friends and acquaintances thought she was Jewish? Did she fool the lot of them?"

Penny smiled. "I had a boyfriend when I was about eighteen, a hairdresser. He was really wet but Mum thought he was wonderful. After a while I broke it off because he was so boring, and anyway he was getting 'too serious'. A few days later *his* mother phoned. She was quite upset and said to Mum, 'I hope Penny didn't break it off because you are not Jewish?'"

We laughed. There was a pause.

Speaking softly, Penny said, "Barry, I know Mum was impossible at times. She was argumentative and confrontational and always had to be right. But don't be too hard on her. She loved you and was very proud of you."

1963

My Son, the Doctor

After my parents split up for good and the family house was stripped of its contents, Penny never went back to Norrice Lea. She met Harry Kay a few days later in a café in the West End. Dad told Penny that when he was left alone in the empty house, sobbing loudly, unexpectedly, there was a ring at the door. He did not want any visitors but opened up to find a smartly dressed man of medium height smiling at him sympathetically.

"I am sorry to intrude," the man said gently. "I was just out for a walk and couldn't help hearing the distressing sounds coming from this house."

Overwhelmed by the man's kindness, Dad, with little hesitation, poured out his heart to him. His name was Lionel Kass. He took Harry back to his own house. Lionel's wife and family then looked after him. They became lifelong friends, eventually setting up a small clothes business together which provided Harry with a decent livelihood for the rest of his days.

The days, months and years after the dramatic split were painful for Harry. Lionel helped him sell Norrice Lea so he had some savings for his old age. Joan Kay Ltd was wound up, the staff dismissed and the lease on the Wells Street premises terminated. Without my mother the business was worthless. She had just walked away, leaving Harry to clean up the mess.

He had another big shock. A few weeks after the marriage broke up Harry received a letter from a divorce lawyer accusing him of *vile and outrageous misdemeanours ranging from serial adultery to gross sexual perversions.* I am in no doubt that these accusations were all fabricated by my mother and that the lawyer simply wrote down everything she said verbatim, taking her word for everything, uncritically and at face value.

Penny slowly settled down to life at the flat with my mother. She confessed she never really liked Norrice Lea ("too suburban, a bigoted ghetto"). She preferred the more cosmopolitan surroundings of St John's Wood. Initially Harry Reuben kept a discreet distance. Penny could not bring herself to have a conversation with him for over a year. Gradually their relationship improved. Penny, still confused about Mum's confession that she was not really Jewish, remained emotionally distraught regarding her identity. Harry Reuben helped her come to terms with this. Eventually they became friends, but Penny still had divided loyalties. She had to keep up the pretence with Harry Kay that Harry Reuben was a monster and a seducer, even though she had begun to like and respect him.

My mother never admitted she had acted wrongly. There was no sympathy from her for Harry or indeed for anyone else she had hurt. All she displayed was self-justification, blaming the whole episode on Harry Kay, refusing to take responsibility herself. Never again did I talk to my mother about that terrible day.

On the train back to Edinburgh many thoughts raced through my head. Did I love my mother any more? Did I even like her? Did her illness affect her relationships with men? Previously it had been the child in me that had rushed down to London to beg my mother not to break up the family when she first ran off with Harry Reuben. Two years later, now aged twenty-three, my attitude had hardened. My mother was not going to affect me emotionally any more. I had to stand back and review the situation more objectively. She was a sick woman. Her mental illness was the cause of her unpredictable, self-centred behaviour. Mum was a patient with little control over what she did. *Don't judge,* I told myself. *Be detached and hope that eventually she will have some insight and seek treatment.*

*

It was in that somewhat defiant frame of mind that I found the strength to face the next eight weeks before my final examinations.

I had several strategies for revision. Firstly, there was the 'card system' which had proved useful before. It was learning by 'lists'. On small, plain cards I would write a question on one side and the answer on the other. For example, *The causes of fever of unknown origin*; *The causes of cough*; *The causes of weight loss*; *Drugs used for hypertension* and so on. I had over a hundred cards and would carry them in my pocket wrapped in an elastic band. I would test myself at bus stops, in coffee shops, walking down the street and at mealtimes.

My second strategy was the paid sessions with hospital registrars. Several hospital doctors, in medicine, surgery, paediatrics, and obstetrics and gynaecology, who were not quite consultants and wished to earn a little extra money, would organise evening classes on how to pass your finals. The advice they gave was worth every penny.

"They are not out to fail you," I remember one of them saying. "You have gone through six years of medicine; your education has cost the government a fortune and the country needs more doctors. You will have to do something really stupid to fail. What is the common mistake that students make in their finals? They guess rather than saying, 'I don't know.' The examiners need to be assured that you are 'safe' and that you will seek advice if you are out of your depth. They will not ask questions about rare diseases, so don't bother swotting up on Muckle-Wells disease or Budd-Chiari syndrome; just make absolutely sure you know how to recognise a stroke, a diabetic coma and a myocardial infarct."

With my card system and the advice obtained in the special evening classes I grew more confident. Something else kept me steady during those critical few weeks. One evening whilst relaxing at the flat of some friends, I met a man called Michael Nelson. He had qualified as a doctor in London and was about five years older than me. We became friends. He became a sort of older brother and a steadying influence. Michael was working hard for his specialist exams in neurology with a view to becoming a psychiatrist. He was also Jewish. I found I could speak freely and openly to him about the traumas I had been through in London. He was compassionate and understanding with a sense of humour. A spare room came up in the digs I was in at the time and he moved in. We had many other things in common besides medicine. Michael was widely read and had an endearing social conscience. We chatted endlessly about politics, world affairs and, of course, girls. Michael talked me through many problems, real and imagined. I began to see things in a different light. The night before my finals I was nervous. Michael taught me relaxation exercises to help me get to sleep. I woke up perfectly refreshed.

The final examinations were straightforward. There were no trick questions, just standard stuff about common medical problems. In paediatrics I was shown a normal chest X-ray – apart from a penny that seemed to be lodged in the small child's oesophagus!

"What's that?" the examiner said.

"The child swallowed a penny," I replied.

"Well done!" he responded with a broad smile.

"What would you do if you were faced with a breech birth at three in the morning?" I was asked in the obstetrics and gynaecology viva.

"Get expert help as quickly as possible," I replied.

"Excellent," they said.

For three days the whole class, all eighty of us, hung around nervously in the Medical Quad waiting for the servitor to come out of the faculty office with the pass list. He took an age to open the big glass case and pin up the notice. We crowded around. I looked for my name. There it was. I had passed. I had made it.

I went back to my digs, walking on air. I picked up the phone, called my mother and told her the news.

"My son, the doctor," she said.

Epilogue

Harry Kay died of coronary artery disease in 1995. After Norrice Lea was sold he moved into a tiny service flat in The White House, a hotel on the edge of Regent's Park which took in a few long-term guests. It suited him and he liked the amenities such as the restaurant, the sitting-out areas, the pool and the doorman. Eventually he made friends with a widow from Maidenhead. I kept in touch and involved him in family events as best I could, but after that terrible day in 1963 our relationship never really recovered.

Harry Reuben suffered more than Harry Kay from my mother's wild outbursts. From the day they married Mum's mental state deteriorated further. She had rapid mood swings alternating between violence and depression and was hospitalised several times. Despite it all Harry Reuben remained loyal and loving. He was basically a kind, rather shy man; cultured, intelligent and trustworthy. Eventually Penny and I had a warm relationship with him. Unfortunately Harry did not declare his earnings to the taxman. He was raided by the customs and excise people and eventually declared bankrupt. Mum then became director of the Lyndhurst Club, although Harry continued to run things from behind the scenes. Finally, in the early 1980s, with deteriorating health and unable to cope with Mum's behaviour any longer, he moved out to live with his brother. He died from emphysema in 1983. Like Mum he had been a heavy smoker for most of his life. Shortly before he died Harry told Penny and me that he had left a considerable sum of money for both of us and that we were to claim it from his nephew, Martin. When we eventually contacted Martin, relaying what Harry had said, he denied all knowledge of the matter. Penny and I were most embarrassed.

During the last years of her marriage to Harry Reuben, Mum's gambling got out of control. She lost thousands of pounds in fashionable London casinos, using the table money gleaned from the Lyndhurst Club. But after Harry passed away and the club was sold, my mother suddenly stopped gambling, joined Gamblers Anonymous and became a 'telephone counsellor' supporting others with the problem she told us she no longer had. Her personality also changed and her violent, disruptive behaviour came to an end, prompting Penny to comment, "She became the mother I never had."

In the 1970s my mother formally converted to Judaism. Her wish was to be buried with Harry Reuben. She attended Hebrew classes at the St John's Wood Liberal Synagogue. Her exercise books from the time have several pages of neat Hebrew script, and in the margins were encouraging comments from the rabbi.

Mum was often witty and funny. For the thirty years she lived on after Harry Reuben died she did her best to be a good mother. She was proud of her children and she loved us, but she demanded demonstrations from us of our love and respect which, for me and Penny, was difficult at times. Behind the open signs of affection with big hugs and kisses there was, unfortunately, a spiteful side to her. Often she seemed to have nothing better to do than to sit alone in her flat, brooding on the perceived imperfections of various family members. Mum loved to corner a friend or relative and hold forth on various subjects such as the virtues of Margaret Thatcher, complementary medicine or royalty, opinions gleaned mostly from the *Daily Mail*. In these situations she was opinionated and tedious.

During my childhood I longed to be with my mother, especially when I could be alone with her and she would love and cuddle me. Sadly, this occurred infrequently. When, as an elderly lady, she eventually had the time and opportunity to be a real mother it seemed too late, although I did my best to return her affection.

Penny had an unhappy first marriage. Her husband was a Greek doctor. Although he had a licence to practise medicine he mainly did locum junior doctor jobs in private hospitals and lived on the fringes of the world of nightclubs and casinos. The more my mother said he was unsuitable for Penny, the more she pushed the two of them together. They lived together in Athens for a while but Penny found his controlling nature unbearable and, one night, packed her belongings and drove her Mini back to London. Her second husband, Gerry Bron, a loving and supportive man whom she married in 1983, died in 2012.

I kept in regular contact with Roland and Lillian Jermy. They retired to Guildford in the 1960s. They always loved a visit and lived a contented life, tending their large garden, into old age. I was in the USA when Lillian died and to my deep regret was not at her funeral. Roland lived on, alone, for a further ten years.

The King's School became comprehensive and co-educational in 1976, but acquired state-funded independent academy status in 2011. Over the years it has enjoyed an outstanding record of success, with the award of beacon status in 1999. I regret that many people connected with the school will be uncomfortable reading that the boarding house was once an unhappy place, at least for some of us. However, this should be set in context. Corporal punishment, bullying and abuse were the norm nationwide during the time I was a pupil. Notwithstanding, virtually all of the staff set high standards. Many recognised my potential and set me on the right path to an academic career. As expected of the very best teaching institutions (and to quote Trevor Elliott, a recent deputy head), "King's is now a pupil-oriented, family-friendly organisation with a robust system to tackle any bullying that might raise its ugly head."

The day after my graduation in Edinburgh I received a letter from Jesus College, Cambridge, offering me a place in 1964–65, the year after my 'house jobs'. It was not easy being an undergraduate again. But it was an extraordinarily stimulating year and I got a respectable upper second, good enough to be accepted for a PhD. I still found time to conduct the college choir, act in the amateur dramatic club and produce a light opera during May Week. One of my classmates, Mark (later Sir Mark) Pepys, became a lifelong friend. Twenty years later I was to succeed his father, Jack Pepys, as professor of allergy and clinical immunology at the Brompton Hospital.

It was with a mixture of elation and apprehension that I reflected on my journey from The King's School, Peterborough to the Edinburgh Medical School. I often thought about the future. Whom would I marry? What sort of a person would she be? Someone quite different from my mother – that was for sure. What I had in mind was a wonder woman; kind, wise, gentle, putting others first, a perfect mother, beautiful of course, a homemaker, a cook, and with things in common with me like music, books and art. Hopefully, she would also be Scottish. And then I found her. "Agreeing to marry you is like jumping off a cliff," she said at the time. Her name is Rosy. We have been married for over fifty years.

I met Rosy (Rosemary) Johnstone a few weeks before my medical finals. She was in her second year of an English MA degree. We got married in 1966 when I started my PhD. Rosy enrolled for a Diploma of Education at Hughes Hall. We lived in a Jesus College flat on Hills Road. Our first daughter, Emma, was born in 1968.

My PhD supervisor, Professor Robin Coombs, a kind and distinguished man (his discovery – the Coombs test – for diagnosing conditions such as transfusion reactions is still used worldwide), suggested that I applied myself to the study of a white blood cell called the eosinophil, which is prominent in allergic diseases. His supervision was very much 'hands off' but I was exposed to a rich scientific environment and quickly learnt how to acquire knowledge by networking. I also worked part-time at Addenbrooke's Hospital to keep up my clinical skills.

I did not get far in the first two years of my PhD but in the final year things came together experimentally. I noticed that some of the most interesting papers in my field came from a group at the Harvard Medical School in Boston, Massachusetts, under the leadership of Dr K. Frank Austen. I wrote to him and he agreed to accept me as a postdoctoral fellow after I completed my PhD. The Royal College of Physicians awarded me a fellowship to cover travel and subsistence for two years in the United States.

Rosy, Emma and I arrived in Boston on a freezing cold day in December 1969. We stayed at the Brattle Inn in Harvard Square before finding an apartment. Dr Austen had insisted that I call him the moment I arrived. After twenty minutes on the phone he had sorted me out, understanding precisely what I had done in Cambridge and how I should proceed in his department. The goals were defined and experiments designed. His was a 'hands-on' form of supervision that suited me well. My two years at Harvard were the most stimulating of my career to that date; the whole department was focused in my area of interest. Frank Austen, small in stature with a high forehead and white hair, was a hard taskmaster. He was competitive, sometimes charming, and often sarcastic. But the work went well and we published several papers together.

Boston was not all work. We had glorious weekends in Maine. Fulfilling a long-term musical ambition, I took up the bassoon and was fortunate to have John Miller, shortly to become principal bassoonist in the Minneapolis Symphony Orchestra, as my teacher.

Returning to Edinburgh in December 1971 I was offered a lectureship in respiratory medicine. My remit was to set up a research group at the City Hospital and provide an allergy diagnostic service. It was an unrealistic challenge. I was too inexperienced to set up my own lab and geographically isolated from other researchers, who were mainly based around the Royal Infirmary near the town centre. However, I managed to attract research funds and build up a small team. I produced little of scientific interest during those first few years. The early 1970s was a difficult time economically with high interest rates, the miners' strike and the three-day week. Whilst my mother was gambling on the roulette tables in London we were having trouble making ends meet in Scotland. We bought our first house, however, and in 1974 our second daughter, Rebecca, was born.

In 1975 I became deputy director of the Edinburgh Blood Transfusion Service with the responsibility of setting up an immunology screening service for patients receiving blood products. I came under the mentorship of John Cash, the director; a charismatic man with enthusiasm, humanity and exceptional organisational skills. I was not trained in blood transfusion medicine and was heavily supported by colleagues when 'on call'. The immunology service was quite easy to set up because I had first-hand knowledge of all the techniques from my Cambridge and Harvard days, but diagnostic hospital laboratory medicine was not something I wanted to do.

I was 'rescued' by Professor Sir Alastair Currie, who offered me the post of senior lecturer in experimental pathology. He gave me a large lab area with state-of-the-art equipment. A five-year grant from the Medical Research Council supported our studies in allergy and asthma. I also taught undergraduates and set up an allergy clinic at the Royal Infirmary.

Our third daughter, Beth, was born in 1976 and we moved out to a beautiful old manse in Heriot, about forty-five minutes' drive from Edinburgh.

Alastair Currie was exceptionally supportive but in Edinburgh at the time there were formidable obstacles to pursuing my real ambition, which was clinical research in asthma and allergy, i.e. experiments on patients. I wanted to study asthma and allergic reactions provoked in a clinical laboratory as others were doing in London and the United States. In the 1970s Edinburgh was not ready for this particular blend of laboratory and clinical medicine.

In 1980 I was appointed professor of allergy and clinical immunology at the Cardiothoracic Institute (later the National Heart and Lung Institute, and now part of Imperial College) and the Royal Brompton Hospital. We had to leave our beloved Heriot and found a house on the borders of Chelsea (later moving to Putney and then to Stamford Brook). I built up a new team with invaluable help from Professor (later Dame) Margaret Turner-Warwick, who remained a lifelong friend. By persuading volunteers to inhale pollen, or whatever they were allergic to, we identified critical cells and chemical messengers which caused asthmatics to wheeze. As well as eosinophils, we highlighted the importance of a subset of T lymphocytes called Th2. Our work in the 1980s and 1990s has eventually resulted in several new treatments of asthma and related allergic diseases, which are now available in the clinic and based on targeting Th2 cells and eosinophils.

I did my share of local and international committee work. In 2006 I was invited to be the specialist adviser to a House of Lords Science and Technology Select Committee enquiry on allergy. We produced a substantial report and many of our recommendations have been implemented. Being president of both the British and European Academies of Allergy and Clinical Immunology was time-consuming but important for promoting high standards in our discipline. In the 1990s I was elected an honorary member of the American Academy of Allergy and Clinical Immunology, and a fellow of the Royal Society of Edinburgh and the Academy of Medical Sciences.

Academically I am delighted by the achievements of the numerous pre- and postdoctoral fellows who passed through my department over the years. Thirty-eight obtained their MD or PhD and eventually were to become either professors running their own research teams, or consultants within the NHS.

I still play the bassoon with the Hounslow Symphony Orchestra and love tennis and country walks.

My three daughters, of whom I am intensely proud, have succeeded in fulfilling their talents: Emma as an artist, Rebecca as a consultant in infectious diseases in Edinburgh, and Beth, a trained architect, now running her own urban regeneration team with Haringey Council. They have managed, in the way of modern young women, to balance the demands of their careers with their commitments to be good wives, mothers and homemakers. They all found wonderful husbands and Rosy and I now have six grandchildren.

So what did happen to Barry Chambers? He survived because Rosy looked after him.

Acknowledgements

The document found in my mother's flat after she died, in which she detailed many facts about her early life of which I was unaware, has provided the main incentive for writing these childhood memoirs. I am grateful to her for not destroying it.

I am indebted to former members of The King's School Boarding House, Peterborough, particularly William 'Bill' Tibbles, Mark Hatton, Martin 'Ginner' Gray, John Uzzell, Roger Boulton, John Roberts, Keith Simpson, Ian Vaughan Arbuckle, Colin Richardson and Gray Jolliffe, for sharing their memories of life at the 'the Pig and Whistle' and commenting so helpfully on early drafts of the manuscript.

Our London writers group ('Not Morley') gave me terrific encouragement and advice at all stages for which I am most appreciative.

Others who have read the manuscript and have given invaluable input, particularly on issues of flow or accuracy (or both), include John Bienenstock, Andrew Wardlaw, Martin Hay, Jean Hay, Elspeth Sinclair and Mark Pepys.

Karl French of The Literary Consultancy provided in-depth critiques and numerous suggestions for improvements.

The former deputy headmaster of the school and chairman of the Old Petriburgians' Association, Trevor Elliott, kindly read several drafts of the manuscript and took great pains to ensure exactness. He also helped me obtain additional information from the school archives and was generally supportive despite his unease on reading about the dark side of school life that some of us experienced in the 1950s.

Two publications, *A History of The King's School, Peterborough* by W. D. Larrett (1966, published by the Old Petriburgians' Association), and *Hornsby Harvest: The Autobiographies of Harry Reginald and Mary Hornsby* (1985, printed privately in Christchurch, New Zealand) have also been important sources of information.

My sister, Penny Bron, provided invaluable details concerning her early life with our mother and Harry Kay. I deeply appreciate her support and perspective throughout this project.

Most of all, I am grateful to my wife Rosy, a published novelist and former English teacher, who spent hours reading and rereading various drafts of the manuscript. She has given advice on all aspects of presentation, and moral support at times when I wondered if I would ever finish this task.